D1429550

SINN FÉIN
1905–2005

IN THE SHADOW OF GUNMEN

SINN FÉIN
1905–2005

IN THE SHADOW OF GUNMEN

KEVIN RAFTER

Gill & Macmillan

Gill & Macmillan Ltd
Hume Avenue, Park West, Dublin 12
with associated companies throughout the world
www.gillmacmillan.ie
© Kevin Rafter 2005
0 7171 3992 1

Index compiled by Helen Litton
Design by Make Communication
Print origination by O'K Graphic Design, Dublin
Printed by MPG Books, Cornwall

This book is typeset in 11.75/14pt Minion.

The paper used in this book comes from the wood pulp
of managed forests. For every tree felled, at least one
tree is planted, thereby renewing natural resources.

A CIP catalogue record for this book is available from the
British Library.

5 4 3 2 1

CONTENTS

ACKNOWLEDGEMENTS

This book started its life as a proposed radio series on the electoral history of Sinn Féin but after some initial interviews were recorded, a conversation with Faith O'Grady of the Lisa Richards Agency quickly turned the project in a very different direction.

In writing this book, I have been able to draw on interviews I recorded with Sinn Féin figures for both journalistic and academic purposes over the last ten years. Where direct quotation is used, the individual is identified in footnotes, although some sources preferred to remain anonymous. I would like to thank Dawn Doyle and Michael Moran from the Sinn Féin press office who were always helpful in setting up interviews with party members and elected representatives.

I have been fortunate in working for several news organisations where priority was given to coverage of events in Northern Ireland. In that regard a debt of gratitude is owed to Joe Mulholland, Ed Mulhall, Michael Good, Sean O'Rourke and Gerald Barry in RTÉ and to Conor Brady and Geraldine Kennedy at the *Irish Times*. The need to stand back and think about the subject was instilled by Dr Jennifer Todd and Professor Tom Garvin at the Politics Department at UCD and also by Dr John Coakley at the Institute for British and Irish Studies.

Some of the material is chapter 7 is drawn from an article which Wesley Hutchinson enthusiastically agreed to publish in *Études Irlandaises*, while Eamon Delaney provided space in *Magill* magazine for some early thoughts which are developed upon in chapter 3.

The staff at the National Library, the National Archives and the RTÉ Reference Library were as always helpful and patient with requests for assistance. I would also like to thank Roger Jupp at Lansdowne Market Research, Willie O'Reilly at Today FM, Yvonne Healy at the Mansion House, and the staff of the House of Commons Information Office. I also grateful to Ashley Taggart and his colleagues at IES Dublin where I have had several opportunities to develop some of the themes in this book.

The book has benefited from conversations and discussions with a number of friends and colleagues, especially Ursula Halligan, Charlie

Bird, Martin Mackin, Martina Fitzgerald, Tom Butler, Colm O'Reardon, Peter Fitzgerald and Miriam Donohoe. Donald Taylor Black and I hope one day to make a television documentary together but in the meantime I have plundered some interviews we recorded about the 1981 hunger strikes. I am also thankful to Noirin Hegarty who came along with her *Sunday Tribune* job offer just as the project needed an injection of energy. I am particularly grateful to Liam Kelly and Ronan O'Brien who read and made some insightful comments on an earlier draft of the manuscript.

Faith O'Grady once again proved that she is the best at helping an idea to be realised while Fergal Tobin and Deirdre Rennison Kunz at Gill & Macmillan battled against a very tight deadline to make the book happen.

As ever the biggest thanks are due to those closest to home. To my parents Bill and Mary, to my boys Ben, Brian and Adam and to my ever patient wife, and best friend, Oorla. This book is dedicated to you.

1

'AN END TO THE ARMED CAMPAIGN', 28 JULY 2005

Séanna Walsh was a natural choice when the leadership of the Provisional Irish Republican Army looked to confirm an end to its war against the British presence in Northern Ireland, in the summer of 2005.

The Belfast man had lived his life through the twists and turns of the modern republican movement. From 'long war' to 'long peace', Walsh had travelled a journey which had started a generation earlier, when the Provisionals emerged out of a split in republican ranks over attitudes to political activism and the use of force in response to loyalist attacks and a failure by the police to protect Catholic areas in Northern Ireland.

Through all the compromises and concessions, through all the successes and defeats, Walsh had remained loyal to Gerry Adams and a strategy that fundamentally transformed both elements of the republican movement—the military, represented by the IRA, and the political, represented by Sinn Féin.

Walsh had a formidable reputation and was known for his unswerving commitment to the republican cause, having spent nearly half his adult life in prison. He also had a strong republican pedigree—his grandfather had been shot dead by the police in Belfast in the early days of the Northern Ireland state, while his own wife was a former republican prisoner. In addition to pedigree, Walsh also had a key association which strengthened the ability of the IRA to convince its own heartland of the merits of its decision.

On 2 March 1981, less than 48 hours into his ill-fated hunger strike, Bobby Sands—who would acquire iconic status within Irish republicanism—wrote in his prison diary, 'My old friend Séanna has also written.' In later years, Walsh would recall meeting Sands: 'I first met Bobby on remand in Cage 8 of Long Kesh before being moved to

Crumlin Road Jail in January 1973. What struck me about him was the cocky self-assuredness of his Belfast dander and his spiky Rod Stewart hair cut. I was a 16-year-old, "thought he knew it all" child of the Short Strand, East Belfast...'[1]

The Provisional IRA was only a handful of years in existence when Walsh, at 16 years old, was arrested while attempting to rob a bank in Belfast. The proceeds from the robbery in 1973 were destined for the coffers of the IRA. For his unsuccessful endeavours, Walsh was sentenced to five years' imprisonment. It was an environment with which he would become very familiar as most of his life over the following quarter of a century was to be spent behind bars.

After his release in May 1976, Walsh enjoyed only three months' freedom. He was arrested, charged with possession of a rifle and given a 10-year prison sentence. He served seven years and seven months of that sentence, but even after his release he was once again back among the ranks of IRA Volunteers. A senior figure in the organisation, Walsh was soon apprehended by the security forces while manufacturing explosives and mortar bombs. A 22-year prison sentence was handed down. By the time he left prison in 1998 as part of the early-release programme under the Belfast Agreement, Walsh had spent over 21 years of his life in prison.

In the seven years after the Belfast Agreement was signed, the IRA issued 24 statements. But not even its October 2001 statement, which confirmed a start to weapons decommissioning, had the historic significance of the statement published on 28 July 2005. In a departure from long-standing practice that generally saw only written statements issued, the IRA leadership decided to get one of its members to appear on camera, reading the statement. Séanna Walsh, with his background, involvement and associations, was an ideal choice.

During the 1980s, this child of East Belfast was one of the republican leaders in the Maze Prison. When he emerged from jail in 1998, he aligned himself with the peace strategy being pursued by Gerry Adams and Martin McGuinness. 'I don't think the ghosts of the past can be exorcised, and to a large extent I still carry a lot of those ghosts on my shoulder,' Walsh said in July 2000.

Five years later, as he read the IRA's statement, Walsh laid to rest the very ghost of the physical force tradition in Irish republicanism:

The leadership of Óglaigh na hÉireann has formally ordered an end to the armed campaign. This will take effect from 4 p.m. this afternoon. All IRA units have been ordered to dump arms. All volunteers have been instructed to assist the development of purely political and democratic programmes through exclusively peaceful means. Volunteers must not engage in any other activities whatsoever.

The decision was the logical outcome of the peace strategy pursued by Gerry Adams. The further that republicans moved into the democratic system, the more their military wing became a political albatross. There had been some early negotiating advantages for Sinn Féin in trading IRA concessions, but the more the peace process deepened, the more the existence of an armed grouping had become incompatible with political advancement. There was only so far that Sinn Féin could travel while the IRA was still in business. The events of 2004 and 2005—discussed in Chapter 2—clearly highlighted the incompatibility of the status quo that had developed within republicanism. Ultimately, a pragmatic decision had to be taken, and as he had done so many times in the recent past, Gerry Adams let pragmatism rule over the traditional core values of Irish republicanism.

Pragmatism has been the defining characteristic of Sinn Féin during the Adams leadership era. No republican principle has been allowed stand in the way of political progress. Even the IRA itself—for so long Sinn Féin's master—came to play the role of servant, a role which ultimately led to an end to the IRA in July 2005.

The statement read by Séanna Walsh—and made available on DVD—hammered the final nail into the coffin of physical force republicanism. This book tells the story of how Sinn Féin in its centenary year emerged out from the shadow of the gunmen of the IRA.

Along with Martin McGuinness, Gerry Adams has rewritten the history of the anti-system Irish republican tradition. To some, these two men have acted out of conviction but to others their historical contribution has been laced with compromise and concessions; others hold them responsible for much of the terrible violence that scarred Ireland after 1969. The Adams–McGuinness leadership axis in the IRA—and its political wing, Sinn Féin—had been unrelenting through more than a quarter of a century of bloody conflict in Northern Ireland.

The so-called 'war' left 3,600 people dead—the majority of them civilians. The Provisional IRA was the single greatest taker of life in the conflict in Northern Ireland. Over the 30 years of the modern Irish troubles, the IRA was responsible for almost half of all deaths.[2]

Martin McGuinness was born in 1950 in the Bogside area of Derry. Gerry Adams was a year older and had grown up in a republican family in Belfast. Both men became active in the Provisional IRA from the start of the contemporary troubles. Very early on in the conflict, they reached positions of seniority within the republican movement.

While different in personality, Adams and McGuinness share the same rock-solid conviction in the correctness of the Irish republican cause, be it achieved through exclusively political or violent means, or a combination of both. The self-claimed purity tradition is central to their narrative for Sinn Féin and the IRA. These republicans trace a direct line of succession from the 1916 Easter Rising right through to their own political and military organisations. The sequence of historical events is arranged to provide a narrative for republican theology.

In this traditional republican story Sinn Féin has inherited the legitimacy of the 1916 rebels. When the majority of Sinn Féin elected representatives backed the 1921 peace treaty with Britain, the party's rejectionist minority became—in republican eyes—the legitimate government in Ireland. The reformers had sold out, sullied the noble cause with their acceptance of a compromise deal that brought something less than an independent Irish Republic encompassing all of the island of Ireland.

The self-appointed authority was passed to the IRA in 1938 and then inherited by the Provisional movement at its foundation in late 1969. Subscribers to this interpretation of Irish history are the purists, those who never deviate, those who never surrender to reformism. They draw inspiration from their direct chain of legitimacy linking Easter 1916 to the Provisionals in 1969.

McGuinness and Adams understood this storyline; they lived it; they preached it. But that devotion to tradition has not prevented them from embarking upon a course of action which would lead Irish republicanism into the biggest compromises, u-turns and concessions of its near century-old tradition. Their journey would by the summer of 2005 see an end of the IRA as an active paramilitary organisation.

Adams and McGuinness started out their careers in the republican movement as men from the militant tradition. Republicans have never been immune to the suffering that their actions inflicted on their own community and on their opponents. But those considerations did little to bring an early end to the violence. One IRA man recalled a prison lecture given in 1973 by Gerry Adams, warning that their war might not have a speedy conclusion:

Adams asked: 'Does anybody here think this war will be over in two years?' There were no takers for that. 'Does anybody think this war will be over in ten years?' No. 'Does anybody think this war's going to be over in twenty years?' Well, we were all getting a bit worried at this stage! . . . He was very much aware that this was a long haul.[3]

Despite this bleak assessment, by the end of the 1970s, both Adams and McGuinness realised that violence alone would not lead to fulfilment of the republican objective of a united Ireland. They were adamant that the republican movement would not be defeated. There would be no surrender. The alternative strategy has been based on the rejuvenation of Sinn Féin, the long-time idle political wing of the Irish Republican Army.

Sinn Féin willingly entered a political deep freeze in 1926. The party was to remain in the wilderness until the early 1980s when, under the leadership of Gerry Adams, modern militant republicans commenced what this book calls their 'era of pragmatism'. The new direction was driven by what a close associate of Adams categorised 'the principle of success'—and he unashamedly defined 'success' as 'the principle that rises above all other principles'.

In seeking to attain this success, Gerry Adams has forced huge change on his organisation, or compromise and concession, as internal critics of his would claim. But whatever description is used, the outcome is the same—over the past two decades, the rulebook of Irish republicanism has been fundamentally rewritten. The trade-off has been between a position of principle combined with isolation or opting for pragmatism married to political success. In the 'era of pragmatism', the Adams leadership ensured which choice was made.

One hundred years after the formation of the original Sinn Féin in 1905, today the party is led by a man who has emerged as an astute political leader. Gerry Adams has seen off all internal—and potentially bloody—challenges to the compromises that he has promoted within republicanism. In the process, Adams has moved Sinn Féin into the lead role in Northern Ireland and positioned his party as a self-styled radical voice of the disaffected in the Irish Republic.

Adams and Sinn Féin have emerged in an era where the policy and ideological distinctions between the main Irish political parties have blurred and where most political figureheads tend to display managerial rather than leadership qualities. There is an enormous contrast between this category of everyday politician and a man who for the past decade has been publicly associated with peacemaking.

Adams has several qualities that have served his party well—in particular, charisma and a whiff of sulphur. Charisma can be an overplayed political quality generally attributed to any party leader who makes even a minimum connection with the public. But whatever the quality that allows political leaders to win sway over not only their own followers but also the middle ground of voters, there is considerable evidence to conclude that Gerry Adams has that quality. 'He has the charisma of a pop star. When you walk with Gerry Adams down any street in Ireland, people flock over to talk to him, to shake his hand,' Aengus Ó Snodaigh, who was elected to Dáil Éireann in 2002, said.[4]

Opinion poll data has continued to show that the peace process has served Adams well on both sides of the border. A *Belfast Telegraph*/BBC survey in 2003 indicated that 93 per cent of respondents in Northern Ireland who backed Sinn Féin believed Adams was performing either very well or fairly well. Two years later, that assessment level declined marginally to 88 per cent. It was a very good result especially as the 2005 poll had been undertaken in the aftermath of the failed devolution talks, the Northern Bank robbery and the murder of Belfast man Robert McCartney.

The years of the IRA's military campaign from 1969 until the mid-1990s provided ample opportunities for the development of a 'republican versus the world' attitude. But the mindset did not disappear with the peace process era. A series of events towards the end of 2004 and into 2005 once more allowed republicans to position themselves as victims, with little acceptance that the power to settle matters often rests within their own grasp.

Republicans have long thrived on a sense of oppression, and many still do. So long as this community sees itself as the oppressed—by either, as they put it, the rejectionist British government or the unionists who do not want Fenians about the place—this community will continue to exist and thrive.

For over 25 years, the IRA was bombing and shooting on an almost daily basis. There was, not unsurprisingly, a very hostile relationship between republicans and the policing authorities, north and south of the border. Claims of police harassment were commonplace and republicans are still quick to air their grievances, as Gerry Adams recalled:

People were vilified. A friend of mine who lived in the Cooley Mountains allowed me put a mobile house on his land. The guy was vilified for it. He got Special Branch attention just because he was associated with me. If a young person became involved with the party, the Branch were at their workplace or around talking to their father. It wasn't socially acceptable. And it was always harder to be a republican in the south.[5]

The homes of republican activists and the homes of their family members were frequently raided by the authorities. Aengus Ó Snodaigh had already moved out of his family home in Sandymount in Dublin in 1985 when gardaí raided his parents' house. 'They took away my address book from when I was in secondary school. And they visited every single person listed in that address book, all my school friends, and they asked them about their connections with me.'[6]

Such events cemented the republican worldview of 'them and us' while also strengthening the internal ties within Sinn Féin, as Ó Snodaigh recalled:

It wasn't difficult because you had the conviction of your belief. But you did become insular. You drank in your own company. We all supported each other. So although we couldn't get venues in Dublin for things like fundraisers there was one venue available to use on Wexford Street [and] all republicans from Dublin went there. We had a little community all of itself.[7]

The republican ability to use attack as a form of defence was evident more recently during the 2005 Garda investigation into money laundering which involved known republicans and those sympathetic to Sinn Féin. The houses of known republicans were targeted and several Sinn Féin members were questioned. The scale of the operation and the money seized surprised many people while claims that Northern Bank notes may have been included in the cash discovered only added to the intrigue. But the initial response of Sinn Féin was to accuse the Garda Síochána of 'politically-motivated harassment'.

The republican community—encompassing both Sinn Féin and the IRA—has always been both sophisticated and highly disciplined. The complex relationship between the two interlinked parts of this community has long been defined by secrecy. Significant membership overlap exists at leadership and grassroots level. The shared objective is the creation of a united and socialist Ireland. The use of violence to achieve this ultimate republican goal has never been an obstacle, and has been the dominant theme for most of the last 40 years.

The exclusion of republicans from the political mainstream throughout the 1970s and 1980s helped to develop an exceptionally strong community spirit within Irish republicanism. With governmental policy driven by a desire to marginalise Sinn Féin and the IRA—because of their support for violence—these organisations existed in a world outside the normal political, and democratic, system.

In late 1983, the Irish government discussed the possibility of proscribing Sinn Féin on account of its role as the political wing of the IRA. The option of a ban was examined after a bloody gunbattle in the Irish Republic had concluded the IRA's kidnapping of supermarket boss Don Tidey, and a garda and an army officer had been shot dead. The following day, the IRA was responsible for a massive car bombing outside Harrods department store in central London, which left five people dead, and another 91 injured.

The ban was not pursued partly on the grounds that it would have provided the republican movement with a propaganda boost while Sinn Féin would only have re-emerged under a different name. The 'them versus us' culture so central to the success of modern republicanism would simply have been even further reinforced, as was seen in the aftermath of the Northern Bank robbery and the murder of Robert McCartney.

Those latter controversies certainly hit Adams's ratings in the Republic as indicated by an opinion poll in *The Irish Times* in early 2005 but the Sinn Féin leader still had overwhelming backing among supporters of his party. Moreover, support for Sinn Féin itself remained remarkably solid in the first opinion polls after the controversies of late 2004 and early 2005. The strength of the Sinn Féin leadership team must take some credit for this performance, with Adams still by far the party's main electoral asset.

There is also more than a whiff of sulphur about the Sinn Féin president. This is both an asset and a liability. There can be no doubt that some people are attracted by this reality. In an era of blandness in political leaders, Adams represents danger, but in the post-IRA ceasefire, post-decommissioning environment it has been presented as controlled danger.

In the summer of 1983, when addressing his supporters at a republican commemoration, Gerry Adams met with resounding endorsement when he saluted those present as his 'fellow gunmen and gunwomen'. This association—denied or otherwise—remains a difficulty for a majority of Irish voters of a certain age. These are the people who clearly recall bombings and shootings sponsored by the IRA.

But for many younger people it is a historical reality that they treat as such while determining their voting choice on contemporary realities, most clearly defined since 1994 by peacemaking.

Opponents of the Sinn Féin president have attempted to counter the apparent peace aura surrounding Adams. Michael McDowell, the Progressive Democrat Minister for Justice, has alleged that Sinn Féin has 'deep and ongoing links to criminality.' The party was, according to McDowell, 'morally unclean.'[8] The revelations in the aftermath of the Northern Bank robbery in December 2004 were the strongest indications that Sinn Féin and the IRA—or at least some members of the two sides of the republican movement—were pursuing a strategy beyond the peace process.

In early 2005, Adams, along with Martin McGuinness and Martin Ferris from Kerry, were named by McDowell as IRA Army Council members. The three men, all long-time republican activists, denied the allegation, saying: 'We want to state categorically that we are not members of the IRA or its Army Council.'

Taoiseach Bertie Ahern offered a somewhat different interpretation from his justice minister saying that he 'assumed' Adams had been a member of the IRA but later remarking, 'I don't know who is on the army council. I was never at one of the meetings.'[9] In the days prior to the 28 July statement from the IRA, it was reported that Adams, McGuinness and Ferris had resigned from the IRA Army Council to be replaced by supporters with no strong attachment to Sinn Féin.

Both McGuinness and Ferris have admitted to having been IRA members in the past but Adams stands apart. He has long denied ever being a member of the Provisional IRA. The issue is raised periodically but the answer is always the same: he is president of Sinn Féin and has never been a member of the IRA.

The denials are difficult to comprehend given Adams's republican career. He came to prominence in republican circles in Belfast in the late 1960s although his family had long-established IRA connections. After the split in the republican movement in 1969–70, Adams sided with the newly established Provisional movement.

His home area of Ballymurphy was one of the PIRA's strongholds in Belfast. The organisation pioneered the use of the car bomb during this time. He quickly moved into a position of influence. In the summer of 1972, the 23-year-old was released from custody to join an IRA negotiating team that was travelling to London for talks with the British government. The request for Adams's release came from the IRA, which would hardly have pursued the issue for an individual lacking seniority, not to mind someone outside its own ranks.

Thirty years later, Dolours Price, who was convicted of involvement in the planting of IRA bombs in London, described Adams as her 'commanding officer' in the mid-1970s. There was ruthlessness on all sides. Adams is said to have ordered the shooting dead of Jean McConville, a widowed mother, who was suspected by the IRA of passing information to the British. It is an allegation that Adams strongly denied.

While in prison in the 1970s, Adams wrote occasional articles for *An Phoblacht* under the pseudonym 'Brownie'. Writing in May 1976, Brownie admitted, 'Rightly or wrongly, I am an IRA Volunteer and, rightly or wrongly, I take a course of action as a means to bringing about a situation in which I believe the people of my country will prosper. The course I take involves the use of physical force.'[10] This would appear to be the nearest Adams has ever come to admitting in public that he was a member of the IRA.

Few of his colleagues actually believe his IRA denials. 'The initial reason for denying membership was simply to make it possible for people to talk to us. But at this stage if he admitted being in the IRA the issue wouldn't end there. If he was to change his story now there would be the inevitable questions: when were you a member, where were you involved and what were you involved in? The pressure on him would be relentless,' one of Adams's advisors privately admitted to the author.

The denials, however, are made all the more ludicrous as many senior republicans within Adams's tightly knit circle have admitted to their membership of the IRA. Leading republicans like Martin McGuinness, Danny Morrison and, indeed, Adams's own press officer, Richard McAuley, have all openly said that they were members of the IRA. But Adams continues to insist that he was not.

Adams has gone to great lengths to dissociate himself from IRA membership, even getting his legal representatives to write to *The Irish Times* in 1983 after an article described him as vice-president of the IRA. The description in the article was, according to the lawyers, a libel, which had 'rendered our client's prestige and integrity in doubt and diminished the pristine temper of his political character'.

Within his own movement Adams commands almost unswerving support and inspires deep loyalty. But to the wider public—and those who have switched their voting allegiance to Sinn Féin—Adams offers an attractive form of political authority. He is the strong leader. He has the quality of decisiveness—the fact that he has never held governmental office, or has never had to make the policy choices inevitable in office, appears to matter little with younger voters. This is especially so when Adams can trade on a résumé that boasts a crucial role in taking the gun out of Irish politics.

Alongside his role in the peace process, Adams has also benefited from the emergence of celebrity culture. Through the medium of rolling 24-hour television news, several Sinn Féin leaders have acquired national and international name recognition. In particular, Gerry Adams and Martin McGuinness are now political celebrities. More importantly for the advancement of Sinn Féin, this recognition has been acquired against the backdrop of the peace process in Northern Ireland. Despite their IRA pasts, Adams and McGuinness have for over a decade now been intrinsically linked in the public mind with the search for peace.

This association with the peace process has undoubtedly diminished what should be a significant negative for the republican leadership. Moreover, opinion poll evidence shows Sinn Féin performing well among the younger age groups and less well with those over 55 years, confirming that there is a correlation between the voter attractiveness of Adams and McGuinness and their links to either past violence or current peacemaking.

The peace process era and the publicity generated for republicans helped the electoral emergence of contemporary Sinn Féin. A party with a handful of seats in Dáil Éireann has been debated and discussed in a manner well out of proportion to its electoral or political size. This situation is unlikely to change even with the end to the IRA's armed campaign and the destruction of its arsenal of weaponry. This increased support for Sinn Féin, on both sides of the border, has met with strong resistance from the party's political opponents.

Several media outlets have been openly hostile, especially in recent times in light of the possibility that Sinn Féin might be a future coalition partner for Fianna Fáil. But just as the party in a way drew strength from the censorship of the Republic's Section 31 broadcasting ban, Sinn Féin representatives appear to thrive on the elevated role afforded them, as Martin McGuinness's remarks about the *Sunday Independent*, the biggest-selling broadsheet newspaper, typify:

I gave up buying the *Sunday Independent* many years ago. I think their vitriolic articles, full of bile, switch people off. Some people may be influenced by the *Sunday Independent* but clearly there are growing numbers of people on this island who are not going to have their politics dictated to them by journalists and columnists who are anti-republican.[11]

Few political leaders control their parties in quite the same manner in which Gerry Adams has presided over Sinn Féin since he assumed the position of party president in 1983. Adams and his kitchen cabinet of key advisers dominate supremely. They cemented control of the IRA in the late 1970s and re-launched Sinn Féin in the aftermath of the 1981 hunger strikes.

None of Adams's predecessors could have introduced the radical changes he has sponsored. This position of total strength is matched by the public persona of the man, who, regardless of how often he has denied being a member of the IRA, was for three decades universally recognised as the leader of contemporary physical force republicanism in Ireland. From the doorsteps of west Dublin to the dining halls in Washington, Adams is the star attraction. In political leadership terms he has box office appeal, and this is fully in the knowledge of his involvement with the IRA and its campaign of violence.

Adams has pursued a strategy that has fundamentally altered the relationship between Sinn Féin and the IRA. With the exception of a brief flirtation with the ballot box in the 1950s, Sinn Féin kept out of electoral politics. The party was, in effect, the poor relation within the republican family, as the IRA and its campaign of violence was given priority. Indeed, in describing Sinn Féin in the 1960s and early 1970s, Adams openly admitted that the party was 'very much the very, very poor second cousin.'[12]

The Adams leadership, however, was convinced of the need for political action to run parallel with a military campaign, although there was no coherent plan indicating the direction republicans would travel. 'I would be telling lies if I tried to give myself powers of vision which saw us precisely where we are today. Not at all. No, I didn't,' Adams said.[13]

Pragmatism has been the defining characteristic of the modern republican movement as its leaders have attempted to redirect their supporters away from physical force action into political activism. They have combined pragmatism with an uncanny ability to respond swiftly to unlikely events. In 1981, the hunger strikes—coupled with the electoral successes of prisoner candidates in Northern Ireland and the Irish Republic—confirmed the leadership's belief that their movement needed to operate a dual strategy of politics and violence. Whatever about past republican doctrine, a pragmatic response was pushed as the only correct policy.

In the 1980s, the leadership around Gerry Adams and Martin McGuinness used their influential positions within the IRA to redirect the organisation's political wing, giving Sinn Féin a more prominent role within the republican movement. But even still there was clarity about the allocation of power between the military and political sides of this organisation—the IRA was the dominant partner.

By the mid-1990s, the balance in the relationship had tipped in favour of Sinn Féin. The Adams-led strategy has seen Sinn Féin emerge as the dominant force in the republican movement, as, especially since its 1994 ceasefire, the role of the IRA was minimised and marginalised.

Since the mid-1980s, there has been a subtle but significant reorientation of Sinn Féin's *raison d'être*. At the party's 1982 Ard Fheis, the Sinn Féin mission was clearly laid out: 'the complete overthrow of British rule in Ireland and the establishment of a democratic, socialist republic based on the Proclamation of 1916.'

Today the party still seeks British withdrawal from Northern Ireland. However, by signing up to the principles in the Belfast Agreement, Gerry Adams and his supporters have accepted that that process must be achieved by peaceful methods. The consent principle, which is central to the 1998 Belfast Agreement, necessitates the agreement of a majority of the people in Northern Ireland for constitutional change.

Under the leadership of Gerry Adams, Sinn Féin has successfully developed its all-Ireland agenda although politically this has required playing something of a 'two-card trick'. In the Irish Republic, the party has tended since 1986 to stress its interest in economic and social issues, while in Northern Ireland the constitutional question dominates the party's agenda. In many ways, this is logical political positioning in response to the different priorities of the respective Sinn Féin constituencies, north and south of the border.

For generations of republicans, politics was a grubby business. Yet, participating in elections was the first step advocated by Adams and his supporters—the second was ending the 60-year-old policy of refusing to take the seats won in the parliament in the Irish Republic. This was a direction that internal critics saw as the first Adams-sponsored sell-out.

A former colleague, Ruairí Ó Bradaigh, who walked away in 1986, smelt pragmatism and compromise.

The Sinn Féin attitude since 1922 was not to accept the two partition parliaments—in Belfast and in Dublin—but in 1986 the Provisionals started out on their reformist road. These people can now hardly call themselves Sinn Féin or claim to be the traditional republican movement of history which was seeking a British disengagement for Ireland and Irish national independence.[14]

The 'era of pragmatism' was dominated by secret talks that had been ongoing since the mid-1980s. The separate discussions between republican leaders and representatives of the government in Dublin and the nationalist Social Democratic and Labour Party (SDLP) have had huge consequences for the cause of Irish republicanism.

The Anglo-Irish Agreement in 1985 provided the republican movement with both linguistic and theoretical challenges. The agreement showed that the British government was prepared to acknowledge the legitimacy of Irish nationalism. The Irish government argued that the British were now neutral participants in the Irish question.

But at that time republicans were still using a language lumbered by history. They talked about the partitionist parliament at Leinster House, about British imperialism and about the necessity for a fixed timetable for British withdrawal. It took republicans time to realise that certain words and language were charged in a very political way. The confidential dialogue between the Irish government and leaders of the IRA spawned almost six years of debate on these fundamental principles.

The language, context and ideology of militant republicanism underwent a transformation not experienced since the peace talks in London in 1921. The August 1994 IRA ceasefire was the first tangible sign that the leaders of the modern militant republican tradition were bringing their movement on a journey involving massive compromise and concession.

In pursuing the contemporary peace process and preventing a significant schism within their ranks, Gerry Adams and Martin McGuinness have emerged as the two most important Irish republicans since Pádraig Pearse, Michael Collins and Eamon de Valera. They have led the modern militant republican movement along a path that initially straddled politics and violence to a point where the political would seem to have emerged triumphant.

The Adams–McGuinness leadership considers the 1998 Belfast Agreement as but a staging post in the republican movement's ultimate ambition to end the partition of Ireland. But what they define as a 'United Ireland' is today no longer clear. Certainly Irish unity remains their central aspiration but it is one that will have to be achieved without violence. The ending of militant republicanism may well be their—not inconsiderable—historical achievement, although the fact that violence continued for so many years after 1969 is also part of their mark on Irish history.

And, yet, it is obvious that physical force republicans have failed to achieve their objectives. They have not secured British withdrawal from Northern Ireland. They have not won a united Ireland. The partition of Ireland remains very much in place, copper-fastened by republican acceptance of the will of the majority in Northern Ireland to determine the future constitutional status of all of Ireland.

The days of physical force republicanism would appear to be over but it may be too early to say they are at an end. The ceasefire in August 1994 promised 'a complete cessation of military operations.' The military campaign may have been closed down but the involvement of the IRA, and some of its members, in illegal activities persisted.

The IRA ceasefire was originally called in August 1994, ended in February 1996 but was reinstated in July 1997. IRA activity declined significantly after the mid-1990s with few killings directly attributed to the organisation and a decline in sanctioned beatings and assaults. But the IRA did not cease to exist. Despite its ceasefire the organisation was not dormant. The paramilitary organisation was active on several fronts in Northern Ireland, including murder, beatings and revenue generation. In addition, there were controversies associated with the IRA including the case of the so-called 'Colombia Three'.

In late 2004, the Independent Monitoring Commission, established by the British and Irish governments to monitor paramilitary activity in Northern Ireland, noted: 'we saw no signs of the PIRA winding down its capability.' Recruitment of new members was said to be continuing, although the numbers were small. Some low-level training had been undertaken while intelligence gathering persisted. Moreover, as will be discussed in a later chapter, the IRA, or senior elements within the organisation, continued to fundraise.

The period since the 1994 ceasefire has been defined by Sinn Féin's slow and often torturous movement along the road from an anti-system grouping on the margins of political life in Ireland to a fledgling participant in the democratic process. No other political party in Europe has undergone such a radical overhaul of its basic principles, not even the former communist parties in central and eastern Europe that transformed themselves into social democratic entities in the aftermath of the fall of the Soviet bloc.

The development of Sinn Féin and the political rise of Gerry Adams present a unique scenario for democracy in Ireland. Indeed, nowhere else in the democratic western world has a political party taken its seats in parliament with the widespread knowledge that outside the walls of that same parliamentary building there was a private army at its disposal.

Sinn Féin presents itself as a radical left-wing alternative to the mainstream political parties in Ireland. But where has this party come from? What does it stand for today? Who are the people driving this project, and who are the people they represent? The answers to these questions will have a significant bearing on the future direction of politics in Ireland as Sinn Féin positions itself to govern in both parts of the island.

In getting from the barricades to the ballot box, the republican movement has made dramatic concessions and diluted so much previously rigid theological dogma. Today Gerry Adams finds himself in a position not dissimilar to that faced by Eamon de Valera back in 1926. De Valera was unable to convince enough of his colleagues in Sinn Féin to back his decision to recognise the institutions established under the 1921 Anglo-Irish Treaty that formally divided Ireland into two separate parts. When Sinn Féin rejected the idea of moving into parliamentary politics, de Valera left to form a new party, Fianna Fáil.

Gerry Adams has, in a way, gone back into republican history in order to bring his party forward. The 'era of pragmatism' has so far brought considerable success for Sinn Féin, whatever one's opinion of the morality of the IRA campaign and its continuation long after many senior republicans had accepted that they had reached a military stalemate in their war with the British.

In early 2005, Gerry Adams wrote to Sinn Féin activists to mark the start of the party's centenary year. But Adams paid no tribute to Arthur Griffith, the party's founding father. With allegations of serious criminality linked to modern republicanism, it is worth recalling that Griffith had little interest in monetary gain. These people had little need for foreign holding companies or cash stuffed into holdalls. Rather, they had their beliefs.

The divergence between the party now led by Gerry Adams and the Sinn Féin of 1905–1916 is huge. Adams and his supporters claim the Sinn Féin inheritance but it is a selective historical legacy. Modern republicans recall the 1916 Rising and the Proclamation. But few Sinn Féin supporters acknowledge that their party's formation is rooted in a monarchy-type solution to Irish independence. Little attention is now paid to Sinn Féin monarchy proposals or, indeed, the party's non-involvement in the 1916 rebellion. Moreover, in the long list of Sinn Féin heroes, many names have been erased, including that of the party's first ideological guru, Arthur Griffith.

But then that is not unsurprising, as the Sinn Féin brand has had a varied and contradictory life over the past 100 years. In his overview of Irish political parties, Maurice Manning observed that between 1905 and 1926 there were at least four successive parties bearing the name Sinn Féin. Another party trading under the Sinn Féin banner may also be added to Manning's list following on from the divisions within the republican movement in 1969–70 that produced Provisional Sinn Féin and Provisional IRA, the organisations that evolved into those today associated with Gerry Adams and Martin McGuinness.

The first Sinn Féin—Monarchical (1905–1917)—was the party associated with the writings of Arthur Griffith who attempted to shape a workable political programme and socioeconomic policy that could peacefully deliver Irish independence from Britain. The second Sinn Féin —Separatist (1917–22)—was the party that emerged after the Easter 1916 Rising and which was closely linked with militant republicanism and the decision to bypass British rule in Ireland.

The tone and the direction of the Sinn Féin party shifted significantly from this time onwards. The name of Griffith's organisation was retained but this was for all intents and purposes a new political entity. The party was more republican in its outlook; the idea for a dual monarchy was sidelined, while the militant side of the separatist movement was working to ensure that its nascent political wing delivered a coordinated message. The subsequent history of Sinn Féin would time and time again see the party's direction being determined by an agenda set by military men.

The second Sinn Féin was in a sense wound up in the latter half of 1922. The doors were closed on the party's head office in Dublin and the warring parties went their separate ways. The third Sinn Féin— Republican (1922–1926)—was the group associated with Eamon de Valera who rejected the 1921 Anglo-Irish Treaty and who opposed the new Irish Free State, politically and, for a time, violently.

The fourth Sinn Féin—Isolationist (1926–1969)—went through various organisational and ideological shifts but always maintained its distance from the institutions established under the 1921 Treaty.

If the split of 1922 checked Sinn Féin's dominant political role in Ireland, the party was consigned to the fringes of Irish political life after the 1926 split which gave birth to Fianna Fáil. Those who remained with

Sinn Féin after the 1926 split were the purists, the diehards, those who refused any compromise on what republicans had proclaimed at Easter 1916. They were an irrelevance to mainstream Irish life. Seventy years would pass before Sinn Féin would tackle its self-imposed strategic time warp. The fifth Sinn Féin—Militarist (1970–today)—was the party that gave political support to the Provisional IRA after the contemporary conflict started in Northern Ireland in 1969.

This fifth-generation party has taken the lead in marking what its members have called 'Céad Bliain Sinn Féin'. In January 2005, Adams addressed a gathering of his supporters in the Mansion House in Dublin. 'Over the past century Sinn Féin has been an idea, a name, a federation of political societies, a national independence movement, a republican campaigning organisation,' Adams declared. What he failed to say was that Sinn Féin is a borrowed term, used and abused by its various owners over the last century for their own particular political purposes.

In truth, Griffith's ideal gave birth to all the main political parties in Leinster House today, directly to Fianna Fáil and Fine Gael; the Progressive Democrats are once-removed cousins, while even Labour has a connection after its 1999 merger with Democratic Left, a party with roots in the 1969–70 republican split. So nobody, and no party, has a monopoly on the legacy of 1905.

It is not that long ago that Adams remarked: 'the strength and character of any guerrilla army is to be found in the calibre of the men and women who make it up. And the calibre of IRA Volunteers is extraordinary.'[15]

Cementing the Sinn Féin hegemony within the republican movement has meant that the Adams leadership has again and again tested the resolve of these men and women. The advancement of the Sinn Féin peace strategy has effectively usurped the IRA, from the 1986 decision to accept the legitimacy of the parliament of the Irish Republic through to the 1994 ceasefire and on to the decision in late 2001 to commence a process of decommissioning of IRA arms.

When Adams addressed the IRA in April 2005, he was again seeking to test its members' 'strength and character' for he was effectively asking the IRA to 'go away'.

In the past I have defended the right of the IRA to engage in armed struggle. I did so because there was no alternative for those who would not bend the knee, or turn a blind eye to oppression, or for those who wanted a national republic.

Now there is an alternative. I have clearly set out my view of what that alternative is. The way forward is by building political support for republican and democratic objectives across Ireland and by winning support for these goals internationally.

I want to use this occasion therefore to appeal to the leadership of Óglaigh na hÉireann to fully embrace and accept this alternative. Can you take courageous initiatives which will achieve your aims by purely political and democratic activity?

A process of consultations between the leadership grouping and republican activists was undertaken throughout May and June, culminating in the historic IRA statement issued on 28 July 2005.

The outcome of our consultations show [*sic*] very strong support among IRA volunteers for the Sinn Féin peace strategy. [...] They and friends of Irish unity through the world want to see the full implementation of the Good Friday Agreement [...] It is the responsibility of all volunteers to show leadership, determination and courage. We are very mindful of the sacrifices of our patriotic dead, those who went to jail, volunteers, their families and the wider republican base. We reiterate our view that the armed struggle was entirely legitimate.

The traditional republican demands were, as always, reiterated in the IRA statement, although the language used was far from uncompromising. In the 1970s, the IRA had predicted early victory over the British who were called upon to set a date for their disengagement from Northern Ireland. But in the summer of 2005, there was no talk of 'Brits Out'.

The IRA is fully committed to the goals of Irish unity and independence and to building the Republic outlined in the 1916 Proclamation. We call for maximum unity and effort by Irish republicans everywhere. We are confident that by working together Irish republicans can achieve our objectives. Every volunteer is aware of the import of the decision we have taken and all óglaigh are compelled to fully comply with these orders.

There is now an unprecedented opportunity to utilise the considerable energy and goodwill which there is for the peace process. This comprehensive series of unparalleled initiatives is our contribution to this and to the continued endeavours to bring about independence and unity for the people of Ireland.

With this statement in July 2005, the IRA signalled its intention to disappear. Individuals with republican associations who were found to be involved in robberies, racketeering, exiling and other criminal acts would no longer have the cloak of political motivation to justify their actions. Martin McGuinness in 2000 envisaged a continuing role for the IRA as a commemorative organisation, a type of old comrades' body.

At such events in future years, even the most diehard of supporters of the Adams strategy may come to accept that the IRA's 'war' did not achieve its basic objective. The British presence still exists in part of the island of Ireland. No date has been set for British withdrawal. There have been significant concessions to core republican dogma. Pragmatism has been the dominant trait in all the strategies pursued by Adams.

In 1986, the former Sinn Féin president—and a former IRA leader— Ruairí Ó Brádaigh warned Adams that, 'the armed struggle and sitting in parliaments are mutually exclusive.' In July 2005, Ó Brádaigh's prediction ultimately came true.

The IRA decision to end its armed campaign, along with the order to its members to dump arms, was the end of a process started in public at the 1986 Ard Fheis which overturned 60 years of republican theology. For almost two decades, Adams displayed little reverence for the sacred cows of the physical force republican tradition.

As the following chapters will argue, there has been little in the republican code which has not been sidestepped by Adams where necessary. Historical principles such as abstentionism and decommissioning—along with the very existence of the IRA itself—have been used as tactics in pursuit of the principle of Irish unity. Sinn Féin now follows an all-Ireland agenda, and, in its centenary year, the organisation is as close as at any time to being described as a normal political party.

The reality of Sinn Féin's electoral dominance north of the border and its growing political presence south of the border means that the party cannot be ignored. But any assessment of the role Sinn Féin may play in political life on the island of Ireland has to be balanced. A great deal of hype surrounds the party, while strong emotions—which are understandable given the linkage with the IRA—often distract from a realistic assessment of the party's policy positions and political prospects.

Standing back from the cut and thrust of contemporary events, the following pages explore the Sinn Féin story over the last one hundred years and examine what type of party is now led by Gerry Adams and Martin McGuinness.

Chapter 2 outlines why, in 2005, the Sinn Féin leadership needed to break a century-old link with the military wing of the republican movement.

Chapters 3 and 4 examine the historical evolution of Sinn Féin as the party moved through a number of different identities, up until the outbreak of the contemporary conflict in Northern Ireland. Chapter 5 examines the attitude of modern Sinn Féin—the party of Gerry Adams and Martin McGuinness—to political activism, and assesses the impact of the 1981 hunger strikes as the party moved to end its abstentionism policy in 1986. Chapter 6 traces the electoral arrival of Sinn Féin over the past two decades, while Chapter 7 explores the impact of the Irish peace process on the party's fortunes. The finances of Sinn Féin are examined in Chapter 8, while the final chapter assesses the policies pursued by the party as it looks to the prospect of governing in Northern Ireland and the Irish Republic at the same time.

THE IRA AND SINN FÉIN: INCOMPATIBLE PARTNERS

The buses started arriving from the middle of the afternoon. The hotel car park filled early. There were many hugs and handshakes inside the Holiday Inn in Letterkenny in County Donegal. Old friends reunited. The mood was a mixture of nostalgia and celebration. The faces had aged but the glint in many eyes showed that more than a touch of defiance lingered.

They had come to Letterkenny—almost 800 people—to mark the twentieth anniversary of an audacious republican prison escape. Gerry Kelly was the star attraction at the celebratory function. Kelly's IRA career was long and varied, taking in bombing campaigns in England and arrests in Amsterdam. He had garnered a reputation as an uncompromising republican, who in the peace-process era emerged as a strong backer of the Adams strategy. But on 23 September 1983 Kelly was one of a group of IRA men who forced their way out of the high-security Maze Prison, outside Belfast.

In all, 38 IRA prisoners escaped after having hijacked a lorry delivering food within the prison. During the operation, a prison officer died; initially it was believed that he died from stab wounds but a subsequent court case acquitted the IRA escapees of murder, leaving open the possibility that the officer's death could have been from a heart attack. Fifteen of the IRA escapees were quickly recaptured while another four were arrested within three days.

Kelly was frequently pressed into retelling the events of September 1983. Twenty years on from the break-out, the gathering of republican supporters heard first-hand accounts of how Kelly and his colleagues masterminded the prison escape. Over supper, they enjoyed a retelling of a story that has attained near mythical status in republican folklore and which is fondly described by republicans as 'the Great Escape'.

At the Donegal dinner dance, three IRA leaders involved in the 1983 prison escape gave a detailed talk on the break-out. Speaking with the assistance of a microphone from the top table, they used a screen to display maps of the prison complex, illustrating how exactly the break-out was planned and orchestrated. *An Phoblacht* later reported that Kelly and his IRA colleagues 'gave their account of the escape in an entertaining and self-deprecating manner that only enhanced the story.'[1]

Presentations were made to the families of IRA men involved in the escape who had died after 1983. A number of these escapees rejoined the IRA while on the run and—according to *An Phoblacht*—'died later on active service'. A special plaque was commissioned for these families with illustrations of a H-Block complex and a prison security tower.

For those involved in the 1983 prison escape, the social gathering in County Donegal was an opportunity to catch up with old friends, swap stories and share in the common solidarity that helps cement republicans in their tightly knit community. The normality of the anniversary dinner for republicans contrasted with the view elsewhere. One unionist politician said that the function was an example of republicans 'glorifying in acts of terrorism'.

As Sinn Féin moved towards greater political respectability, and as the 'era of pragmatism' extended beyond the 1986 abstentionism decision, there was an increasing realisation—although not necessarily acceptance—that broadening the Sinn Féin voter appeal would require less prominence for the party's militant republican associations. The logical outcome of the republican peace project required the end of the IRA, as Adams began to indicate more strongly in early 2005.

But even with the formal end of the IRA, events like the Letterkenny function, now marked as celebratory anniversaries, will continue. They are—and in a post-IRA world, will still be—very important for Sinn Féin as the party seeks to maintain a real sense of internal cohesion. These functions lock republicans into a shared sense of community, a world that embraces them all.

Gerry Kelly described the Letterkenny function as 'a massive event in republican history . . . It's a big calendar event for republicans and we are here to enjoy the night.' Every week, dozens of these types of events are held, allowing republicans recall their traditions, history and experiences. Throughout every year, republicans have an opportunity to participate in talks, ballad sessions, protests and sporting events. These functions and meetings are also important fundraisers for local Sinn

Féin organisations. Hardly any night of any week goes by without a fundraising event being organised somewhere in Ireland to benefit republican coffers. The classified section of *An Phoblacht* each week contains listings for these fundraisers, which help to pay for the activities of local branches of Sinn Féin.

The republican social calendar is also full of reunion functions to mark the whole range of IRA attacks and activities over the last 30 years. The Letterkenny Maze Escape dinner dance was not an exception. For example, in October 2004, a dinner dance was held to mark the thirtieth anniversary of the IRA escape from Portlaoise prison. Other key republican dates, including the deaths of IRA members killed 'on-active-service', are remembered in a similar way.

This busy calendar of events and commemorations helps unite republicans, but the marches, meetings and social functions also involve Sinn Féin in a celebration of the IRA's recent history. It is at these anniversary events that the near perfect symmetry between the military and political wings of the republican movement becomes most publicly evident. The presence of Adams or McGuinness at events celebrating the IRA and its members dispels any lingering doubts about the separateness of the two organisations. But Sinn Féin could not sustain this relationship with the IRA indefinitely in a post-ceasefire, post-Belfast Agreement era. The value of the link had a diminishing return as Adams and his colleagues finally accepted in early 2005.

Over the past three decades, Adams has sponsored a fundamental rewriting of republican core dogma, so much so that the modern Sinn Féin is a party of many contradictions. At the core of these contradictions has been the party's involvement in democratic political activism, while maintaining a close relationship with the clandestine IRA.

The IRA Army Council ruled the military wing of the republican movement. The Sinn Féin Ard Comhairle decided the tactical direction of the political section. There was considerable overlap between the two organisations although there was a lack of clarity about the exact demarcation line between Sinn Féin and the IRA. Nevertheless, senior members of Sinn Féin held membership of the IRA and this allowed them significant influence over the direction of the IRA.

The relationship went beyond organisational links, or so critics of the republican movement believed. The IRA had access to significant funds. A substantial amount of this income came from smuggling and other criminal activity, as is discussed in Chapter 8 where Sinn Féin's financial records are also examined. The extent to which illegal funds benefited republican political activism remains a matter of considerable dispute.

The Irish Minister for Justice, Michael McDowell, claimed Sinn Féin had 'deep and ongoing links' with criminal activities and was financed in part by the proceeds of IRA criminal involvements. Not unsurprisingly, Caoimhghín Ó Caolain—Sinn Féin's senior political representative in the Irish Republic—rejected the allegation as 'scurrilous slights' on the integrity of his party. Where the truth is found is difficult to determine as the republican movement is a tightly knit community marked by deep secrecy, although as long as Sinn Féin had IRA fingerprints, the party remained outside the democratic club.

The emergence of Sinn Féin as a political force in Northern Ireland and a growing political presence in the Irish Republic altered the internal dynamic within the republican movement. The Irish peace process generated a significant electoral dividend for Sinn Féin but the party's ability to develop was dependent upon a relatively acquiescent military wing.

Adams delivered an IRA ceasefire in August 1994 and, in July 1997, he secured a restoration of that original ceasefire which had broken down in February 1996. But in truth, the Sinn Féin peace agenda was not hampered by the continued existence of the IRA until late in 2004 and early in 2005 when the contractions of a political party having links to an illegal private army became a permanent impediment to progress.

In 1982, leading IRA man Brian Keenan wrote from Leicester Prison in England, 'We must never forsake action but the final war to win will be the savage war of peace.'[2] Two decades later, that very same 'savage war of peace' threatened to tear asunder the political project meticulously constructed by Adams and his supporters in both Sinn Féin and the IRA. The historic IRA decision in July 2005 had in reality a strong sense of inevitability about it.

As is discussed in later chapters, the peace process years have produced considerable political gains for the republican movement. Doors have opened that previously were firmly shut tight; votes have been cast where previously there was no mark made beside the name of a Sinn Féin candidate. Adams and McGuinness have gone from despised paramilitary outcasts to welcomed political figures. But the transition has not been a smooth one as a series of controversial events—all associated with the IRA—has repeatedly dogged the Sinn Féin transition into a purely democratic political party.

In June 1996, a group of IRA men set out to rob a post office in Adare in County Clare. Their operation led to the murder of Garda Jerry

McCabe. The IRA initially denied any involvement but Sinn Féin representatives would some years later find themselves arguing for the early release of the McCabe killers as part of a deal to achieve the full implementation of the Belfast Agreement.

In August 2001, three Irishmen were arrested at Bogotá's main airport as they stepped off an internal flight that had arrived from southern Colombia. All sorts of claims followed. Forensic tests were reported to have found traces of explosives and drugs on their clothing; they were also reported to have been teaching anti-government rebels to make bombs.

The three men had strong links to the republican movement but the IRA denied that their trip to Colombia, travelling on false passports, had received official sanction. Gerry Adams put immediate distance between the three men and his party. 'They were not there to represent Sinn Féin. I would have had to authorise such a project and I did not do so. Neither was I or anyone else asked,' Adams said.[3] But shortly afterwards it emerged that one of the men, Niall Connolly, was acting as Sinn Féin's representative in Cuba. The party responded by saying that the appointment had never gone through proper channels.

But it has not just been the activities of the IRA in a peace process environment that have caused problems. The words that emanated from the IRA leadership were at times contradictory and frequently did not help the republican cause. In 1998, just after the parties involved in the multi-party negotiations sealed the deal that was the Belfast Agreement with its commitment on arms, a spokesperson for the IRA bluntly declared, 'let us make it clear that there will be no decommissioning by the IRA.'[4]

Nevertheless, later that same year, the IRA established contact with the International Independent Commission on Decommissioning. Adams continued to maintain that his party's role was to use whatever influence it had to ensure that decommissioning took place, although few accepted the distance he sought to put between the two wings of the republican movement.

Even without IRA movement on arms, the Ulster Unionist Party decided to enter government with Sinn Féin in Northern Ireland in November 1999. Martin McGuinness and Bairbre de Brún were the two Sinn Féin ministerial nominees. But in the absence of serious progress on decommissioning, David Trimble resigned in February 2000 and the institutions were suspended. Three months later, the IRA promised to put its weapons completely and verifiably beyond use. The institutions were re-established. The first IRA move on decommissioning came in October 2001. A second act of decommissioning was confirmed in April 2002.

But the fragile institutional framework in Northern Ireland came unstuck once more in October 2002 with the allegations that a republican spy-ring was operating at Stormont. The bizarre episode was not enough to end Adams's commitment to the peace process. In April 2003, the IRA said, 'we are resolved to see the complete and final closure of the conflict. The IRA leadership is determined to ensure that our activities, disciplines and strategies will be consistent with this.'[5] Later that year, Adams said that Sinn Féin's position was 'one of total and absolute commitment to exclusively democratic and peaceful means of resolving differences.'[6]

Progress was, however, painstakingly slow. Despite several attempts to revive the political institutions, before and after the 2003 assembly elections, there was no advancement. Even the emergence of Ian Paisley's Democratic Unionist Party as the dominant force within unionism had little real impact either way. More negotiations broke down in late 2004, this time over the provision of photographic evidence of weapons decommissioning as well as the future intentions of the IRA.

The proposed deal had tantalisingly promised an end to the IRA but the organisation had not been acting as though it were about to go out of business. There had undoubtedly been a significant decrease in IRA military action as confirmed by the reports of the Independent Monitoring Commission in 2004 and 2005. Indeed, the IRA had all but ended its war against the British presence in Northern Ireland. As one leading republican figure put it to the author early in 2005, 'Even if the IRA wanted to go back to war, who would they fight, such has been the decrease in the British military presence on the streets?'

While the IRA retained the capacity to restart its campaign of violence, there was little support within the wider republican community for such action. Nevertheless, IRA violence continued to be a feature of the landscape in Northern Ireland. Shootings just short of murder, exiling people from Ireland and robberies had become the norm for the IRA in its post-ceasefire world.

There were over 1,200 so-called punishment attacks in the post-1995 period which were attributed to the IRA. These brutal attacks—which underlined the IRA's self-adopted role as judge, jury and near executioner—frequently left people crippled or limbless. One victim in 2004 was beaten by IRA men wielding pickaxe handles, after which he was shot nine times in the lower legs. It is impossible to find any political motive for such violence.

Indeed, little action undertaken in the IRA's name in recent years could have qualified as politically motivated violence. Shootings, beatings and exilings simply allowed republicans to cement control over certain areas. Some of the proceeds from robberies may have funded political campaigns but self-enrichment became the main motivation behind many of the activities of certain IRA figures. Personal gain was never what the IRA campaign was supposed to be about. The Adams leadership had long heaped praise on IRA members for their commitment and discipline. Successive Sinn Féin Ard Fheiseanna passed motions commending their military associates.

The massive contradiction at the heart of the post-Belfast Agreement republican movement—still maintaining a military organisation as a component of a political strategy—was dramatically exposed in late 2004.

On Sunday, 19 December, armed men abducted two employees of the Northern Bank along with members of their families. The hostages were warned that failure to comply with certain instructions would result in serious violence. Over the course of the following day, the two bank employees delivered cash to the robbers. After the heist, the men and their families were released.

Up to 20 gang members were involved in the operation that was planned and executed with military precision. The gang gained entry into one of the homes of the bank officials by pretending to be police officers.

The two bank officials were held separately and questioned in detail about security at the bank. They were ordered to behave normally at work the following day. To do otherwise would have met with swift and bloody consequences for their immediate family members. At six o'clock that evening, one of the officials walked out of the bank building with a holdall containing £1m in sterling notes. He walked a short distance to a street corner where the money was handed over.

To describe internal security at the bank as lax would be an understatement. The raiders had substantial knowledge about considerable security loopholes at the bank which were then exploited to the fullest possible extent. With their successful trial run completed, the gang proceeded with their audacious plan. Over the following two hours, the bank officials put more cash into plastic containers and wheeled their load out of the building on trolleys. They were met at the rear entrance by a white transit van which a few hours earlier had been driven across the border from the Irish Republic. The gang made two trips to the rear entrance of the Northern Bank headquarters without any suspicion being raised by bank security.

As news of the massive raid was digested, republican sources immediately insisted that the IRA was not responsible. 'We are dismissing any suggestion or allegation that we were involved,' the IRA declared on 23 December 2004. That same day, a Sinn Féin spokesperson told the media, 'Of course, Sinn Féin accepts what the IRA is saying, that it was not involved.' Over the Christmas period there were police raids on several houses in republican areas in Belfast. Gerry Adams was quick to criticise the police investigation, labelling the raids 'a clearly orchestrated effort by the securocrats in the British system who are intent on wrecking the peace process.'

Although nobody had been charged with the robbery, a few days into the New Year, PSNI Chief Constable Hugh Orde in the strongest terms identified the IRA as the chief suspect. 'On the basis of the investigating work we have done to date, the evidence we have collected, the information we have collected, the exhibits we have collected, and putting them all together and working through it, in my opinion the Provisional IRA were responsible for this crime, and all main lines of inquiry currently undertaken are in that,' Orde stated.

There was an angry response from the republican leadership. 'Hugh Orde's comments are nothing more than allegations and politically based allegations at that. He has not produced one scrap of evidence,' Martin McGuinness replied. The IRA issued a statement explicitly denying any involvement. 'The IRA has been accused of involvement in the recent Northern Bank robbery. We were not involved.'

Despite the lack of tangible evidence—and the failure to arrest and charge anyone in connection with the crime—the IRA denial was given less credence by the two governments than was Orde's assessment. On 9 January 2005, Taoiseach Bertie Ahern went as far as to suggest that senior Sinn Féin leaders must have been aware of what was planned. 'This was a Provisional IRA job. This was a job that would have been known to the leadership, this is a job that would have been known to the political leadership. That is my understanding,' Ahern concluded.

He went on, 'The thought that we were trying to negotiate a comprehensive deal that others, and perhaps others who were closely associated, were getting ready to have one of the biggest Christmas robberies that ever took place does nothing to help anybody's confidence.'[7]

Sinn Féin again denied the claims linking republicans to the bank heist. Adams reacted angrily to the suggestion that he was privy to the planning of the raid. 'If he [Ahern] believes that I was involved in a criminal conspiracy to rob, and that I withheld information, then he has a civic responsibility to make sure that I am subjected and Martin McGuinness is subjected to due process,' Adams said.

Senior republicans privately conceded that there was huge anger in Sinn Féin and IRA ranks. The failure to conclude a deal with the DUP in late 2004—compounded by Paisley's language of humiliation—had left Adams and McGuinness exposed, internally and externally. The offer from the IRA to disarm completely was considered of such historic consequence within the republican movement that failure to agree a final deal made many republicans question the Adams–McGuinness strategy. There was no serious challenge to their leadership but their assurances about unionism's commitment to cross-community power-sharing were now open to scrutiny.

There was also increased focus on just what the Adams–McGuinness strategy was seeking to achieve. The uncertainty over who carried out the Northern Bank robbery, and who knew about the operation, only added to the confused situation. 'Whoever robbed the Northern Bank didn't give a damn about the peace process, or give tw'penny about the work Gerry Adams and I have been involved in for the last 10 years,' Martin McGuinness said.[8] But if the two governments pointed the finger at the IRA, while Adams and McGuinness insisted that the IRA was not involved, the possibility was left open that the latter two republican leaders had been kept outside the loop. If this had been true, it would have been a sinister development within republicanism.

A further—and highly ambiguous—IRA statement warned the two governments not to 'underestimate the seriousness of the situation.' Some commentators took this statement as an implicit threat of a return to violence but it also signalled the deepening internal difficulties within the secretive organisation. It was not clear who was directing the IRA at this stage, and the military side of the republican movement appeared somewhat out of step with the political direction favoured by the Adams–McGuinness leadership axis.

There was little sympathy for the Northern Bank in republican circles. There were, however, questions about the motivation behind the lucrative raid. Information was sought on whether the action had official sanction, and the purpose for which the money was intended. There was great speculation about the latter issue, with everything from the creation of a retirement fund for some IRA men to the seed capital for an Adams bid for the presidency of the Irish Republic in 2011. Republicans were talking in private and comments were appearing on Internet websites. One entry on the Anthony McIntyre-organised Blanket website was a typical example.

I have been keeping a vague eye on this bank robbery business. I say 'vague' because to tell you the God's honest truth I've had it up to here with the goings on with Provisional Sinn Féin and the Provisional IRA (the latter being an Army I once proudly belonged to). Call me old fashioned if you like, but there used to be standards, codes of conduct, that sort of thing when I was a Volunteer. Robbing a bank, various methods, go in ask for the manager, tell him you were 'liberating funds on behalf of Óglaigh na hÉireann', that things go well so long as he did as you requested. That worked as soon as you showed him your 'credentials' tucked in waistband. Jump over the counter, announce who you were and do the job. These methods saved P O'Neill the bother of putting out a statement claiming responsibility. The 'liberated' funds would buy weapons, feed Volunteers on the run, help look after the families of those in gaol and keep the war machine ticking over ... The War is over, we are told. Guns paid for from those bank robberies are to be melted down, some already have been. So this 'big one' [the Northern Bank robbery] is not about buying guns, Provisional Volunteers are not on the run nor are they in prison (with the one or two embarrassing exceptions), so what is all this money needed for?[9]

The robbery was unprecedented in both its scale and audacity. The aftermath left the already troubled peace process reeling. Trust in the intentions of Adams and his colleagues plummeted in a manner not previously experienced. Murders, beatings and robberies had been attributed to the IRA since 1994 but the process had continued to edge forward. But planning for the theft of what would total £26.6m in sterling notes had to have taken place at a time when talks to normalise political life in Northern Ireland were under way. Criminality was now publicly elevated onto a par with decommissioning as a barrier to forward movement. As will be discussed in Chapter 8, the discovery of almost £3m in raids in the Irish Republic—some of which, it was alleged, was linked to the Northern Bank robbery—only added to the pressure on Adams.

Yet, whatever internal debates were under way—and probably also considerable internal recriminations—the Sinn Féin leadership continued to defend the wider movement. 'The IRA are not criminals, never were criminals, and in my opinion, never will be criminals,' McGuinness said. But the Irish and British governments preferred to accept the view of the International Monitoring Commission when it concluded that the robbery had been 'planned and undertaken' by the IRA.[10]

In a deliberate and coordinated move, Sinn Féin decided not to comment on—or offer any explanation of—the second IRA statement. 'The days of Sinn Féin interpretating IRA statements are over; they're gone. Our focus is on getting the Good Friday Agreement implemented. We're going to defend our democratic mandate against all-comers,' McGuinness said.[11] But the contradiction of having an illegal paramilitary organisation in a peace process environment was about to engulf Sinn Féin in a manner not previously experienced in the period since the first IRA ceasefire was called in August 1994.

On 30 January 2005, Belfast man Robert McCartney left a local gym where he had been lifting weights. The forklift truck driver was the father of two sons, aged two and four. He was planning to get married to their mother, his partner Bridgeen Hagans, later in the year. After his session in the gym, McCartney went for a drink in Magennis's bar in the Short Strand area in East Belfast.

The Short Strand is home to about 3,500 Catholics. Around 60,000 Protestants surround the enclave of red-bricked houses that is a republican heartland. The area gave birth to the Provisional IRA when the organisation first laid claim to be the protector of the besieged Catholic community in Northern Ireland. On 27 June 1970, a group of IRA men stood their ground in the Short Strand as a loyalist mob threatened to burn Catholics out of the area. One IRA man was shot dead in the gun battle that also claimed the lives of three loyalists. Over the following years, the Short Strand community gave IRA members shelter. Former IRA volunteer Anthony McIntyre recalled a local population that was 'tough, resilient and generous . . . These people were outstanding; their hospitality always something to be remembered.'[12]

There was a good crowd in Magennis's bar when Robert McCartney arrived for his drink. The bar was a favourite of republicans from Sinn Féin and the IRA. It was no different on 30 January, with a group that had just arrived back from a Bloody Sunday commemoration in Derry. According to one version of events, an IRA man accused McCartney of making a rude gesture to a woman in his circle. 'Do you know who I am?'

the IRA man is said to have asked.

McCartney knew the man and his reputation, but he refused to apologise, saying that he had done nothing wrong. A row followed. A knife was produced. Brendan Devine who was sitting with Robert McCartney had his throat slit. The mêlée continued out onto the street where McCartney was beaten and stabbed. He was left lying in a pool of his blood while the men responsible went back into the pub and oversaw a forensic operation of military precision. Doors were locked, the room was thoroughly cleaned, and CCTV tapes were removed. The people in the bar were warned to forget what they had seen and heard. All the while, Robert McCartney lay outside on the street, dying, just half a mile from his home.

Police officers woke Bridgeen Hagans at 1.20 a.m. Other members of the McCartney family were also contacted. They all rushed to the Royal Victoria Hospital where they were met by the news that their fiancé and brother had been anointed. Robert McCartney had been badly beaten and repeatedly stabbed. He died several hours later, shortly after eight o'clock in the morning.

Belfast is a relatively small city. The Short Strand is smaller still. It was, therefore, not long before the McCartneys were aware of what exactly had happened in Magennis's bar. The names of the people who had murdered their brother quickly spread. The men responsible for the stabbing, beating and clean-up operation all lived near the McCartney family. They were neighbours in the Short Strand. More importantly, they were members of the republican movement.

The murder of Robert McCartney was not unique. IRA members had been responsible for several bloody murders in the ceasefire years. Since the July 1997 ceasefire, about 20 people had been victims of the IRA. Most of these deaths involved Catholics who had fallen foul of leading republican hard men. These killings had nothing to do with the republican 'war' against the British presence on the island of Ireland. With the ending of full-scale military activity, but not an end to the IRA as an organisation equipped with weaponry, its members drifted in a variety of different activities. Many IRA men have traded on their association with the organisation for personal financial gain or enhanced local prominence.

The murder of Andy Kearney provided one example of the thuggery the republican leadership was prepared to tolerate. Three months after the Belfast Agreement was signed in April 1998, Kearney from Belfast intervened in a pub dispute when a senior IRA figure threatened a

mother and her son with violence. Kearney was 33 years of age and the
father of a new-born daughter. The row moved outside the pub. Punches
were thrown. Kearney got the better of the IRA man whose pride also
obviously took a bashing. Two weeks later, as Kearney lay in bed with his
infant daughter, the front door of his Belfast flat was broken down. A
gang of men overpowered him with chloroform before shooting him
three times in the leg. Kearney bled to death. Another man, Mark
Robinson, also met a similar bloody death, beaten with scaffolding poles
before being stabbed to death near his home in Derry in April 2001. He
also had fallen foul of a local IRA commander.

The British and Irish governments had chosen not to allow these and
other murders to derail the peace process. But by 2004 this stance was
becoming increasingly difficult to sustain. On 20 February 2004, four
masked men entered Kelly's Cellar, a bar in Belfast. The men were all
dressed in white forensic suits, balaclavas and surgical gloves. The
clothing was chosen to prevent contamination of a crime scene. The men
were clearly intent on confronting one man, Robert Tohill. He was
severely beaten and then dragged out onto the street where he was
bundled into a car. But some people in Kelly's Cellar had rung the police
on their mobile phones. A police car quickly arrived on the scene,
intercepted the kidnapper's vehicle and arrested those responsible. The
Irish and British governments accepted that the operation was planned
and undertaken by the IRA. Political sanctions on Sinn Féin followed but
the peace process trundled on.

What was obvious was that the IRA was killing—or trying to kill— its
own. There was no political motivation involved, but the governments in
Dublin and London generally turned a blind eye as they attempted to
bed down a lasting political framework in Northern Ireland. Whatever
about the attempted killing of Tohill, the murder of Robert McCartney
was different for two particular reasons—timing and the dead man's
siblings.

The period since the collapse of the political negotiations in early
December 2004 and the massive Northern Bank robbery left the Irish
and British exasperated with Adams and his colleagues. The peace
process had reached a defining moment with Sinn Féin and the IRA
under huge pressure to complete their transition from an anti-system
movement to a fully committed participant in democratic political life.

Sinn Féin was slow to appreciate the seriousness of the McCartney
murder or the extent to which it would engulf the party in the aftermath
of the collapsed political talks in December 2004 and the Northern Bank

robbery. Local Sinn Féin councillor Jim O'Donnell blamed a 'knife culture' for the death. Alex Maskey condemned the police for their reaction to rioting which followed attempts to search the homes of several suspects to the murder. The party's candidate in a by-election in early March in the Irish Republic unwittingly summed up the Sinn Féin reaction. 'Those who carried it out should take responsibility for their actions. People accept it was not organised by republicans; it was a drunken brawl in a pub which makes it all the more sadder that a family should lose someone because of drink,' Joe Reilly said.[13]

However, the murder outside Magennis's bar was not a pub brawl. It once more involved IRA men throwing their weight around, with many members of the republican community turning a blind eye to the event and to its consequences. But the sisters of Robert McCartney were not about to allow his death go unnoticed.

The McCartneys' greatest strength was their straightforward demand —justice. This had been for so long a core word in the Sinn Féin vocabulary.

> Go round to their houses and tell them to hand themselves in. We want them charged with murder. The two crucial ones, the one who did the murder and the one that got the knife, we want them done for murder, the rest can get a few years for grievous bodily harm . . . and the rest of them would probably get a few months for doing the clean up . . .[14]

The McCartneys became a focal point for discussions about the future direction of the republican movement. The manner in which the father of two, who voted for Sinn Féin, was murdered highlighted the massive contradictions in the post-ceasefire world inhabited by the republican movement.

The sisters knew their community and they knew their history. Catherine McCartney drew on her training as a history lecturer to condemn a movement that had strayed from its self-declared origins. 'Wolfe Tone and Henry Joy McCracken must now be turning in their graves,' she said.[15]

Sinn Féin made no attempt to contact the McCartney family, so, three weeks after the murder, they decided to approach Gerry Kelly, the senior republican figure who was also a Sinn Féin assembly representative for North Belfast. Kelly had little to offer the McCartneys, repeatedly responding to their many questions with, 'I can't answer that'. But the sisters were not fading away. Media interest in the McCartney case intensified. Adams made contact and arranged a meeting.

The Sinn Féin president was well aware of what had happened in Magennis's Bar. Many of those in the bar were closely associated with the republican movement, the IRA and Sinn Féin. But Adams did not reveal all he knew as the sisters told *Village* magazine in March 2005:

> We believed what he said because it was what he said on TV, that what had happened was insupportable. But we believe now . . . that he was coming to suss us out. Gerry Adams already had the names of all the people involved. He wanted to find out what we knew and what we didn't know. So, we were sitting here, giving names to him that he wasn't supposed to know and he was supposed to be going off to help, while in fact we believe now that he knew all along [who was involved]. There was one name we had and he said he didn't know who he was. Yeah, but we've seen a photo of [this person] standing shoulder to shoulder with him [Adams] at Joe Cahill's funeral. He was his bodyguard [Adams's bodyguard]. [This person] was the one who got rid of the knife.[16]

Several Sinn Féin activists had been enjoying a night out at Magennis's Bar on the evening Robert McCartney was murdered. The various groupings in the pub included two local election candidates. Their presence in the pub was slow to emerge but, on 30 January, Deirdre Hargey was among several Sinn Féin members 'suspended without prejudice' as the party started its own investigation. The identification of Sinn Féin figures like Hargey and another party election candidate, Cora Groogan, only increased the pressure on Adams to resolve the matter.

Representatives of the IRA also met with the family. 'They thought they were going to meet a bunch of hysterical women. They were gob smacked. One of them was sitting here, hyperventilating nearly. They said they were Army Council. One was from Belfast, and one was a Southerner,' the sisters recalled.[17] The meeting lasted for five-and-a-half hours but there was little to show from all the talking.

The IRA also suspended members but the meeting was notable for the solution offered—the McCartneys were told that the organisation was 'prepared to shoot those directly involved'. The family of the dead man declined the offer and when the IRA made public its offer, there was utter revulsion from all sides. A decision to extract revenge with further violence—and in the absence of genuine justice for those responsible—

was the hallmark of IRA policing, sentencing and punishing. Sinn Féin said that the offer was 'a huge mistake'. That there was confusion within republican ranks was all too evident.

In March 2005, the McCartneys took their campaign to the United States. The welcome that awaited them in Washington was in stark contrast to the frosty reception given to Sinn Féin. For the first time in several years, Gerry Adams found doors firmly closed. Along with President Bush, political figures like Senator Edward Kennedy—who had championed republicans in the post-ceasefire environment—felt it necessary to send a strong message to the Sinn Féin leadership. The cold-shouldering of Adams was as much symbolic as anything else, but the message was cleared delivered—the future in Northern Ireland had to be delivered without the IRA or IRA-related activities.

The association with the IRA has provided Sinn Féin with an added dimension, unique among all mainstream political parties in Ireland, north or south of the border. The link in the peace process era meant that Sinn Féin has been elevated to a political status well beyond its voter strength, a fact that has facilitated the party's electoral growth. Without the IRA, there would have been no peace process for Sinn Féin to become involved in, and without the peace process, the doors of government in Dublin, London and Washington would never have been opened to Sinn Féin and its leadership.

The peace process has been the party's principal calling card for well over a decade. The end of the IRA and the transition of the peace process into a political process in effect dilutes the importance of Sinn Féin. In such a scenario, the party is faced with the very real prospect of simply being a normal political party. There is no way of telling how Sinn Féin will develop without the obvious benefit that is the IRA's whiff of sulphur. The party will remain a political force in political life in Northern Ireland, but power south of the border necessitates a full commitment to democratic life. The Adams strategy—as discussed in subsequent chapters—has been defined by acute pragmatism, with all areas of republican strategy and thinking being considered in purely tactical terms, with the aspiration of Irish unity remaining the only principal objective of contemporary Sinn Féin.

THE BIRTH OF SINN FÉIN, 1905–1926

In April 1900, an elderly Queen Victoria arrived in Dublin, a city festooned with Union Jacks. The flag of the British Empire flew from buildings and lampposts throughout the capital city of Ireland, then a country ruled from London and presided over by a monarch in the sixty-second year of her reign. Palace officials let it be known that the visit was a private one, driven not by any political motivation but rather by a desire on the ailing queen's part for a 'change of air'.

This early twentieth-century 'spin' from Buckingham Palace cut little ice with a prolific journalist named Arthur Griffith who was emerging as a leading theorist behind a new strand of Irish nationalism. Griffith was unhappy not only with the ineffectual performance of the Irish Parliamentary Party (IPP), whose constitutional drive for devolved power for Ireland had delivered little, but he was also unconvinced that independence could be achieved by the military alternative favoured by the secretive Irish Republican Brotherhood (IRB).

Griffith had concluded that the majority of Irish people were not separatists and would not back a rigidly separatist policy. In his written output, he propagated a new vision for Irish nationalism which he believed offered the possibility of independence while maintaining the unity of the country. The Griffith vision was called 'Sinn Féin'.

Short in stature, fair-haired with sea-blue eyes, Arthur Griffith was somewhat elusive to those who frequented nationalist circles in Dublin in the early days of the twentieth century. But he garnered deep loyalty from a new class of nationalists, many of whom were galvanised into protest by the royal visit. They saw the monarch's presence in 1900 as a part of the British army's Boer War recruitment drive to attract Irishmen to their campaign in South Africa. Offence was also taken at the timing of the visit, which coincided with the 100-year anniversary of the British abolition of the last Irish parliament.

The mood of this small separatist group was not helped by the fact that to welcome Queen Victoria a Union Jack had been draped over the statue of Henry Grattan in Dublin city centre. Grattan had led the opposition to the ending of the Irish House of Commons in 1800. A century after that unsuccessful campaign, the monarch of Britain and Ireland came to visit Dublin. It was the third time Queen Victoria had travelled to Ireland. The first trip had been made in 1848 in the aftermath of the Great Irish Famine when the queen declared that while the sufferings of the Irish 'really were too terrible to think of', they were 'a terrible people'.[1]

These sentiments had been expressed in private after the monarch had left Ireland where she had received an enthusiastic welcome. Half a century later, Victoria was still on the throne but some in Ireland planned a less welcoming response to her latest Irish visit. Griffith allowed the pages of his newspaper, the *United Irishman*, to be used to attack the royal visit. Few punches were pulled as Victoria was labelled the 'Queen of the famines, of the pestilences, of the emigrant ships, of the levelled homesteads, of the dungeons and the gallows.'[2]

These sentiments were, however, not shared by very many of the people of Dublin who, whatever about their desire for greater independence and their nationalist spirit, lined the streets to greet the queen and her entourage. The monarch was obviously impressed and was prompted to revise the judgement she had reached after her 1848 visit. On her return to Britain in April 1900, Victoria wrote: 'I can never forget the really wild enthusiasm and affectionate loyalty displayed by all in Ireland, and shall ever retain a most grateful remembrance of this warm-hearted, sympathetic people.'[3]

The queen was, by April 1900, experiencing failing eyesight which—when combined with the protectiveness of her court officials—may explain her lack of reference to booing from boisterous nationalists who succeeded in tearing down some Union Jacks in central Dublin. But the protestors were in a clear minority and they failed to generate much heat with their actions. The uninspiring protest movement left its mark on Griffith. The next time, the nationalist response would be more vocal, better organised and would be underpinned by a clearly understandable policy prescription for achieving independence.

Within a year of her Irish visit, the reign of Queen Victoria ended. Upon her death, Britain, Ireland and the rest of the Empire got a new monarch. Edward VII hoped for a new relationship with Ireland. On 21

July 1903, huge and excited crowds greeted the king in Dublin. The *Cork Examiner* wrote: 'No sovereign visiting our shores ever met with anything like the hearty good will, the honest, unaffected welcome extended by the people of all classes . . . '[4] But newspaper articles also reported equally noisy protests.[5] Once more, the pen of Arthur Griffith was at work: 'To the Irish Nationalist the King is as foreign as the Akond of Swat, but, unlike that potentate, he claims to be the sovereign of this country.'[6]

Opposition to the 1903 royal visit took many forms. The monarch's accession oath—which nationalists claimed was anti-Catholic—was printed on posters plastered all over Dublin. Griffith was one of the leading figures in the newly established National Council, which succeeded in stopping Dublin Corporation from giving the king a loyal welcome.

The decision on the issue left the Lord Mayor of Dublin in a quandary. Three years earlier, Tim Harrington—who was also a Westminster MP for the Irish Parliamentary Party—had opposed the visit of Queen Victoria. But he remained tight lipped on his view about the 1903 royal visit despite huge National Council pressure on Dublin Corporation to snub the new king. The irrepressible Maud Gonne was involved in the campaign and remarked to William Butler Yeats: 'Harrington is completely gone over to the enemy . . . I hear he frequents the castle.'[7]

A month before the royal visit, the IPP held a fundraising meeting at the Rotunda in Dublin. The event was going to schedule until Maud Gonne and other members of the National Council arrived. She demanded to be allowed to ask a question of Harrington who was in attendance. The hall erupted as tempers frayed. Fists and chairs were thrown before the police arrived to quell the mêlée. Responsibility for the incident rested—according to *The Irish Times*—with Maud Gonne, 'that most picturesque but impractical of lady politicians.'[8]

Maud Gonne may have enjoyed the headlines but the successful campaign organised to coincide with the 1903 royal visit—and even the less eventful 1900 protests—helped to establish Arthur Griffith as a leading figure in nationalist circles. Moreover, the two royal visits in part contributed to the emergence of a new political organisation in Ireland as the National Council outlived the royal visit and was two years later reconstituted as the Sinn Féin party.

An emerging Irish writer named James Joyce was one of many people within the small nationalist community in Dublin who were taken by the writings of Arthur Griffith. In September 1906, Joyce wrote of Griffith:

> ... so far as my knowledge goes, he was the first person in Ireland to revive the separatist idea on modern lines ... He wants the creation of an Irish consular service abroad, and of an Irish bank at home ... He said in one of his articles that it cost a Danish merchant less to send butter to Christiania and then by sea to London than it costs an Irish merchant to send his from Mullingar to Dublin. A great deal of his programme perhaps is absurd but at least it tries to inaugurate some commercial life for Ireland ... [9]

Absurd or not, Griffith was not easily dismissed by Joyce. Two months later, in correspondence with his brother, the novelist again returned to the ideas propagated by Griffith: 'For either Sinn Féin or Imperialism will conquer the present Ireland. If the Irish programme did not insist on the Irish language I suppose I could call myself a nationalist.'[10]

The two men had met at the Martello tower at Sandycove in Dublin which had been built in the early nineteenth century to withstand Napoleonic invasion. The tower—some 40 feet high—offers breathtaking views out over the Irish Sea, and was home for a short time in 1904 to Joyce. Arthur Griffith was another visitor to the tower. Joyce thought Griffith unassuming and he liked his ideas for advancing the cause of Irish nationalism.

Indeed, Joyce was sufficiently impressed that when he came to write his masterpiece, *Ulysses*, Griffith was alone among the political figures of the time given favourable mention. Work on *Ulysses* started in 1914, and the book was published in Paris in 1922. The novel's action all takes place on a single day (now celebrated by Joyce devotees as Bloomsday), 16 June 1904. In the Dublin of that time, the original Sinn Féin platform was appearing in weekly instalments in Griffith's *United Irishman* newspaper, which Joyce once observed was 'the only newspaper of any pretensions in Ireland'.

The character Leopold Bloom is given a central role in the creation of Griffith's vision for Ireland. In a scene in the novel, set in a pub in Little Britain Street, John Wyse Nolan asserts that Bloom gave Griffith the idea that inspired Sinn Féin. Leopold Bloom applauds Griffith's description of the insignia of *The Freeman's Journal*, which supported the Irish Parliamentary Party, as a home rule sun rising up from a laneway behind the Bank of Ireland. Moreover, in the final section of *Ulysses*, Molly Bloom makes not the most flattering reference to Griffith as someone who is supposed to be the coming man but does not look it.

Leopold Bloom and the other characters in *Ulysses* lived in the Ireland of 16 June 1904. In the real-life Ireland at that time, only a minority of people sought outright rejection of the union with Britain, although many liked the idea of greater political freedom. Griffith was looking for a way to tap into the latent nationalism of this majority. Sinn Féin was among a plethora of political, cultural and literary groups established at the tail end of the nineteenth century and the dawn of the twentieth century, all seeking to promote an Irish nationalist agenda. There was considerable overlap in membership and also in the causes and campaigns that interested this small coterie of individuals. For example, those active in the separatist movement campaigned against the royal visits to Ireland in 1900 and 1903. They also found common cause in supporting the Boer farmers in Transvaal who were fighting the British.

Griffith had first-hand experience of the Boer situation having spent 18 months in Transvaal between 1897 and 1898, working first as a journalist and later as a machine supervisor at a gold-mining company in Johannesburg. When he returned to Dublin, he threw himself back into nationalist agitation, joining the Irish Republican Brotherhood and establishing a republican newspaper. The first issue of the *United Irishman* was published on 4 March 1899. The list of those who contributed articles to the newspaper over the following years is impressive—leading names from Irish history such as Pádraig Pearse, Maud Gonne and Roger Casement.

Alongside his newspaper, Griffith was involved in Cumann na nGaedheal, established in September 1900 with aims that included encouraging the study and teaching of Irish culture, the promotion of national games and the discountenancing of everything leading to the Anglicisation of Ireland. Griffith's organisation numbered among a collection of other cultural, political and literary groups, all with a broadly similar aspiration towards greater Irish independence from Britain, and all of which shared an overlapping membership. Included among the organising committee of Cumann na nGaedheal were leading Fenians, John O'Leary and Thomas Clarke. Maud Gonne served as a vice-president.

The organisation made little impact and when, in 1903, protests against the royal visit were being planned, a new body—the National Council—was established. It is fair to conclude that out of these groups, Sinn Féin emerged, but not before Griffith displayed the innovative political thinking that so bowled over individuals such as James Joyce.

Arthur Griffith was a talented journalist. But he was more than just a wordsmith; he was also a man of ideas. In the first half of 1904, he published his manifesto for a new Ireland, in effect a political programme. The Griffith blueprint first appeared in the *United Irishman* as a series of articles entitled 'The Resurrection of Hungary'.

Every week between 2 January and 2 July 1904, Griffith expanded on his separatist vision which would offer a genuine and unique alternative to the polar opposites on offer from the Fenians and the Irish Parliamentary Party. The articles were spread out over 27 weeks— interest was strong and, in November 1904, the collected work was published in a single volume of 99 pages and costing one penny.

Griffith was not opposed to a military solution to obtain independence but he saw little prospect of success from that route. Unlike many nationalists at the time, Griffith sought out a workable solution that would win popular support. It was not a full-blooded republican programme—central to the programme was acceptance of the sovereignty of the British monarch in Ireland. Griffith proposed a 'Dual Monarchy' arrangement within which Ireland would adopt a parliamentary system similar to that at Westminster but would agree to share a monarch with Britain.

This acceptance of royalty was later dispensed with as the Sinn Féin party adopted a more hardline republican agenda but another of Griffith's original ideas was held dear in the extreme. Griffith proposed that the Irish elected representatives at Westminster withdraw from the London parliament. This group would meet instead in Dublin and constitute themselves as an Irish parliament. It was hoped that the British authorities would accept this new arrangement, which was a step further than the Home Rule plans, which had been thwarted so often at Westminster. The policy of parliamentary abstentionism would within a few short years take on near infallibility status for republican purists.

The 1904 Griffith plan drew on the solutions proposed to deal with the difficulties in the Austro-Hungarian Empire in the 1860s and sought to draw parallels for the relationship between Ireland and Britain. The *United Irishman* articles were written not by a professional historian, rather by a propagandist seeking a workable solution to the Irish question. Griffith neatly sidestepped the collapse of a similar dual-monarchy system involving Sweden and Norway while, in drawing on Friedrich List's writings on economic nationalism to support his case, he failed to record List's approval for the union between Britain and Ireland. But Griffith was not interested in the rigours of academic theorising; he was proposing what looked like a simple and effective alternative to what was being offered by both the Fenians and the Irish Parliamentary Party.

Griffith worked from an untidy office at Fownes Street in Dublin. His steadfast dedication to the Irish cause was much admired. He had little interest in monetary gain, and on a meagre income he supported his mother, wife and two children while his publishing endeavours experienced constant financial difficulties. The separatist cause was not fashionable beyond a small cabal of dedicated, diehard enthusiasts.

The vision of a new Ireland may have been given life on the pages of the *United Irishman*, but Griffith's room—as one colleague recalled—had the appearance of 'hopeless confusion . . . The desk, the floor, the window recess, the mantel-piece, all full of files of papers— even the visitor's chair had to be apologetically cleared; against the wall at his left hand, bound files of his own paper, and in the middle of all this print, dust and quiet, this one man.'[11]

One day in December 1904, Arthur Griffith's work was interrupted by the arrival of a young woman named Máire de Bhuitléir and her sister. As was normal, their discussion turned to Griffith's doctrine of self-sufficiency, passive resistance and parliamentary abstentionism from Westminster. The blueprint for achieving Irish independence from British rule impressed the young women.

As she listened, Máire de Bhuitléir recalled the early motto of the Gaelic League: 'Sinn Féin, Sinn Féin, amháin'—that is, Ourselves, ourselves alone. The slogan neatly summed up the distinctive form of nationalism that Griffith was describing, and suddenly de Bhuitléir remarked: 'The policy of Sinn Féin, in fact.' Griffith was taken by the name because, as de Bhuitléir later recalled, he 'pounced upon the saying with delight. "Sinn Féin", he said, 'are exactly the two words to express my meaning.'[12]

The Sinn Féin party was born on Tuesday, 28 November 1905, in a shabby room of the old Rotunda in Dublin with fewer than a hundred men and a handful of women in attendance. Arthur Griffith sat at the top table with a sheaf of papers in his hands. One account recalled an audience—many unaware of the speaker's name—listening in rapt attention to Griffith who was 'very tranquil, very modest, very unaggressive—yet also full of suppressed flame and ardour.'[13]

The meeting that day was the first conference of the National Council while the slogan adopted was, in fact, Sinn Féin, the name which would shortly become the catch phrase for separatist politics in Ireland. The National Council had been in existence since the royal visit in 1903. It was not a political party, rather it was more like a small club which met to debate issues and which published occasional pamphlets.

The National Council was linked by shared objectives to another group, the Dungannon Clubs in Northern Ireland. In April 1907, the Dungannon Clubs merged with Cumann na nGaedheal and the new entity adopted the name 'the Sinn Féin League'. That was the first time the term was used as the name of an organisation in its own right, as over the two previous years it had been a phrase that described individuals and programmes that favoured Irish independence from Britain, as well as being the title given in 1906 to a new Griffith newspaper.

Despite his recognition in nationalist circles as the author of the Sinn Féin programme, Arthur Griffith steered clear of the new venture for several months. So the first organisation that called itself Sinn Féin did not in fact number Griffith among its members. It was, however, a short absence as in September 1907 the National Council merged into the Sinn Féin League with Griffith as the dominant figure in the new grouping.

While it was not a structured political party as we see today, even in its early days Sinn Féin demonstrated an ability to garner votes. Seats were won on Dublin Corporation, and by 1908 12 of the body's 60 councillors could be described as supporting the Sinn Féin cause. Among those elected under the Sinn Féin banner were William T. Cosgrave, who became the first head of government of the Irish Free State in 1922, and Sean T. O'Kelly, the second President of Ireland.

The party's first significant electoral outing was a Westminster by-election in the Leitrim North constituency in February 1908. The vacancy was caused by the resignation of C. J. Dolan, the sitting Irish Parliamentary Party MP. Dolan was so disillusioned with the performance of his own party that he deliberately resigned to force a by-election in which he ran as a Sinn Féin candidate. It was a contest for which Griffith had not planned but nevertheless his party threw itself into the campaign. Interestingly, in light of more contemporary funding allegations, Sinn Féin had little difficulty raising significant amounts of money for this by-election contest. The campaign budget was boosted by a sizeable donation from the United States, which was to become a long-standing source of money for republican activity.

Despite the resources at its disposal, Sinn Féin lost the 1908 North Leitrim by-election. The party received 27 per cent of the vote while the IPP romped home with 73 per cent although its victory was somewhat tarnished by the reality that the win had been secured by tactical voting by those of a unionist persuasion. Griffith put a positive spin on the outcome and in the process displayed his talent as one of the first Irish spin-doctors: 'Ireland's resurrection would be dated from the day when 1,200 Irishmen in the poorest and most remote county in Ireland voted for Sinn Féin.'[14]

The loss in North Leitrim was in fact the zenith of Sinn Féin's electoral record before the Easter 1916 Rising. Parliamentary arithmetic at Westminster once more pushed Home Rule for Ireland back onto the British political agenda. Sinn Féin did not contest the Westminster elections in either January or December 1910. In truth, the party had no real national presence. Moreover, it lacked a genuine popular base, as Tom Garvin points out: 'Nominally a political party, Sinn Féin was, before 1916, actually little more than a coterie of Dublin journalists, minor politicians, politicised students and office-workers with some contact with similar groups in provincial centres and with some connections with small agrarian and republican groups . . . .'[15]

Indeed, Sinn Féin had failed to develop a strong organisational base. The annual secretary's report made for bleak reading when it was published in August 1909. Almost half of the party's 106 branches had failed to pay their affiliation fees while only 581 members had sent in their one-shilling annual subscription. There was impatience about the party's progress and most members drifted into other nationalist groups. The decline continued unchecked. By 1915 one of Griffith's supporters wrote that the party was 'on the rocks' and could not pay the rent for its headquarters in Harcourt Street in Dublin.[16]

Still the party had decent name recognition. The words 'Sinn Féin' came to define a certain political outlook—a tendency towards separatism. Newspapers and government officials in describing those seeking greater independence from Britain tended to use the label 'Sinn Féin' as a form of shorthand. The words 'Sinn Féin' appeared in police reports as a generic description for those believed to be harbouring separatist views.

The irony was, of course, that Sinn Féin from 1905 to 1916 was far from a revolutionary movement, nor indeed was it a vibrant organisation on the move. Indeed, had it not been for the activism of Arthur Griffith, the party might simply have faded away. Griffith continued to publish and, in turn, his journalism—and the ideas he advocated—helped to maintain what was no more than a loosely connected coalition.

The results of the 1910 Westminster elections pushed Home Rule back up the British political agenda. The Liberal government was dependent for its Westminster majority on the votes of Irish Parliamentary Party members. Home Rule was the price of this support. Legislation to establish a devolved legislature for Ireland was introduced and, with the abolition of the veto powers of the House of Lords, this proposal looked a firmer guarantee of becoming reality than previous ill-fated attempts at Irish devolved government.

Opponents of the measure, however, were not going to accept the will of parliament so easily. Historian Michael Laffan acknowledges as much: 'The Conservative opposition and its unionist allies realized that they could no longer block Home Rule by constitutional means. They resorted to treason.'[17]

In January 1913, unionists, led by Edward Carson, established a paramilitary force and threatened a violent response to the Home Rule plans. A counter organisation was formed in November of the same year to defend the Home Rule idea. It was not too long before elements of this movement were being erroneously described as the 'Sinn Féin Volunteers'. Among the ranks of its members was Arthur Griffith.

The Home Rule Bill was enacted in September 1914 but immediately suspended for the duration of the First World War. The delay in introducing the devolved institutions, coupled with the strength of the unionist lobby, undermined the Irish Parliamentary Party. The pendulum swung the way of those who sought a fully independent Irish republic, and were prepared to use violence to achieve their objective.

The latest in a long series of armed risings against British rule took place at Easter 1916. About 700 republicans were involved on Easter Monday, while about the same number again joined their ranks over the course of the six days of fighting. In military terms, the rebellion was a failure. When the fighting was over, the British still remained in place. Over 450 people had been killed, with another 2,500 injured. The centre of Dublin was left in ruins. As an exercise in reawakening the nationalist spirit in the wider public, the rebellion was initially unsuccessful. There was no universal upsurge in public support for those responsible for the military operation.

But a series of events in the weeks after the quashing of the rebellion started a process during which public sentiment turned in favour of radical nationalist politics. Resentment against the British increased with the execution of 15 rebel leaders. There was also unease over the internment of another 2,000 volunteers.

It was not just the treatment of the rebels that angered the public. Disaffection spread with the failure to implement the long-promised devolution of power to a new parliament in Dublin, while speculation persisted about the extension of conscription to Ireland to assist with the war in Europe.

The Irish Republican Brotherhood through its infiltration of the Irish Volunteers—a movement established in response to the unionist show of arms against Home Rule—was responsible for the Easter Rising in 1916. Certainly individual members of Sinn Féin participated in the rebellion but the party itself was not involved despite the event's later being commonly labelled the Sinn Féin Rising.

Griffith may not have overseen the formation of a formidable political organisation—if he even had that objective—but in his prolific writings he had created a concept that was now universally understood. On 10 June 1916, the British Liberal Party politician, David Lloyd George, wrote: 'Sinn Féinism is for the moment right on top.' Later that same month, General John Maxwell, who had been given responsibility to restore order in Ireland, admitted that the Irish people 'now think that Sinn Féinism and Irish patriotism are synonymous terms.'[18]

This acknowledgement of the spread of 'Sinn Féinism' was not confined to the British establishment. One colleague of Arthur Griffith later wrote: 'As Ireland became pro-insurrection she became Sinn Féin, without knowing what Sinn Féin was, except that it stood generally for Irish independence in the old complete way, the way in which the Irish Party had not stood for it.'[19]

It is an oddity of Irish history that today's supporters of Sinn Féin are strongly attached to the legacy of Easter 1916 and yet their party was not even involved in the rebellion. In truth, Sinn Féin as an organisation was a carpetbagger. Indeed, Sinn Féin was peripheral not only to the 1916 Rising but also, at that time, to Irish life in general.

The divergence between the party now led by Gerry Adams and the Sinn Féin of 1905–16 is huge. Adams and his supporters claim the Sinn Féin inheritance but it is a selective historical legacy. Modern republicans recall the 1916 Rising and the Proclamation of a Republic. But few Sinn Féin supporters acknowledge that their party's formation is rooted in a monarchy-type solution to Irish independence. Little attention is now paid to Sinn Féin monarchy proposals or, indeed, the party's non-involvement in the 1916 rebellion. Moreover, in the long list of Sinn Féin heroes, many names have been erased, including that of the party's first ideological guru, Arthur Griffith.

The Sinn Féin organisation was transformed during the period after the Easter Rising although it was several months before it was clear that the party had the ability to respond to its new-found national prominence. Indeed, throughout the latter half of 1916, there was actually little evidence to suggest that Sinn Féin was on the cusp of considerable political achievement.

In the aftermath of the 1916 Rising, Arthur Griffith was among those detained by the British authorities because of their known separatist leanings. In Griffith's absence, Sinn Féin was run by someone who had been a unionist supporter until a few years previously, and who by 1918 had actually returned to that political persuasion. 'My well-meaning but feather headed friend Herbert Pim seems to be muddling up Sinn Féin a bit,' Griffith wrote from Reading Jail in November 1916. The party published a number of pamphlets during 1916 but—while generally ineffective—its most important asset remained its name.

The release of republican detainees in December 1916 provided the party with a membership intake necessary to establish itself as a national force. The following February, a police report in County Clare observed: 'in each place where an interned prisoner has returned, the Sinn Féiners have begun to meet, use seditious expressions and up to a certain point defy law and authority.'[20]

Sinn Féin was no longer an elitist party of intellectuals. Its membership base was widened. In 1906, the party had 21 branches. There was steady growth and the figure increased to 128 by 1909 although almost half of these branches failed to pay their annual affiliation fee. But in the months after the Rising—and especially in 1917—this position was transformed. Sinn Féin now came to represent the new confident calls for political change, and a year following the Rising the party is reported to have had 1,240 branches across the island.

Public support for Sinn Féin was tested in a series of by-elections in 1917 and 1918 although it was by no means obvious that the Irish Parliamentary Party was about to be swallowed up in an imminent Sinn Féin rise. In early 1917, a Westminster vacancy arose with the death of the Irish Parliamentary Party MP for North Roscommon. A by-election was held in February 1917.

Roscommon was home to Michael O'Flanagan, a Roman Catholic priest with a passion for republican politics. He had returned to Ireland towards the end of 1914 having spent a decade in the United States raising money for the Catholic Church and promoting the objectives of the Gaelic League, an organisation for which he acted as special envoy. Back in Ireland he gained notoriety for organising his parishioners at Cliffoney in County Sligo, over their right to local turf banks. His grievances against the authorities were to expand, as during 1915 and 1916 he became a familiar figure at republican gatherings. He officiated at the funeral of the veteran Fenian, O'Donovan Rossa, and also delivered the oration at a commemoration in Belfast for the Manchester Martyrs.

It was not unusual for members of the clergy to be involved in nationalist political activity but few were as publicly active as Michael O'Flanagan. His energetic involvement in the 1917 North Roscommon by-election was the start of an ongoing role with Sinn Féin that would continue for over 30 years; the Roman Catholic priest even served as party president for a time in the mid-1930s.

'The quarrel between Ireland and England will go on until Ireland is completely separated from England under that beautiful tricolour flag of the Irish Republic,' O'Flanagan once declared. Ten thousand people allegedly gathered at Ballyjamesduff in County Cavan to hear that speech, which was probably just as well since the British authorities censored reporting of the meeting.[21]

The British were not the only ones who wanted to quieten O'Flanagan. The priest's own religious superiors were also intent on silencing their overtly republican member. But they could only look on as O'Flanagan deepened his involvement with Sinn Féin—he was even appointed a judge in the short-lived republican courts established by the first Dáil in 1919.

O'Flanagan was, in fact, suspended for a time from his priestly duties, an action he openly condemned.

> It is true that I am a priest. But I was an Irishman 24 years before I became a priest. Almighty God made me an Irishman and put upon me the duties of a citizen of Ireland and the duties that the law of God and the law of Nature have placed upon me, the law of no institution, even if it be a Divine Institution can take away from me.[22]

Some years later, O'Flanagan was even more explicit in his condemnation:

> And I say to every Bishop in the Catholic world that if you accept your politics from the Pope you are unworthy of the citizenship . . . of any country in the world with the exception of the Vatican City. I say also to the Pope, you are not infallible in anything but purely religious doctrines . . . .[23]

When it came to republican infallibility, however, O'Flanagan was one of those who stuck rigidly to the Sinn Féin ideology that emerged in the 1916–18 period. He was a purist in a party that at the time of the 1917 by-election in North Roscommon was less of a formalised political organisation and more of a group of like-minded individuals doing their best without any real agreement about their intended end-objective.

O'Flanagan managed to borrow £400 to finance the Sinn Féin campaign and acted as the chief organiser for George Noble Plunkett, the party candidate. Plunkett was a hereditary papal count whose son had been one of the signatories to the 1916 Proclamation and had been executed for his part in the rebellion. Plunkett allowed Sinn Féin to garner a sympathy vote deriving from the failed rising but he was a peculiar mixture, with a background steeped in the fine arts and two failed applications for the position of under-secretary in Dublin Castle to his name. This association with the republican cause made some sections of his former social circle unhappy and, in response to his republican connections, Plunkett's name was removed from the membership of the Royal Dublin Society.

The North Roscommon by-election campaign in February 1917 was contested in blizzard-like conditions but the biting snow did not prevent a Sinn Féin success, with Plunkett securing 3,022 votes against the 2,395 votes won by the other two candidates. Whatever about the victory, the campaign itself was vitally important to the breakthrough of Sinn Féin, as Michael Laffan observes in his study of the 1916–23 Sinn Féin:

> The greatest achievement of the campaign was the emergence of a sense of cohesion and common purpose among a disparate group of people who, until then, had often suspected or disapproved of each other. It was through the informal and almost accidental process of working together in Roscommon that they initiated the formal and deliberate policy of reviving the separatist movement. An organisation was developed and close links were established between different parties and individuals.[24]

The victory in North Roscommon elevated Plunkett within Sinn Féin and he saw himself as the de facto leader of the party. Over the following months, around the country Griffith and Plunkett shared platforms together. Griffith was not troubled by Plunkett's success although many in Sinn Féin found their new abstentionist MP difficult and impractical. His tenure as the principal Sinn Féin spokesman was, however, short-lived because, by the autumn of 1917, a new leadership was readying itself to take control of the organisation and its objectives.

Despite the prominence of Sinn Féin in 1916 and 1917, it was not altogether clear that the majority of the population would have been unhappy with delivery by Britain of the long-promised devolved government in Dublin. There was still ambiguity about the Sinn Féin policy platform. Griffith and his supporters clung to their favoured dual-monarchy prescription but a more republican membership was now advocating complete independence for the island. Both groups were at this point still, if somewhat uncomfortably, co-existing within the same movement.

One story involving Griffith and the republican leader Michael Collins indicates the obvious conflict between the different versions of the Sinn Féin party that existed before and after the Easter 1916 Rising. Ahead of a by-election in South Longford in May 1917, a group of Sinn Féiners including Griffith and O'Flanagan sat in the party's offices in Harcourt Street in Dublin.

The Roscommon-born priest was reciting some poetry that he had written when suddenly Michael Collins burst through the door, shouting loudly at Griffith: 'I want to know what ticket is this Longford election being fought on . . . If you don't fight the election on the Republican ticket you will alienate all the young men.' Griffith remained silent as a blazing row developed, with Collins rejecting the idea that winning the election was the most important objective. Voices were eventually lowered as Fr O'Flanagan put aside his poetry and sought to act as a calming influence.[25]

This was a time when there were great changes in how election campaigns were run. Not unlike 75 years later, Sinn Féin was to the fore in adopting innovations such as organising the canvass, managing personation agents at polling booths and sharing the workload between local and national sections of the party.

Tom Garvin has observed: 'The almost military centralisation of the new party was very noticeable and contrasted with the localist and decentralised structure of the Irish Party . . . .'[26] Three-quarters of a century later in Northern Ireland, the SDLP would fill a similar role, crushed by the confident onward march of contemporary republicans. Modern Sinn Féin also aims—as discussed in Chapter 9—to inflict a similar fate on Fianna Fáil in the Irish Republic.

There are other similarities with more recent times. Following the South Longford by-election contest, the *Irish Independent* observed: 'the Sinn Féiners have shown more remarkable organising powers. Their posters are displayed at every crossroad and village in the constituency and their colours float from treetops and the roofs of houses. Pamphlets are being handed out by the thousand . . . .'[27]

If those comments about the visibility of the party organisation sound familiar, comments about the well-funded campaign will not be surprising in the context of contemporary Sinn Féin. The party's by-election campaigns in 1917 were without doubt backed by generous resources, with one observer in South Longford recording: 'they have a fleet of motor cars and are all put up in the best hotels in town and are spending money freely.'[28]

All the campaigns were keenly contested—speakers were stoned and pelted with eggs. The count in South Longford generated considerable controversy with the candidate for the Irish Parliamentary Party being briefly declared the winner until a bundle of misplaced ballot papers was discovered. After the recount, a margin of 37 votes separated the two leading candidates, with the Sinn Féiner in pole position. It was a crucial victory but the narrow winning margin clearly indicated that Sinn Féin was not about to be automatically swept to power in Ireland.

Two months after the Longford contest, Eamon de Valera made his first foray into electoral politics. One of the leaders of the 1916 Rising, the American-born de Valera was still in prison when he was nominated as the Sinn Féin candidate for the East Clare by-election. He was released several days later along with other republican prisoners.

The tone and the direction of the Sinn Féin party shifted significantly from this time onwards. The name of Griffith's organisation was retained but this was, to all intents and purposes, a new political entity. The party was more republican in its outlook; the idea of a dual monarchy was sidelined, while the militant side of the separatist movement was working to ensure that its nascent political wing delivered a coordinated message. The subsequent history of Sinn Féin would time and time again see the party's direction being set by an agenda determined by military men.

This membership overlap was visible during the East Clare campaign in the summer of 1917. As he made his way around the constituency, de Valera was escorted by armed members of the Volunteers, or the Irish Republican Army as they would later be known. The Sinn Féin campaign was noted for its discipline and the involvement of young men, many carrying revolvers. De Valera secured some 70 per cent of the vote in a famous victory. More success followed. A month later, W. T. Cosgrave topped the poll in a by-election in Kilkenny. Cosgrave was a long-serving party member who also sat on Dublin Corporation. In the splits and divisions that would come in later years, Cosgrave and de Valera would lead different political off-shoots of the original Sinn Féin established by Arthur Griffith.

These electoral tests in 1917 allowed Sinn Féin to build its political machine. The party was on an electoral roll. There was considerable excitement and energy associated with Sinn Féin. It was attracting members and money to its cause. The party's headquarters in Harcourt Street in Dublin was abuzz with activity. There was huge demand for information about membership. New branches were being established in parts of the country where the organisation had previously been patchy. Sinn Féin representatives were also in demand to speak at party meetings in every corner of Ireland. Arthur Griffith's wife remarked in November 1917 that her spouse: 'has had so little time rushing about the country . . . it is now 9 months since he's been home a weekend.'[29]

Arthur Griffith was witnessing the transformation of his party. Around 1,700 delegates attended a party convention in October 1917 at which de Valera unanimously replaced Griffith as Sinn Féin president. It was a logical move with de Valera's record during the 1916 Easter Rising and his electoral success in East Clare. Moreover, his elevation sidelined Count Plunkett who also lost out as vice-president, with Griffith and O'Flanagan filling the two available positions.

All sides accepted the policy of parliamentary abstentionism. The adoption of a republican platform was less easily agreed. There was some straight talking in the small hours of the morning between the party strategists as they sought to clarify what exactly Sinn Féin stood for. Griffith and his supporters held out for their dual-monarchy idea. The more radical grouping wanted the creation of an Irish Republic. Eventually a compromise was reached, with the new party constitution committing Sinn Féin to securing independence, and then, once freedom had been won, the Irish people could choose in a referendum the type of system they wished to govern them. The second Sinn Féin— the separatist version—was born.

The fragile nature of the Sinn Féin political advance was clearly evident in the early part of 1918 when the party's solid progress was brought to a definite halt. In three successive by-elections in the first half of the year, Sinn Féin candidates were beaten. There was still life left in the Irish Parliamentary Party, or so it seemed. Ironically, in light of the strength of Sinn Féin in what is now Northern Ireland, two of those defeats in 1918 were in the northern part of the island. South Armagh was a nationalist constituency and the voters—including unionists who cast their ballots tactically—sided heavily against Sinn Féin. The voters of East Tyrone were also not minded to back Sinn Féin.

In between these two losses, Sinn Féin experienced another setback in Waterford in a by-election caused by the death of the IPP leader, John Redmond. The campaign was heated, with Sinn Féin taking the worst of the stone and bottle throwing. There was an obvious sympathy vote for the IPP and Sinn Féin found itself tasting another defeat.

There had been seven contested by-elections, from North Roscommon in 1917 through to East Tyrone in April 1918. Whatever momentum—and sense of electoral invincibility—that Sinn Féin had built up in 1917 was lost in the first four months of 1918. In terms of votes cast in these seven contests, Sinn Féin received 13,569 to the 10,964 for the Irish Parliamentary Party. At just over 55 per cent of the total vote, Sinn Féin's performance was a clear indication of the dramatic upturn in the party's progress, but the figure did not provide grounds to forecast the total disappearance of the IPP. But then the British authorities unwittingly aided the republican cause on several fronts, particularly a failure to deliver on Home Rule, the threat of conscription and the treatment of republican prisoners.

In late 1917, a dispute arose over political status, which led republican prisoners in Mountjoy Jail in Dublin to call a hunger strike. The dispute —its causes and its consequences—was all too similar to that which occurred in the Northern Ireland prison system in the 1976–81 period— yet another reminder of the failure to learn the lessons of republican history.

Republican prisoners in 1917 refused to wear prison clothes or to do prison work; the authorities refused to accept their self-claimed status of political prisoner, and force-fed those who in protest refused food. Prisoners were strapped to a chair and an 18-inch rubber tube was inserted through the mouth or the nostrils down the throat.

Thomas Ashe—who had worked as a national school principal before the 1916 Rising—organised the hunger strike in Mountjoy Prison, for political status. On 25 September 1917, Ashe died after having been force-fed. His funeral became a public statement of opposition to British rule. The emotional response led many who would ordinarily have been happy with devolved government within the British Empire to harden their attitude towards a continuation of the link with Britain.

This fact was acknowledged openly in the pages of the British media. The *Daily Express* wrote: 'The circumstances of his [Ashe's] death and funeral have made 100,000 Sinn Féiners out of 100,000 constitutional nationalists.' In a similar vein, the *Daily Mail* noted: 'Sinn Féin today is pretty nearly another name for the vast bulk of the youth of Erin.'[30]

The balance within the nationalist constituency was tilted further in the direction of Sinn Féin not by any action of the politicians in Ireland but rather by a decision taken in London. In April 1918, the British government announced plans to introduce conscription in Ireland. The British forces in France had suffered heavy casualities and the extension of conscription to Ireland was seen as one means of getting replacements. In the region of 200,000 Irishmen were believed to be available with the introduction of conscription.

The policy met with widespread opposition in Ireland, drawing criticism from diverse quarters, including the Catholic Church, the trade unions and the IPP, which, in protest, withdrew from Westminster. The party of constitutional nationalism that had monopolised Irish politics for so many years was left floundering—it had failed to deliver on Home Rule and now it had to adopt a Sinn Féin strategy, having unsuccessfully prevented legislation on conscription from being extended to Ireland. Griffith, it seemed, had been proven correct in his warning that 'the one place that England can never be defeated is on the floor of the British House of Commons.'[31]

Conscription, coupled with a failure to implement Home Rule, led many people to conclude that the only viable option was Irish independence from Britain. Sinn Féin was ready to welcome this new support. The party led the campaign against conscription as its own membership base expanded. In May 1918, the British moved against Sinn Féin, rounding up 73 senior party members on the pretext that the party was involved in a plot with Germany to mount another rebellion in Ireland.

Griffith was among those detained. Although imprisoned, he was selected as the Sinn Féin candidate for a by-election in East Cavan, which took place in June 1918. Public hostility to conscription—and the arrest of its party leaders—assisted the Sinn Féin effort. The campaign allowed the party to recover from the by-election reverses earlier in 1918. Griffith was elected, winning by 3,785 votes to 2,581. In truth, the conscription crisis in 1918 allowed the party to face into the Westminster election of that year with considerable optimism. The Irish Parliamentary Party was increasingly looking like a spent force. The actions of the British government were driving the nationalist voters of Ireland into the ranks of Sinn Féin.

The previous general election to the Westminster parliament had taken place in December 1910. An election was overdue, with the life of the incumbent parliament being extended repeatedly because of the war in Europe. In the period between these contests, the political world had altered dramatically in Ireland. The franchise had been significantly widened between the 1910 and 1918 elections, while the emergence of Sinn Féin signalled a shift in the public mood.

Public discord with British policy in Ireland was measured by the results of the December 1918 general election. The outcome delivered a dramatic victory for Sinn Féin, with a mass public conversion to the party. The political landscape in Ireland was transformed. The election results soon took on near religious meaning for Irish republicanism and, long after the 1918 contest, republicans continued to argue that the majority of Irish people had expressed support for British withdrawal from the island of Ireland, and had given their endorsement for the Republic as proclaimed at Easter 1916.

Sinn Féin contested as a separatist party and nominated leading figures from the republican movement to contest seats across the island. In mid-September 1918, Liam de Róiste observed that he was the only Sinn Féin candidate so far selected who had never been in prison or on the run. The British duly intervened. In late September, as the police sought to arrest him, de Róiste fled into hiding.

The authorities targeted Sinn Féin for unfavourable treatment— party headquarters was raided several times, activists were arrested, meetings disrupted, and posters and leaflets seized. The continued harassment disrupted the activities of the party but failed to halt the Sinn Féin advance. Indeed, the authorities only added to the grievance culture, which Sinn Féin took advantage of, so as to generate publicity and sympathy. The party emphasised the glories of the Easter Rising, denounced the British treatment of Ireland and stressed the threat of conscription.

With so many senior figures in prison, the irrepressible Fr Michael O'Flanagan spearheaded the campaign. It was said that he addressed 97 meetings in the four-week period before polling day. In a 15-page pamphlet published in September 1918, the Roscommon-born priest wrote: 'Sinn Féin wants no unthinking mob to rush blindly to the polls. Sinn Féin desires and expects the Irish people to use the brains that God gave them and to give intelligent consideration to the case it submits.'[32] His involvement with Sinn Féin met with disapproval from his superiors and they duly suspended him from his priestly duties. In protest against this decision, his parishioners locked the doors of the village church against his successor, while many travelled to a nearby village to attend Sunday mass.

Sinn Féin won 73 of the 105 Irish seats in the 1918 Westminster Parliament although there were only 68 Sinn Féin MPs as five of them represented more than a single constituency. A study of the geographical spread of the Sinn Féin seats shows that 70 of its seats were won in the area that subsequently became the 26 counties, where there were 75 seats available.

The election was a Sinn Féin whitewash in terms of seats won although, despite its sensational successes, the party actually failed to secure an overall majority of the nationalist vote. The Sinn Féin candidates received a total of 485,105 votes with the IPP securing 237,393 votes. Overall, Sinn Féin won just under 48 per cent of the available vote, which had been augmented with non-property owners (all men over 21 years) and women over 30 years of age being given the right to vote for the first time. It was a pattern that would be repeated over 80 years later in both Northern Ireland and the Irish Republic when newly mobilised groups were enthused to back Sinn Féin candidates rather than stay at home on election day.

One of the consequences of the party's monopolising of the nationalist constituency was the ruin of the moderate, pro-Home Rule, Irish Parliamentary Party. Public sentiment had moved away from a devolution-type solution as an answer to Ireland's future. Interestingly, in 26 constituencies—accounting for almost one-quarter of the total electorate—Sinn Féin candidates were unopposed as the IPP failed to nominate candidates. The IPP had dominated Irish politics for over 35 years and, in the previous Westminster election, the party had won 68 seats. After all the votes were counted in the 1918 contest, the IPP was left with a mere six seats, four of which were won in Ulster, thanks to a pact with Sinn Féin.

The election results were considered a vote in favour of the Sinn Féin policy platform. Sinn Féin promised to make 'use of any and every means available to render impotent the power of England to hold Ireland'. The party proposed achieving this aim through a withdrawal of Irish representation at Westminster and appealing to the Paris Peace Conference for recognition of Ireland's right to statehood.

Sinn Féin was true to its election pledge. The party's first act after the election was to establish a separatist assembly in Dublin. With the exception of its new MPs who were still in prison, Sinn Féin's elected representatives gathered at the Mansion House on 21 January 1919, and the first Dáil declared an independent republic. The economic and social programme was based on the ideas propagated by Griffith but, in truth, the party was far from the organisation he had formed fourteen years earlier. In the aftermath of the 1918 election results, one Sinn Féin vice-president remarked: 'The people have voted for Sinn Féin. What we have to do now is explain to them what Sinn Féin is.'[33]

Whatever about its republican programme, few people were fully aware just how their vote connected with Sinn Féin's military relation. The fact was that Sinn Féin—while a separate organisation—played a secondary role to the wishes of the military men within the wider republican community. There was considerable membership overlap, a situation illustrated by Michael Collins who was both the Sinn Féin Minister for Finance and also the IRA's Director of Intelligence. This relationship between the political and the military has remained an important aspect in the history of the republican movement. It was only in the 1990s that the political side reached a superior position and controlled the direction of what can best be described as anti-system republicanism.

In the aftermath of the meeting of the abstentionist assembly in Dublin in early 1919, military conflict between the republicans and the British began. The republican strategy during the War of Independence was based on the use of guerrilla tactics. The British had a vastly superior military advantage over the IRA but destroying their enemy would have required a wholescale military campaign in Ireland, which was not a favoured option. The war was bloody. It is estimated that between 1919 and 1921, 1,400 people were left dead due to the conflict, of whom 624 were members of the British security forces and 752 were IRA volunteers and civilians.[34]

A truce came into effect on 11 July 1921. Negotiations between the British and Irish delegations followed. An independent 32-county Irish Republic—true to the Easter 1916 Proclamation and the results of the 1918 general election—was the Sinn Féin objective in the peace talks.

Michael Collins ruled out accepting any partition of the island: 'We do not intend to have Lloyd George put a little red spot on the map of one corner of Ireland and call it part of England, as he does Gibraltar. We want a united Ireland.'[35] Eamon de Valera was equally blunt in establishing the republican negotiating position: 'Sinn Féin will conduct no peace negotiations that do not provide for the full recognition of the Irish Republic and complete separation of Ireland from England.'[36]

Neither Collins nor de Valera was, however, taking full account of the changed constitutional reality on the island. While the republicans were waging their military campaign against the British, the Government of Ireland Act had been passed at Westminster. This legislation—which became law on 23 December 1920—had already fundamentally altered the political reality in Ireland, as it allowed for the creation of two new jurisdictions, each with its own parliament.

The division of the island had taken place with the creation of the six-county Northern Ireland and allowing provision for a 26-county Southern Ireland. The long-promised Home Rule had been delivered but the unionist veto had prevented its application to a unitary Ireland. The Act hoped for an eventual reunion of Ireland—but only with the consent of the two parliaments, and given the in-built unionist majority in Northern Ireland, it was difficult to envisage such a scenario arising in the short term.

Northern Ireland was a cold place for nationalists. Between July 1920 and July 1922, 557 people were killed—303 Catholic, 172 Protestant and 82 members of the British security forces. Thomas Hennessey records that 'although Catholics formed only a quarter of Belfast's population they had suffered 257 civilian deaths out of 416 in the two-year period. Catholic relief organisations estimated that between 8,700 and 11,000 Belfast Catholics had been driven out of their jobs and 23,000 forced out of their homes, with about 500 Catholic businesses destroyed.'[37]

For half a century, the unionists who ran Northern Ireland were guilty of corrupt and anti-democratic practices. The nationalist community faced discrimination in electoral politics and state employment—as well as in housing and public service allocation. In truth, the seeds of the contemporary post-1969 conflict were sown in the early years of the new state's existence.

In the early 1920s, it was not just supporters of the new Northern Ireland state who pursued a deliberate campaign of violence against their neighbours. The IRA also took its campaign against the British presence on the island into Northern Ireland. Between July 1920 and July 1922, republicans were responsible for killing 254 Protestant and security force members.

The other wing of the republican separatist movement was also active in Northern Ireland. Elections to the new Northern Ireland parliament took place in May 1921. Sinn Féin dominated the nationalist vote—securing 104,716 votes (21 per cent) against 60,577 (19 per cent) for the

Irish Party, although each party won six seats while 40 unionist candidates were also returned.

De Valera saw the opportunity to participate in elections as allowing the Irish people again to prove their loyalty to the principle of Irish independence: 'You who vote for Sinn Féin candidates will cast your vote for nothing less than the legitimacy of the republic, for Ireland against England, for freedom against slavery, for right and justice against force and wrong here and everywhere.'[38]

This approach was, however, to be superseded by events in London where Irish and British representatives met in the latter half of 1921. The peace talks involved compromise and concession. The treaty that emerged from the negotiations fell short of the pure republican position. What was on offer was dominion status for 26 counties within the British Commonwealth, with parliamentarians having to swear an oath of allegiance to the new Free State that included being 'faithful to H.M. King George V, his heirs and successors . . . .' The new state, its institutions and symbols were laced with reminders of the British inheritance while the continued presence of British naval defence facilities at several Irish ports was a reminder of another kind.

Dáil Éireann debated the peace deal in December 1921 and in early January 1922. The Pro-Treaty grouping within Sinn Féin argued that the military campaign had delivered substantial political rewards, while accepting that these were less than the demands in the party's 1918 manifesto. They saw the Treaty as a dynamic text, which would open up other opportunities in the future for advancing independence and creating political unity.

The dissenting minority took its direction from the 1916 Proclamation and the declarations of the first Dáil established by Sinn Féin representatives in the aftermath of the 1918 election. In the view of those opposed to the Treaty, a 32-county state independent of Britain had already been declared. As one military expert recorded: 'From the point of view of the doctrinaire republicans, the Anglo-Irish War had never been about fighting for something—concessions, negotiating positions, compromises, etc.—but for safeguarding a pre-existing entity.'[39]

The opponents of the Treaty argued that it was no return for the sacrifices endured by republicans. But this was a minority view as, on 7 January 1922, the Treaty was accepted in the Dáil by 64 votes to 57. The decision meant that the first split in the ranks of the republican movement, and in the Sinn Féin party, was not far away.

AN INSIGNIFICANT LITTLE GROUP, 1926–1969

When Queen Victoria visited Dublin in 1900, she stayed in the Mansion House, an exceedingly fine building near the fashionable Stephen's Green end of Dawson Street. It is likely that Arthur Griffith, who led the campaign against the royal visit, was among those who protested outside the house which had been the official residence of the city's Lord Mayor since the early eighteenth century. Given her positive assessment of the 1900 trip, the queen probably did not hear the catcalls. The history of the house added a certain touch of irony almost two decades later when Griffith and other like-minded nationalists gathered inside the Mansion House for the first meeting of the Sinn Féin-led abstentionist Irish parliament.

The building has long been associated with the historical evolution of the Sinn Féin party. In the Round Room of the house—built in 1821 to host a gala dinner for George IV—the triumphs and tribulations of the party have been played out. The abstentionist Sinn Féin MPs met there on 21 January 1919. Fr Michael O'Flanagan, in his role as self-styled priestly guardian of the republican cause, was also involved. To hushed silence, O'Flanagan is said to have 'recited the prayer of the Holy Ghost for wisdom and guidance.'[1]

The newly elected Sinn Féin politicians pledged themselves to the republican cause: '. . . we, the elected Representatives of the ancient Irish people in National Parliament assembled, do, in the name of the Irish nation, ratify the establishment of the Irish Republic and pledge ourselves and our people to make this declaration effective by every means at our command.'

The unity on that day was later shattered with the Anglo-Irish Treaty, and those divisions were laid bare inside the Mansion House as parliamentary debate indicated that Sinn Féin colleagues were prepared to go their separate ways. The 1922 split was formalised at a Sinn Féin Ard

Fheis in the Mansion House—such gatherings in the Dawson Street mayoral residence would become a familiar ocurrence as differences over republican ideology continued to divide the Sinn Féin party—most famously in 1926, and also again in 1986.

It was only in the early 1990s when a ban was placed on Sinn Féin using the Mansion House facilities that the party moved to other venues for its annual conference. Certaintly the ghosts of Sinn Féin's past walk the steps from Dawson Street into the Round Room of the Mansion House. Historical figures like Eamon de Valera, Arthur Griffith, Maud Gonne and William T. Cosgrave. Contemporary names like Ruairí Ó Brádaigh, Gerry Adams and Martin McGuinness.

Thousands of party members have passed through the double doors into the building's single entrance, walking over the black and white floor tiles into the Round Room with its imposing dome-shaped ceiling. Many Sinn Féiners would have pushed through the narrow staircase up to the balcony which surrounds half the Round Room.

All these meetings shared common elements—an electric mood amongst the delegates, bitter disagreements and powerful speeches from political figures of historical importance. And it was no different when, in the aftermath of the Treaty decision, an Extraordinary Ard Fheis met on 22 February 1922. Three thousand Sinn Féin delegates crammed into the Round Room of the Mansion House. One writer remarked that the gathering 'promised to be the most important and the most divisive Ard Fheis in the history of Sinn Féin.'[2]

Several party leaders sought support for the Treaty. But the delegates were of a different mind. When Arthur Griffith rose to speak, he found himself competing with jeers from the body of the hall. The party he had founded in 1905—and which had been transformed in the period after the 1916 Easter Rising—was once more metamorphosing into an entirely different beast.

The anti-Treaty side saw the future of the republic as being at risk in a sell-out of the Sinn Féin cause. They were fired up to defend the republican ideal, whereas many among the pro-Treatyites were ambivalent about the peace deal and had come to accept it only reluctantly. In the Mansion House in February 1922, it was obvious which grouping had been most energised by the Treaty agreement.

Those opposed to the Treaty were not only most vocal but their numerical presence over the moderates was aided by IRA intimidation. One pro-Treaty republican described the upshot of the threat of violence in County Mayo in the west of Ireland:

The reports I have received show that the great majority of voters are pro-Treaty [.] On the other hand while the organisation has only been started within the last few days, and not a single meeting has been held, the anties have held two or three meetings in every parish and have been most arduous in their canvass. They are about the streets and round the country all day. Undoubtedly some conversions have been made. The real danger is coercion by the IRA . . . and terrorism threatened to such an extent the Ballina people (who do not seem to me very courageous) fear to hold a meeting. I regard it as bluff but it has an effect in two different directions. It makes many anti republican and frightens others into taking no action. The only real danger I see is that IRA . . . will be sent to the country polling boothes [*sic*] to help people sort out and also that the ballot boxes may be seized either during or after the voting . . . Letters were sent out to call a pro-Treaty meeting two days ago of rep[resentative]s of parishes but the letters were not delivered . . . .[3]

Despite the mood at the February 1922 Ard Fheis, a vote on the Treaty was avoided as the leaders from the diverging sides sought to preserve some semblance of unity. This was, however, only a temporary postponement of the inevitable split. The divisions between the former colleagues in the republican movement were effectively formalised in March 1922. A majority of members of the IRA opposed the Treaty and, at a General Convention, the IRA rejected the authority of Dáil Éireann. Military conflict resumed in Ireland, only this time between two groups who had soldiered together in the 1916–21 period. The civil war lasted for almost a year, ending in May 1923, and leaving between 800 and 4,000 people dead.

But it was not just in the military domain that those opposed to the Treaty were defeated. The results of the June 1922 general election showed a clear public preference for the pro-Treaty grouping within Sinn Féin although support for the de Valera faction was not insignificant.

A pact was agreed between the pro-Treaty and anti-Treaty sides of the party to try to prevent an electoral split. Some hopes for a reconciliation lingered. Each side nominated in each constituency only as many candidates as it had members of the outgoing Dáil. Eight of the 28 constituencies were not contested. The results, however, produced victory for the pro-Treaty side—in the contested constituencies they won 41 seats to only 19 seats for the anti-Treaty side. The victors moved into government in the new Free State.

The pro-Treaty grouping had attempted to preserve Sinn Féin—at a minimum for the continuity that the party's name provided—but eventually in the absence of compromise with their erstwhile colleagues, in party political terms, they were obliged to disown the name Sinn Féin. It would be another 80 years before the party, although as an entirely different entity, would next get anywhere near holding parliamentary or political power in either part of Ireland.

The second Sinn Féin was in a sense wound up in the latter half of 1922. The doors were closed on the party's head office in Harcourt Street in Dublin and the warring parties went their separate ways. There was still, however, the matter of funds held by the party. The outgoing officers supported the Treaty and acted to ensure that de Valera and his supporters did not have access to those monies. They argued that, since the split, the party called Sinn Féin no longer existed. The not insubstantial sum of £8,610 was eventually lodged with the High Court in February 1924 and was to remain under court protection until a case was taken to determine its ownership over 20 years later. That case, as discussed later, delivered an interesting judgment on the nature of the republican legacy.

So, out of the split in 1922, the third Sinn Féin emerged. Despite their electoral losses—and the subsequent defeat in the civil war—those on the anti-Treaty side re-grouped as the Sinn Féin party to which the 'republican' classification can be attached. The new version of the party was formally inaugurated in the Mansion House in June 1923. In reality, however, this third Sinn Féin existed from the period after the Treaty split in early 1922 to late in 1926 when divisions emerged over recognition of the institutions of the new Free State. It was a coalition of highly diverse interests drawn from political and military backgrounds.

Sinn Féin—or as its members were known, 'Republicans'—contested the 1923 general election to the parliament of the new Free State on an abstentionist platform which was consistent with the party's refusal to recognise the legitimacy of the new state or its institutions. They argued that democratic authority still remained with the Second Dáil. Successful Sinn Féin candidates pledged to establish a parallel state and institutions in a manner similar to that in which republicans operated in the aftermath of the 1918 Westminster election. The big difference between 1918 and 1923 was, however, that Sinn Féin was in a majority in the former year but by the latter was operating as a minority.

Nevertheless, anti-Treaty Sinn Féin performed well in the 1923 Dáil election. The party nominated 85 candidates and won 44 of the 153 seats available in the new parliament. By way of comparison, the pro-Treaty side—which had in April 1923 restyled itself as Cumann na nGaedheal—won 63 seats. Richard Sinnott observes that 'the party's performance in that election (just over a quarter of the vote) could be interpreted as a considerable achievement in the wake of the civil war defeat and with many of its activists in jail.'[4]

Despite the decent Sinn Féin performance in the 1923 election, the tide was against a party whose primary aim was to undermine the new Free State. Whether this stated objective allows those on the anti-Treaty side to be automatically classified as anti-democratic is not so easily determined. Certainly Tom Garvin divides the two camps into democrats and dictators:

> In 1923, after the Civil War, the electorate again voted preponderantly for pro-Treaty parties and the message was unambiguous this time. The entire IRA campaign of 1919–21 had been legitimised in the minds of the Dáil and the IRA leaderships as being in accordance with the will of the electorate as expressed in December 1918. It was difficult for most IRA to ignore that electorate when it turned on them . . . .[5]

A more subtle interpretation of the republican strategy is provided by John Regan who stresses the role played by the threat of British violence should the Irish people have decided to express their aspiration for national self-determination in a manner contrary to British interests.[6] The leading anti-Treaty IRA man, Liam Mellows—who was executed by the Free State during the civil war—remarked that the backing given to the Treaty represented not the will of the people but the fear of the people.

It is near impossible to measure the democratic strand in the anti-Treaty Sinn Féin. Nevertheless, this grouping largely ended armed conflict in 1923 and thereafter edged slowly towards participation with the institutions of the newly created state. But the hardliners persisted with an ideological position that was increasingly at odds with the will of the people in the Free State.

Sinn Féin performed poorly in a series of by-elections between 1923 and 1927, winning only four of the 21 contests. The party also polled disappointingly in electoral contests in Northern Ireland. No Sinn Féin candidates were elected at the October 1924 Westminster election, while the following year republican representation (albeit of the abstentionist kind) in the Northern Ireland parliament fell from six to two seats.

These electoral setbacks were matched by financial troubles with unpaid bills and debts becoming a common occurrence. By 1925, an internal reassessment was underway within Sinn Féin, with many attributing the electoral failure to abstentionism coupled with an absence of radical policies to address the all-too-obvious socioeconomic problems in the Free State.

The matter came to a head at a meeting of the party's standing committee in May 1925. The internal differences on abstentionism were evident in the resolution passed at that meeting, which determined that de Valera as Sinn Féin president could ' . . . act on the assumption that the question of Republicans entering the Free State parliament if the oath were removed, is a question to be decided on its merits when the question arises as a practical issue.'[7] This position of fudge was considered so contentious that the resolution was not made public.

The IRA was also engaged in its own form of reassessment—its relationship with Sinn Féin. Speculation that some anti-Treaty Sinn Féiners were rethinking their strategy and were considering ending their parliamentary isolation pushed the IRA to sever its link with the political wing.

An IRA resolution noted that:

The Government [Sinn Féin] has developed into a mere political party and has apparently lost sight of the fact that all our energies should be devoted to the all-important work of making the Army efficient so that the renegades who, through a coup d'etat, assumed governmental powers in this county be dealt with at the earliest possible opportunity.[8]

It was not just a change to abstentionism that prompted the IRA decision. Sinn Féin's financial position had gradually worsened after a cash-rich period in 1923–24. One consequence of this poor financial health was an inability to provide funds for the IRA. In addition to the lack of Sinn Féin money, the party had not delivered on its early electoral promise and was further than ever from attaining power in Ireland. The IRA leadership determined that the organisation was gaining little, if anything, from the association with its political cousins in Sinn Féin.

The break with the IRA did not remove Sinn Féin from the realm of violence. The party refused to accept the existence of the new constitutional arrangements on the island and left open the option of supporting military action to achieve its stated goals. There was also a continued overlap in membership between the two organisations. This close relationship was illustrated in April 1927 when the police raided Sinn Féin's offices on Dawson Street in Dublin. Documents seized in Dawson Street led the authorities to search the home of a Florence McCarthy. During that search, more documents were discovered, including the names of people who had sat on a Central Criminal Court jury the previous February and a circular which had been sent to each member of the jury, signed 'Ghosts'. Florence McCarthy was subsequently sentenced to a six-month term in prison.

The republican fundamentalists wanted the party to continue to stand aside from the new state. At the 1925 Sinn Féin Ard Fheis, two days of debate took place on a motion from the party's Caherciveen cumann (branch) in County Kerry, which proposed making a commitment to abstentionism until such time as an all-Ireland Republic was formed. De Valera opposed such a rigid interpretation of the policy advocated by Arthur Griffith many years previously to attain his monarchical solution to Ireland's relationship with Britain. Another compromise was reached at the 1925 Ard Fheis—the policy remained but with further discussion planned before any change would be brought to a future party conference.

In any event, de Valera had come to accept that an unchanged position meant permanent isolation on the margins of political life. He was further confirmed in his view after the Boundary Commssion Agreement was published in late 1925, leaving partition in place, in the short term at the very least.

De Valera decided the time had come for the party to consider the possibility of parliamentary participation. He made his first public move at a meeting of the Ranelagh cumann of Sinn Féin on 6 January 1926. The Sinn Féin president told the gathering that he was prepared to take his seat in Dáil Éireann if the oath of allegiance was removed. He was no longer prepared to remain in the world of ideological purity awaiting the return of the all-Ireland republic. Five years of self-imposed isolation were about to end.[9]

The departure from the position of republican purity was formalised at the Sinn Féin Ard Fheis in March 1926. The numbers attending were much depleted compared with the Sinn Féin gatherings prior to the 1922 split, but still 500 delegates packed into the Round Room of the Mansion House in Dublin. De Valera proposed that with the abolition of the oath of allegiance, abstentionism would be treated as an adaptable tactic rather than an immovable principle. To the purists, however, this was a position that was incompatible with the principles on which Sinn Féin was based.

Fr Michael O'Flanagan led the opposition to the de Valera proposal. 'The staunchest priest, who ever lived in Ireland' was how Cathal Brugha described the County Roscommon-born cleric. O'Flanagan had opposed the Treaty but had spent the early 1920s in America and Australia, from where he was deported after spending three weeks in prison due to—in his own words—'some compliments paid to St George on the occasion of his feast.'[10]

De Valera is said to have invited O'Flanagan back to Ireland and to have asked him to chair a Sinn Féin sub-committee appointed to prepare a new policy programme for the party. The controversial matter of electoral strategy was soon, however, occupying all minds, with O'Flanagan leading the campaign against the change and even proposing counter-motions to those favoured by de Valera.

The debate ran for two days before the main protagonists—de Valera and O'Flanagan—wound up the proceedings with each man delivering a final 15-minute speech. When the votes were counted, it became apparent that the new policy had been defeated. A narrow majority (223 votes to 218) opposed de Valera's position.

The Mansion House emptied just before midnight with the realisation that another split had occurred in the ranks of the Sinn Féin movement. The following morning, de Valera made his final address as Sinn Féin president. If he had won the vote, it was probable that the successful faction would have retained the name Sinn Féin and the defeated traditional republican minority would have departed. With a handful of votes more for de Valera, it might well be that Fianna Fáil might never have come into existence. But as it was, de Valera and his supporters were the ones to leave to form their new political organisation.

The fault lines in Sinn Féin in 1926 were between pragmatists and idealists. After the split was confirmed, it seemed that the numbers would divide evenly between the two groupings. Indeed, de Valera took with him 21 of the 47 Sinn Féin TDs while there were 17 resignations from the 37-member party standing committee. But as Fianna Fáil gathered momentum—and showed an enthusiasm for power—more and more Sinn Féiners switched their allegiance to the new party. The idealists were offering no new vision; there was a complete inability to consider the value in revising what the party represented and the means used to achieve its objectives.

Arthur Griffith had bequeathed abstentionism to Sinn Féin but he had never intended this policy to impinge on the party's development. It worked successfully in the aftermath of the 1918 Westminster election because Sinn Féin won a majority of the seats on offer and was in a strong position to utilise the policy. In truth, abstentionism can be effective only where those adopting the policy are in a majority. But for over half a century, Sinn Féin held abstentionism as a core value. The policy became a non-debatable principle. Crucially during these years, the party was always in a political and parliamentary minority. It was a position from which republicans could not win. The unmoveable stance hurt Sinn Féin's progression and it has been only in the 'era of pragmatism' under Gerry Adams that republicans have been prepared to act on the matter.

If the split of 1922 checked Sinn Féin's dominant political role in Ireland, the party was consigned to the fringes of Irish political life after the 1926 split. Initially, the IRA was favourably disposed towards de Valera's new party, hoping that it would continue with an abstentionist policy. The IRA was still estranged from Sinn Féin and Smith observes: 'for a while it seemed that the movement would recognise the party [Fianna Fáil] as its de facto electoral arm.'[11]

The IRA sought a commitment that Fianna Fáil members would pledge, 'not to enter any foreign controlled Parliament as a minority or a majority.'[12] But having broken from Sinn Féin, de Valera was unwilling to take advice from the military wing of the anti-system republican movement. In any event, political circumstances were to change with the assassination of senior cabinet minister, Kevin O'Higgins.

There had been limited IRA activity after the ending of the civil war in 1923, primarily sporadic attacks on police and army barracks. The killing of Kevin O'Higgins, therefore, qualified in IRA terms as a 'spectacular'. In the aftermath of his death, the Free State government introduced legislation that required all election candidates to agree at the time of their nomination to take the oath of allegiance and also to take their seats if elected to parliament. Under protest, Fianna Fáil TDs entered Leinster House on 12 August 1927.

Despite the departure from doctrinaire purity, the IRA leadership still saw benefit in Fianna Fáil's political advancement although this was primarily in the hope that the party would treat the organisation and its objectives more favourably than the Cumann na nGaedheal government.

But there was little advantage forthcoming from Fianna Fáil after the party first entered government in 1932. Initially, de Valera adopted a policy of 'killing the IRA with kindness'. Republicans were released from prison while state pensions were offered to those who had fought in the civil war, regardless of which side. Moreover, the new government pursued constitutional changes, such as abolishing the parliamentary oath, downgrading the position of the monarch's representative and refusing to pay annuities due to the British from the various land acts.

All these measures help to diminish the republican leadership's argument that the new Free State was not worth supporting. The rationale for their rigid ideological position was further diluted with the introduction of a new constitution in 1937, which transformed the Free State into a republic in everything but the name. The 1937 Constitution removed all aspects of British identity that had been incorporated from the Anglo-Irish Treaty into the original constitution of the Free State.

Whatever empathy Fianna Fáil had with the IRA—latent or otherwise —it ended with the 1937 constitution as, in Fianna Fáil's view, it was now unacceptable to withhold loyalty to the Irish state. Moreover, the republican aspiration for reunification with what was now Northern Ireland remained in place and was explicitly recognised in a constitutional claim of ownership over the entire island. Within Fianna Fáil there was now little sympathy for former colleagues and when IRA violence reappeared, de Valera acted swiftly and banned the organisation. Nobody was too concerned about Sinn Féin.

The fact of the matter was that the fourth Sinn Féin had little relevance to mainstream Irish life. Those involved with the organisation after the 1926 split were the purists, the diehards, those who refused any compromise on what republicans had proclaimed at Easter 1916. Fr Michael O'Flanagan continued his involvement and served as party president in the mid-1930s. It was a role also filled by other traditionalists like J. J. O'Kelly who succeeded de Valera as party president in 1926. O'Kelly wrote about Irish language and Irish history using the name 'Sceilig' and also served as president of the Gaelic League. After five years as Sinn Féin president, O'Kelly stood down in favour of Brian O'Higgins, a veteran of the 1916 Rising, participant in the Dáil Treaty debates and anti-Treaty Sinn Féin TD for Clare until the June 1927 general election. O'Higgins was uncompromising in his republican outlook and parted with Sinn Féin in 1933 over the issue of taking Free State pensions, which he opposed.

In truth, de Valera left behind a motley crew whose strategy for dealing with the Ireland that emerged out of the 1921 peace treaty was fundamentally flawed. Opposition to the new institutional arrangements was mounted from an ideological bunker inhabited by individuals like O'Flanagan, O'Kelly and O'Higgins. They wanted to turn the clock back to the world before the Treaty, and the only political tools they wanted to utilise were those honed and sharpened in a different era. In truth, after de Valera and his supporters departed, the party that emerged—the fourth Sinn Féin, the Isolationist model—had no alternative vision to offer.

Seventy years would pass before Sinn Féin would tackle its self-imposed strategic time warp. In the meantime, it was led by well-meaning individuals like Margaret Buckley who, from her late teens at the birth of the twentieth century, was involved in every organisation established to progress the cause of Irish independence from British rule, although it was the Sinn Féin organisation that was to consume a great deal of her energies for almost 50 years.

Born Margaret Goulding in County Cork, she was still a teenager when she became a founder member of the local branch of Maud Gonne's Inghinidhe na hÉireann (Daughters of Erin) set up around the time of Queen Victoria's visit to Ireland in 1900. The young Cork woman quickly became a strident member of the emerging separatist movement.

A move to Dublin came after her marriage to Patrick Buckley, and their home in the north Dublin area of Glasnevin became a cradle of republican activity. The Buckley house was a regular venue for meetings where strategies were planned and schemes plotted. It was also a safe place where arms were stored and, for that reason, dawn raids by the British—and later Free State—forces were not uncommon.

Buckley was known for her sharp wit and biting put-downs of opponents, and her voice was heard from Sinn Féin platforms for nearly half a century. A powerful public speaker, she never lost her distinctive Cork accent. In truth, she is one of the less-known witnesses and participants in the struggle for Irish freedom. Indeed, Margaret Buckley is interesting because her life very much paralleled the story of the Sinn Féin movement over the first half-century of its existence.

Buckley was involved in the 1916 Easter Rising, imprisoned by the British and released in the general amnesty in 1917. The term in prison did little to cool her enthusiasm for republican politics. In the Sinn Féin drive to usurp British power in Ireland after the 1918 Westminster election, Buckley was appointed as a judge in the newly created Republican courts in Dublin. These arbitration courts were intended to supplant the British system in Ireland and were an important part of the abstentionist system favoured by Sinn Féin.

While not a leading name in the republican movement, Buckley was well known to the British authorities and was eventually arrested in December 1920. She spent the subsequent six months in Mountjoy Jail. The War of Independence formally ended with the acceptance of the Anglo-Irish Treaty in 1921 but Buckley sided with those opposed to the peace deal. Her involvement with the anti-Treaty republicans led to another prison term, only this time courtesy of the government of the new Free State.

She was one of about 400 women imprisoned during the Irish civil war of 1922–23. Many women were detained in the North Dublin Union, a former workhouse that was filthy and lacked any proper washing facilities and other basic amenities. The women were treated harshly but still ran the internment centre along military lines, as Buckley later recorded:

There was plenty of open space about the rambling buildings, and here Lily McClean drilled her troops in great style. I have never seen any woman call out orders and enforce them like Captain McClean ... There were rumours of peace moves outside, but we were far more isolated in this camp than we were in the jails. We had little, if any, communication with the outside world ... It was about this time that I was dealt a bitter blow. A paper, some weeks old, had been found somewhere, and a group of the girls were eagerly scanning it. Presently one of them called out to me: 'What is the number of your house?' I told her. 'They've got your dump,' she called back, and read out a long list of 'stuff' which I thought was safe for ever, considering that it had escaped the search on the night of my arrest, in January, and subsequent raids. I sat down and cried . . . .[13]

Throughout her life, Buckley would refuse to recognise the institutions that emerged out of the 1921 peace deal. It was this hardline opposition that led her to remain with Sinn Féin after 1926. Buckley was the first woman to lead a political party in Ireland—a feat that was not again achieved until Mary Harney was elected leader of the Progressive Democrats in 1994. One chronicler of Buckley's life observed: 'Margaret Buckley was foremost of the really faithful few who maintained the Sinn Féin organisation intact during the difficult years of the 1930s, '40s and '50s . . .'[14] This was the political life lived by the purest of the pure of diehard republicans. These were the people who kept the flame burning from the Republic proclaimed at the General Post Office on Easter

Monday 1916, voted for that Republic in the Sinn Féin landslide election victory in 1918 and saw their beloved Republic surrendered by 'traitors' at Downing Street in 1921.

In a way, Margaret Buckley and her colleagues in Sinn Féin kept alive a political brand name that could be handed on to other republicans. As such, the label Sinn Féin had proven to be hugely flexible, for the party that Margaret Buckley joined in 1905 was very different from the party she served as president between 1937 and 1950, as vice-president until 1958 and as honorary vice-president from 1958 until her death in July 1962. The party had transformed itself again and again, and would do so to an even greater degree in subsequent decades, most particularly under the leadership of Gerry Adams from the early 1980s onwards.

From the 1920s onwards, the rump band of republicans who numbered the membership of the IRA and Sinn Féin pursued a lonely path. A form of self-imposed exile marked their grim existence which was only made worse by their own destructive divisions. After the break between the IRA and Sinn Féin in November 1925, it would be another 23 years before the twin elements of the republican movement would again co-exist together. The departure of de Valera in 1926 stripped Sinn Féin of credibility and relevance.

Michael Laffan has observed of the 1926 split: 'Most of the politically talented republicans followed de Valera into Fianna Fail, and—as subsequent events proved—so did most republican voters.'[15] The bleak early life of the fourth version of Sinn Féin was to be an indication of the direction the party would travel for many years that followed.

Only around 200 delegates registered for the Sinn Féin Ard Fheis in late 1926. But it was not just members who were in short supply— money was also tight. A loan was required to pay the rent due on the party's headquarters. In a pamphlet history of Sinn Féin, written as a propaganda exercise at the time of a new IRA campaign in the late 1950s —Margaret Buckley recalled Sinn Féin's precarious existence:

We were left without resources—there being only about £26 left in the Treasury—and we soon had to evacuate the expensive headquarters in Suffolk Streetand move to 16 Parnell Square. Those premises were burnt out and many of our historic documents lost. We led a roving existence for some time . . . and were subjected to raids by Free State troops who searched, or attempted to search those present, and confiscated documents and literature which was never returned.[16]

This much-depleted fourth Sinn Féin contested the June 1927 general election on an abstentionist platform but found it was eclipsed by its recently departed colleagues in Fianna Fáil. The party received a mere 3.6 per cent of the vote, winning only five seats to the 44 seats secured by de Valera's new grouping.

A second general election was held later in 1927. The new rule requiring all candidates to pledge in advance to take their seats if elected was introduced for this September 1927 election. Abstentionism was incompatible with the new legislation, and so Sinn Féin withdrew from electoral participation. It was another 30 years before the names of Sinn Féin candidates would again feature on ballot papers in southern Ireland.

In a blunt but accurate summary of the party's role in subsequent years, Maurice Manning observes that 'from this point on, Sinn Féin ceased to have any real influence, existing merely as a minor organisation on the fringe of Irish politics, growing more extreme, more intransigent, with the passing of time, until eventually it had little more than a shadow existence.'[17]

The rump Sinn Féin may not have been near achieving its goals but it clung to the knowledge that it was consistent with the doctrinaire purity while others deviated into the corrupt world of political activism.

In his address as party president in 1928, J. J. O'Kelly noted: 'the most obvious results of the Fianna Fail apostasy have been the inevitable drift and shelving of principles that everywhere follow political compromise . . . The movement prospered while it was kept on a place too exalted for the corrupt to thrive in . . . we have no prospects to offer but the old unrequited service to a deathless cause.'[18]

In truth, however, the fourth Sinn Féin was an irrelevance. The adherence to the abstentionism policy lessened the party's public profile. To add insult to injury, when the Cumann na nGaedheal government banned the IRA and several other republican organisations in 1928, Sinn Féin was not even placed on the proscribed list.The weakened Sinn Féin was run by a small number of aging fundamentalists, like Margaret Buckley. The party suffered from a small and declining membership, and it had no money. Moreover, republican militarists had little time for Sinn Féin—senior IRA men were said to have been disparaging Sinn Féin up and down the country.

On several occasions during the 1930s, when militant republicans rekindled their interest in politics, they chose to do so without their former party. One such example was Cumann Poblachta na hÉireann, established in 1936 amid some unease in the IRA about any political participation.

The existence of this new party caused many republicans to switch their allegiance away from the little that was left of the local Sinn Féin organisations. The Mallow branch was wound up when its membership —all IRA members—defected to Cumann Poblachta. But political action remained a secondary endeavour for these republicans and it was no surprise when the new party, having failed miserably in two by-elections in 1936, was quietly disbanded.

Two years later, the flame of republican purity was vested not in Sinn Féin but in the IRA. In an act of symbolism, the seven surviving anti-Treaty members of the second Dáil, elected in 1921, transferred their authority to the Army Council of the IRA. These republicans believed that the democratic mandate of the second Dáil had been usurped by the Treaty settlement and that they—and not the Free State administrations —were the rightful government of Ireland. The IRA was now—in traditional republican terms—the inheritor of the spirit of Easter 1916 and the body vested with preserving the separatist mandate. In republican terms, the move made the IRA Army Council the de jure government of the Irish Republic, and thereby gave the organisation the right to use force and levy for war.

The seven anti-Treaty republicans included names long familiar with Sinn Féin history—Count Plunkett, J. J. O'Kelly, Mary MacSwiney, Brian O'Higgins, Cathal O'Murchadha, Tom Maguire and Professor William Stockley. Despite the close and recent association that these individuals had with Sinn Féin, the party was not even informed of the decision to bestow the mantle of government on the IRA Army Council. This can be taken only as an illustration of just how marginal, by 1938, the party had become to the business of republican activism.

Interestingly, 31 years later when the IRA split in 1969, Tom Maguire, as the last member of the 1938 group, declared that the Provisional IRA was the successor body and the one which would wield authority as the de jure government of the 32-county Irish Republic. This action by Maguire was long heralded as legitimising the actions of republicans associated with Gerry Adams in the Provisional IRA and Provisional Sinn Féin.

Their lineage of republican purity from the all-Ireland Dáil in 1921 was removed, however, in 1986, in a division over the recognition of the parliament of the 26-county Irish Republic. Ironically, Maguire, who by that time had reached his ninety-fourth birthday, turned his back on those who altered the traditional course of republican politics.

Adams was snubbed as, instead, the elderly republican nominated Republican Sinn Féin as the legitimate Sinn Féin and therefore as the inheritors of the mandate and authority of the 1921 all-Ireland government.

The rigidities of the republican ideological position dominated Sinn Féin. Within a decade of the 1922 split, the party that had briefly dominated politics in Ireland was a marginal influence even within the republican movement. Shunned by its former friends in the IRA, rejected by the public, Sinn Féin seemed to be in terminal decline. Party membership by the 1940s was about 100. In May 1948, the Sinn Féin joint secretary, Diarmuid O'Leary, remarked of the party's members: 'they are just getting old, you know.'

The following year, only 50 delegates attended the party's Ard Fheis. At the time, one republican newspaper observed of this declining group of aging diehards: 'for years Sinn Féin has been content to pursue its way quietly and unobtrusively, relying on the small band of loyal stalwarts who have kept the organisation going, in good times and in bad.'[19] The party organised republican lectures in the winter and spring months and maintained contact between former comrades through the annual Wolfe Tone commemoration at Bodenstown in County Kildare.

Their main task was refusing recognition to what they saw as a sham creation, the 26-county state. Bizarrely, they tried to live their lives by bypassing the institutions of that state. There were bitter rows in their ranks in the mid-1930s when the party chose to allow its members to take the republican pensions introduced by the Fianna Fáil government. For some in Sinn Féin, taking this pension was akin to supping with the devil. Mary MacSwiney—one of the surviving members of the Second Dáil—resigned in protest, as did Brian O'Higgins who had taken over as party president in 1931.

The resolve of the Sinn Féin membership was again tested in the 1940s with a court case that went to the very core of the republican theology. The case revolved around the monies held by Sinn Féin at the time the party split in 1922 over the Treaty. The pro-Treaty party officers succeeded in preventing de Valera from getting his hands on the money by vesting the total amount of £8,610 with the High Court until its ownership was determined. The money remained under court control until a court challenge in the early 1940s.

By that time, the balance had grown to £24,000, and ironically de Valera was fundamentally opposed to the money being claimed by the leadership of the party which saw itself as anti-Treaty Sinn Féin. In

March 1947, he told the Dáil, 'To say that an insignificant little group, no matter what technical grounds they may put forward, could be regarded as entitled to the possession of these national funds is just absurd.'[20]

This was an interesting twist as the money had been entrusted with the High Court in the first place to prevent de Valera from getting his hands on it. The 1926 split in Sinn Féin, however, shifted relations and de Valera did not want the group he had parted from to receive the money. Jeannie Wyse-Power had been involved with Sinn Féin before the 1916 Rising and had held the position of joint treasurer since 1909. She ran a restaurant in Henry Street on the north side of Dublin city, which sold only Irish produce. Wyse-Power supported the Treaty and it was her actions—along with those of fellow treasurer, Eamonn Duggan—which deprived de Valera of access to the money. One supporter of the de Valera faction subsequently admitted: 'The difficulties created by the withholding of the funds at this critical time can not be overestimated ....'[21]

After the death of Mrs Wyse-Power in January 1941—Eamonn Duggan had died in 1936—her brother approached de Valera with a suggestion that the funds be used to help those who had been involved in the republican movement between 1916 and 1921 and who were in financial difficulties.

With the prospect that the money would be dispersed—money that they considered theirs of right—Margaret Buckley as Sinn Féin president was forced into responding. The decision to take a legal case was not without its difficulties for Buckley and her colleagues. This was the group which a few short years previously had only very reluctantly agreed that Sinn Féin membership was compatible with taking a civil war pension from the Free State. Now they were proposing to go before one of the state's highest institutions—the legitimacy of which they refused to recognise—to, in effect, ask for their money back. Some republican diehards resigned from Sinn Féin over the decision but four party members, including Buckley as the incumbent president and J. J. O'Kelly, a previous party president, opted to proceed with the case.

This group claimed that as the contemporary leadership of Sinn Féin, it had legal entitlement to the money held by the High Court. Legal proceedings dragged on for several years, during which time the Fianna Fáil government introduced legislation to deal with the funds held by the courts. The Sinn Féin Funds Bill was introduced in the Oireachtas in March 1947 and was, to say the least, an unusual development, with the government moving legislation on an issue that was before the courts.

The opposition parties in Dáil Éireann taunted de Valera, claiming that he feared being called as a witness in the case. Across the Dáil chamber, one Fine Gael TD confronted de Valera: 'He does not want to stand up and take his oath and give evidence because his conscience will be in conflict with history.'[22] Naturally enough, the Fianna Fáil leader rejected the accusation and claimed he was motivated by the fact that, in the absence of legislation, the 'funds would be frittered away in legal costs.'[23]

The legislation was eventually passed but the court case continued. In the end, Mr Justice Kingsmill Moore found against Buckley and her colleagues based on the fact that when de Valera and his supporters had formally reconstituted Sinn Féin in 1923, they had bypassed the individuals who held officer positions at the time of the split and who were the only people with the authority to call the 1923 meeting.

The case was lost and costs were awarded against Sinn Féin, but Buckley and her supporters were able to take some comfort from the judgment handed down by Mr Justice Kingsmill Moore. He found that there was no continuity in legal terms between the second Sinn Féin party (Separatist SF, 1917–22) and the third version of the party (Republican SF, 1922–26). This was a conclusion that republican purists could never accept.

There was, however, some satisfaction in the judge's determination that the anti-Treaty Sinn Féin party that emerged after the split in 1922 was the same party that they represented in 1948. That is, using our categorisation, the third Sinn Féin (Republican SF, 1922–26) was legally at least the same party as the fourth Sinn Féin (Isolationist SF, 1926–69).

Judge Kingsmill Moore observed of Margaret Buckley and her Sinn Féin colleagues that they:

. . . appeared to me perfectly sincere, believing not only in the righteousness but also in the rightness of their claim. Moreover they adduced considerable evidence to show that they faithfully represent one approach to the Irish Republic which was prevalent in the Sinn Féin of 1917–22 . . . which I have termed transcendental . . . It would appear that all the required steps were taken to preserve the continuity of the organisation and that present-day Sinn Féin is legally the same organisation as that which was born in 1923.

The republicans may have lost their case and access to the money but they could take some semblance of victory from the judgment. The High

Court had determined that legally Sinn Féin—and not Fianna Fáil —continued the line of republican purity.

It was at best a shallow victory. Politically and militarily, the republican movement was a motley crew, and an unsuccessful one at that. During the Second World War, the government in Dublin tolerated no resistance from the IRA that would interfere with the policy of neutrality. Republicans were arrested, executed and allow to die on hunger strike. Sinn Féin meetings were banned and the authorities even censored reporting of the party's Ard Fheis. The 1939–45 period indicated just how severe Fianna Fáil in government was willing to be with its former colleagues from the early years of the Free State's existence.

After the Second World War was over, in the late 1940s a reassessment of the direction that the entire republican movement was taking led to a policy reorientation and a new interest in re-establishing IRA links with Sinn Féin. A number of disparate events indicated not insubstantial support for republican politics. There was also the enthuastic response to the establishment of the Anti-Partition League in late 1945, which united all the various groups opposed to partition.

The Anti-Partition League was followed by the emergence in the Free State of a new political party with strong republican leanings. That supporters of the republican cause backed both organisations in significant numbers was food for thought for those hardline republicans who had shunned the political process. In particular, Clann na Poblachta offered a model of sorts for republican advancement. The new party was led by former IRA men and drew on a republican constituency for its electoral successes in the 1947–48 period. The party joined a multi-party government in Dublin after the 1948 general election.

There was renewed thinking about republican strategy, although what was interesting was that it took place within the narrow parameters of traditional republicanism. So, electoral participation and political activity were not warmly embraced; rather they were considered a temporary tool usefully to assist a new IRA campaign. For the first time since the 1920s, however, there was a significant change of emphasis. The target was no longer the Irish Free State but rather the British presence in Northern Ireland.

An Easter statement from the IRA's Army Council in 1950 signalled an end to military action against the newly proclaimed Irish Republic: 'in order that no excuse may be provided for using coercion and to define quite clearly that the Irish Republican Army had only one enemy,

England, no sanction will be given for any type of aggressive military action in the Twenty-Six County area.'

While hardly a radical departure, the mantra of this anti-system cabal was in the 1950s narrowed even further to a straightforward demand for British withdrawal. But republicans proceeded with absolutist demands for Irish unity with little consideration about the merits of political action to achieve their goals. There was an unwillingness to consider using the constitutional process to progress republican objectives.

The IRA still did not recognise the legitimacy of the Irish state but with its new thinking came a renewed desire to start a military campaign in Northern Ireland. Sinn Féin was to play an ancillary role as the republican movement briefly re-entered the world of electoral politics.

In the late 1940s, Sinn Féin was restored as the IRA's political wing. While they had been parted, both organisations shared the same aims — an end to partition, non-recognition of the institutions established by the 1921 Anglo-Irish Treaty and an openness to the use of violence to achieve those aims. The alternative for the IRA was to set up a new body. But given the pitiful condition of the Sinn Féin party, the IRA was able simply to take over Sinn Féin without any fuss and, in tandem, obtain a long-established political brand name. This option had the added attraction of re-establishing historic lineage and continuity through linkage of the traditional militant and political wings of Irish republicanism.

Once the IRA had determined that Sinn Féin as a political organisation would again be useful to its overall objectives, membership overlap was actively encouraged. An order was issued that all IRA members were to join their local Sinn Féin cumann. Suddenly Sinn Féin was relevant again and the influx of new members was to revitalise an organisation that had been morbid for nearly two decades.

At the annual Bodenstown commemoration in 1949, one senior member of Sinn Féin said: 'The Republican movement is divided into two main bodies—the Military and the Civil Arms, the Irish Republican Army and Sinn Féin. Each has an important task to do. In the final analysis the work of either is as important as that of the other.'[24]

The reality, however, has traditionally been very different. Sinn Féin undoubtedly has long operated as the weaker component in the republican movement. This imbalance between political activism and military action was to persist until the Adams-led Sinn Féin made a decisive shift in favour of politics in recent times.

The re-adoption of Sinn Féin was made on IRA terms. The militants moved to take control of the political organisation at the Sinn Féin Ard Fheis in 1950. Margaret Buckley, who had served as Sinn Féin president for thirteen years, stood down. She was by then in her mid-sixties, and the length of her tenure as Sinn Féin president said much about the lack of new blood in the party. Buckley—who remained as vice-president— was replaced by Pádraig MacLogain, another veteran of the War of Independence but, significantly at that time, a senior figure in the IRA.

MacLogain had been an abstentionist member of the Stormont Parliament, representing the South Armagh constituency from 1933 to 1938. By the time he came to lead Sinn Féin in 1950, he was based in County Laois where he ran a public house. He was an advocate for IRA action in the 1950s and during these years provided the necessary linkage between the Sinn Féin Ard Comhairle and the Army Council of the IRA.[25] He was not the only senior individual with dual membership— several other members of the new Sinn Féin executive also had strong IRA connections, including the party's new general secretary, Charlie Murphy, who subsequently served as the IRA's adjutant-general.

This new leadership proceeded to draft a new Sinn Féin constitution, although not before sympathetic Catholic Church clergy vetted the document to ensure that the contents did not clash with Catholic teachings. The new constitution was a restatement of the traditional objectives of post-1921 republican hardliners. The main objectives remained: 'The complete overthrow of English rule in Ireland . . . to bring the Proclamation of the Republic, Easter 1916, into effective operation and to maintain and consolidate the Government of the Republic, representative of the people of all Ireland, based on that Proclamation.' Abstentionism retained its central place in the traditional republican doctrine although no barrier was placed on Sinn Féin members taking seats in local government authorities in the Irish Republic.

The revival of the IRA and the renewal of Sinn Féin took several years to gain public attention. Electoral success was achieved in the 1955 Westminster elections in Northern Ireland, and two years later in Dáil Éireann elections in the Irish Republic. In between, in 1956, the IRA commenced a new military campaign. However, within the world of Irish republicanism there were some individuals who were prepared to stretch their political positioning and ideological outlook beyond that established in the 1920s.

As the IRA re-evaluated its strategy, some republicans broke ranks to test the republican cause at the ballot box. The County Tyrone republican Liam Kelly, who parted with the IRA in late 1951, offers an interesting example of an early willingness to adapt the rigid strategic position pursued by the militant republicans. The County Tyrone man had moved from the purist republican view as articulated by the IRA. He accepted the legitimacy of the 1937 Irish Constitution but still vowed to overthrow British rule in Northern Ireland using violent methods. Political participation was also something Kelly did not oppose although he still favoured abstentionism as a core belief in relation to the Stormont parliament. In a way, Kelly's position was similar to the one that the Gerry Adams-led Sinn Féin followed in the 1986–98 period.

Kelly established a splinter militant republican group, Saor-Uladh (Free Ulster) with a political wing, Fianna Uladh (Soldiers of Ulster). He famously staged an occupation of his hometown of Pomeroy on Easter Monday 1952. The exercise involved Kelly and a number of enthusiastic supporters setting up roadblocks and cutting telephone wires before proceeding to read the 1916 Proclamation in the centre of the town. Bizarre as the episode was, it involved open defiance of the unionist government at Stormont which had banned such gatherings.

In the 1953 elections to the Stormont parliament, Kelly ran as an independent candidate in the Mid-Ulster constituency. Mid-Tyrone was a nationalist area. The outgoing nationalist MP had held the seat for almost five years. In the 1949 Stormont election, he had a comfortable two-to-one victory margin over his unionist opponent, the first unionist to run in the constituency and also the first time in seven elections that the seat had been contested.

The voters were left in no doubt about Kelly's refusal to recognise the legitimacy of Northern Ireland:

> I will not take the Oath of Allegiance to a foreign Queen of a bastard nation. I took an Oath of Allegiance to the Irish Republic when I was sixteen. I have kept that oath and I intend to keep it. I do not believe in constitutional methods. I believe in the use of force; the more the better, the sooner the better. That may be treason or sedition, call it whatever the hell you like.[26]

The voters in Mid-Tyrone were obviously receptive to Kelly's brand of hardline republicanism. They gave him 4,178 votes, a majority of 802 ahead of his nationalist opponent. The authorities in Northern Ireland were, however, unimpressed with his vocal outbursts during the election campaign. The new abstentionist member of the Stormont parliament was—shortly after his election—arrested and charged with making a seditious speech.

Kelly was convicted and, having refused to pay a fine and give an undertaking to keep the peace, he was given a twelve-month sentence. He was eventually released in August 1954 and was met by 10,000 supporters upon his return to Pomeroy. A pitch battle ensued between republicans and the RUC, which left twelve policemen and 40 civilians injured.

At the time of his release, Kelly held the distinction of being a member not only of the Northern Ireland parliament but also of Seanad Éireann in the Irish Republic. His appointment to the Upper House of the Irish parliament had been orchestrated by Sean McBride, the former IRA man who subsequently became the founding leader of the constitutional party, Clann na Poblachta.

In the negotiations that led to the formation of the second inter-party government in Dublin in 1954, Sean McBride's party had opted to offer the new administration external support. Despite being outside the new government, Clann received some of the spoils of office in return for this support. With McBride's backing, Liam Kelly achieved membership of Seanad Éireann. The Clann leader hoped that other republicans would follow Kelly's attitude to abstentionism and come to participate in the electoral process.

The new senator, however, made little use of his position in southern politics. It was the end of 1955 before he made his first contribution. That speech on the development and preservation of Irish-language-speaking areas was also his last.

Kelly pursued a dual political strategy—participating in elections on both sides of the border but taking his seat only in the parliament on the southern side—the legitimacy of the Oireachtas was recognised but the institutions in Northern Ireland were still avoided. Indeed, Kelly advanced an early version of what became the modern republican parallel strategy of combining political involvement with military activism.

The Irish senator and Stormont parliament member was involved in actions against RUC barracks at the end of 1955. He led a raid on the police barracks at Roslea in County Fermanagh which left two dead, a republican and a police officer. Kelly was to serve single terms as Stormont MP and Irish senator and, like many republicans before and after, he subsequently emigrated to the United States. His election victory was important in signalling the existence of an untapped constituency which was prepared to vote for republican candidates, and obviously keen to do so in numbers.

Nevertheless, the republican dilemma about linking participation in elections with recognition of the entire system continued to bedevil militant Irish republicanism. Only in the early 1980s could it be said that the issue was adequately aired and that the merits or otherwise of this facet of republican ideology were fully debated. In the 1950s, the success of Liam Kelly aided the nascent debate about electoral participation but only in terms of what use politics was to the military cause.

Two IRA men were nominated to contest the 1950 Westminster elections but this was not Sinn Féin returning to electoral politics in Northern Ireland; rather it was an opportunity to raise the profile of a campaign on the treatment of republican prisoners. Neither candidate —both of whom were interned in Crumlin Road prison at the time of the election—was elected.

The 1950 contest was a trial run of sorts for Sinn Féin, as the political party moved back into the electoral arena in May 1955 when it contested Westminster elections in Northern Ireland. Most of the party's candidates were in prison, serving sentences for IRA activities. The Nationalist Party stood aside and nominated no candidates, thus giving Sinn Féin a clear run at the Catholic vote. Sinn Féin collected 152,310 votes, and two candidates were elected on an abstentionist platform. Historian Thomas Hennessey has described the result as 'the biggest anti-partition vote since 1921 and nearly fifty thousand more than the total anti-partition vote in 1949.'[27]

The two successful Sinn Féin candidates were both serving ten-year prison sentences related to an IRA raid on an army barracks in Omagh in 1954. Doubts were raised about their eligibility to be elected because of their convictions under the Treason Felony Act, passed by the Westminster parliament in 1848. Unionists successfully petitioned to have Phil Clarke's election in Fermanagh–South Tyrone overturned, and their candidate was awarded the seat.

Moreover, the British government proposed that a fresh election be held in the Mid-Ulster constituency where republican prisoner Tom Mitchell had won the seat by 260 votes. Mitchell increased his majority to 806 votes in the second poll in Mid-Ulster, but on a subsequent petition the seat was awarded to the unionist candidate. In a bizarre turn of events, the unionist candidate was himself deemed ineligible, as he was a state employee. So, for the third time, the voters of Mid-Ulster were asked to choose who they wanted to represent them at Westminster. This time there was a conclusive result because the nationalist vote split with the nomination of a Nationalist Party candidate, and so a unionist won the seat.

The unionist-controlled government at Stormont had long taken steps to mute any electoral involvement by hardline republicans. So, while Sinn Féin contested the Westminster elections in 1955, the party did not nominate any candidates when elections were called in 1958 to the Stormont parliament, where different rules applied.

A number of legislative measures sponsored by unionists combined to prevent Sinn Féin participation in parliamentary elections in Northern Ireland. Legislation from the 1920s required candidates to take an oath foreswearing organisations which were outlawed in Northern Ireland. As this list included the IRA, an automatic difficulty arose for Sinn Féin candidates, although it has to be noted that in the period after 1922, several abstentionist republicans stood for—and were elected to—the Stormont parliament.

Further measures were introduced in the 1950s with the increased possibility that abstentionist republicans would enter the electoral arena to generate propaganda for their aims. Legislation was introduced in 1953 that required candidates to take an oath of allegiance before they were nominated. Moreover, on the back of Sinn Féin's Westminster successes in 1955, the following year the unionist government at Stormont proscribed Sinn Féin. In truth, republicans would not have been too aggrieved at their exclusion, given, in the first instance, their lack of commitment to the political process itself.

Republicans took a very restricted message from their electoral performance at the Westminster contest in 1955. Rather than viewing it as a manifestation of broad Catholic unhappiness in Northern Ireland —and a popular base to be tapped towards achieving specific republican objectives—they saw the result, instead, as an endorsement of military action.

But it was not that militant republicans felt they needed public endorsement for their actions. Indeed, during the 1955 Westminster campaign, a Sinn Féin spokesman warned a public meeting in Belfast: 'If our constitutional campaign fails then inevitably there will be nothing for it but the use of physical force—the gun, rifle and hand grenade in an effort to take back by force what was taken from us by force.'[28]

Since the end of the Second World War, the IRA had been exploring the feasibility of a new military offensive. The organisation, however, was in no condition to mount any serious campaign, lacking money and arms. To counter part of this problem, a series of raids on army barracks in Britain and Northern Ireland was undertaken from 1951 through to 1955. The IRA was edging closer towards military action against the British presence in Northern Ireland.

The 1950s were an incredibly active decade for the republican movement as the IRA commenced its new military campaign and Sinn Féin contested its first election in almost 30 years. On 12 December 1956, the IRA started a border campaign directed exclusively at targets in Northern Ireland. The campaign, which lasted until 1962, was a complete disaster.

The plan, named Operation Harvest, was built around the idea of mobile flying columns attacking targets in Northern Ireland from bases in the Irish Republic. High on the list of targets were communication links—rail, road and telephone sites, as well as army and police barracks. Over 100 IRA members were involved when the organisation's border campaign commenced in mid-December 1956. During the first month, bombs destroyed a BBC transmitter in Derry and an army building in Enniskillen. A police hut in Newry and several bridges in Fermanagh were also damaged. It was the start of a six-year campaign that involved 500 incidents and seventeen deaths, including six RUC officers and eight members of the IRA.

When the campaign commenced, the IRA issued a public statement outlining its aim of creating 'an independent, united, democratic Irish Republic'. Interestingly, Sinn Féin was also the vehicle through which the republicans chose to generate propaganda for their cause: 'Irishmen have again risen in revolt against British aggression in Ireland. The Sinn Féin organisation say to the Irish people that they are proud of the risen nation and appeal to the people of Ireland to assist in every way they can the soldiers of the Irish Republican Army.'[29]

On New Year's Day in 1957, a number of IRA members were involved in an attack on an RUC station in Brookeborough, a small town in County Fermanagh. Among those leading the attack were Fergal O'Hanlon, Sean South and Daithi Ó Connell. Nineteen-year-old O'Hanlon had a brother, Einachan, who later that year was elected to Dáil Éireann by the voters of Monaghan. Ó Connell would subsequently rise to prominence in the republican movement in the 1970s and, along with Ruairí Ó Brádaigh, would lead the two strands of the republican movement, holding senior positions in both the IRA and Sinn Féin. The bomb the IRA men were delivering to the RUC station failed to explode, while, in a hail of police fire, O'Hanlon and South, a 27-year-old from Limerick, were fatally shot.

The border campaign reactivated support and sympathy for the IRA and Sinn Féin in traditional republican areas. The circumstances were created for Sinn Féin to return to electoral politics in the southern Irish state after an absence of 30 years. Having been restored as the political wing of the IRA at the start of the 1950s, the party had tested the electoral waters in Northern Ireland with some success. Now the time was correct—the republican leadership believed—to return in the south with the clear intention of seeking endorsement for the IRA's border campaign.

The party made a tactical decision to contest the 1957 general election in the Republic. Abstentionism was still the hallmark of the republican electoral strategy which itself was subservient to the military campaign. The decision to contest in 1957 was by no means a signal that hardline republicans were contemplating a full-scale commitment to politics—in truth, the campaign was built around the traditional republican objective of British withdrawal, while Sinn Féin was once more operating to the agenda set by the IRA.

Sinn Féin polled well, receiving 5.3 per cent of the vote (65,640 first preferences) and four of the party's candidates were elected to Dáil Éireann although, in keeping with traditional republican dogma, they did not take their seats. The party won seats in republican heartlands— Sligo–Leitrim, Monaghan, Kerry and Longford–Westmeath.

Among those elected in 1957 was a 25-year-old schoolteacher named Ruairí Ó Brádaigh who had been a republican activist for over a decade and was involved in the IRA's renewed military campaign in Northern Ireland. Ó Brádaigh was interned in the Republic shortly after his election. He subsequently became a senior republican figure, serving on the IRA Army Council during the 1970s and as Sinn Féin president from 1970 until 1983.

Ó Brádaigh had little time for the parliament to which he was elected: 'Well the Sinn Féin attitude since 1922 was not to accept the two partition parliaments which supplanted the All-Ireland First Dáil and Second Dáil. . . .'[30] It was a view that typified republican attitudes to the political reality that had been accepted by the vast majority of people since the 1922 peace settlement.

Like all republican purists, Ó Brádaigh refused to accept the legitimacy of Dáil Éireann or any parliamentary body elected in Northern Ireland. He believed that political participation should be driven by a pick-and-choose strategy, with republicans contesting elections only when there was an opportunity to use politics to advance overall republican objectives.

Despite his contemptuous attitude to the institutions in both the Irish Republic and Northern Ireland, Ó Brádaigh had no difficulty with electoral participation by republicans:

The Republican attitude is that the election machinery belongs to the people and that the election machinery has been used to assemble an All-Ireland parliament before and indeed it can be done again. What we are calling for is an All-Ireland election to a 32-county assembly, which in the context of a British declaration to quit Ireland would debate and work out a new constitution for the whole of Ireland which would then be put to the people in referendum.[31]

While Sinn Féin polled well in the 1957 general election, the real victors were Fianna Fáil. De Valera was returned for a final term as Taoiseach and one of his first acts was to quash the nascent republican threat. The outgoing government had, in fact, targeted leading republicans in early 1957, but many of these individuals were released by the middle of the year. A more effective measure to remove leading republicans from active control of the IRA and Sinn Féin was required. Internment without trial was introduced in July 1957.

The Sinn Féin headquarters was included on the list of premises to be raided by the Garda Síochána. Most of the party's Ard Comhairle members were arrested although the authorities thought it sensible not to detain the former Sinn Féin president, Margaret Buckley, who at 78 years of age soon found herself the only member of the party executive not held by the state. Buckley may no longer have been party president but she was still an active member.

The party's publicity committee published a short history of Sinn Féin, written by Buckley—'a proud history' the title claimed of the 1905 to 1956 period. Interestingly, Buckley acknowledged the value of ending electoral isolationism, writing of the 1955 Westminster contest: 'the propaganda value of the campaign was enormous.'[32] There was also some satisfaction to the heavy-handed response to the renewed republican activity, as Buckley concluded: 'this panic counteraction is the greatest compliment that could be paid to Sinn Féin. . . .'[33]

With internment policies in place in the Irish Republic—and also in Northern Ireland—the IRA was stripped of its leading members. Moreover, the organisation's border campaign was suffering from a lack of funds, weapons and public support. The campaign peaked in 1957 when there were 341 IRA operations. In fact, three-quarters of all the 450 IRA operations mounted between December 1956 and February 1962 took place in 1957.

Despite the emotionalism surrounding the deaths of O'Hanlon and South—and the Sinn Féin performance in the 1957 Dáil elections—there was little public enthusiasm for the IRA campaign. The voters delivered their verdict in two further sets of elections. The Sinn Féin vote collapsed at the 1959 Westminster elections—the party received 73,415 votes, down from 152,310 in 1955. No seats were won. At the Dáil general election in 1961, all four Sinn Féin seats were lost. The party's vote declined from 65,000 first preferences in 1957 to 35,000 in 1961. The wave of republican emotion in the aftermath of the O'Hanlon and South funerals had undoubtedly contributed to the vote for Sinn Féin candidates in 1957. Four years later, in the absence of an emotional focus during the 1961 campaign, the voters saw no real reason to back republican candidates.

Something more fundamental was also involved in the collapse of the Sinn Féin vote. By continuing with its policy of not taking seats won, Sinn Féin failed to make adequate use of the political platform which parliamentary membership—especially of Dáil Éireann—would have provided. Moreover, with the continuation of armed conflict, there was an obvious limit to the electoral advance of traditional republicanism. Many people were sympathic to the republican cause—as evidenced by their support in the ballot box—but were less receptive to the violence associated with the IRA, which in turn tended to reduce their willingness to back Sinn Féin candidates. This reality would also later shape the thinking of Gerry Adams in the 1980s.

In any event, republicans had taken a short-term view of electoral participation, trading on tradition and emotion. No attempt was made to establish Sinn Féin as a significant political party. There was no distinct policy platform on offer besides ending partition. If anything, Sinn Féin, as represented by its republican leaders, was a conservative organisation driven by classic Irish Catholic orthodoxy. The adoption of even mild left-wing radical politics was not an option for these traditional Catholics who feared any association of their cause with the slur of communist sympathiser.

The decision to participate in electoral contests was merely to bolster the IRA military campaign. Republicans were simply not interested in developing a strong political movement. They took the results as an endorsement of their border campaign. But the 1957 electoral performance—just like the 1955 Westminster result—was transitory.

The electoral performances did not lead to any immediate or radical overhaul of the traditional republican attitude to political action; rather there was a reversion to type. The conclusion reached by Seán MacStiofain, who later became IRA Chief of Staff, would have been widely shared:

> This result confirmed my belief that a revolutionary organisation must be extremely careful about the timing of any involvement in parliamentary elections. Revolutionary political action is necessary. But it should not always include the contesting of elections, though there are times when it is advantageous to do so. The best strategy is to go all out in local elections, build up from that base and then wait until you can put enough candidates in a general election to give the people a clear choice between straight Republican and Free State policies.[34]

Whatever about waiting for the day when the Irish public would again flock to republican politics in numbers reminiscent of 1918, the reality for Sinn Féin was much bleaker. In terms of getting its objectives implemented, the party was politically and ideologically bankrupt. When it came to policies outside the national question, Sinn Féin had nothing to offer the electorate. It was a lesson from history that many contemporary republicans failed to appreciate. Republicans like Gerry Adams and Danny Morrison initially believed that Sinn Féin would continue to capitalise after 1981 on the electoral triumphs achieved during that turbulent year by prisoner and hunger-strike candidates in Northern Ireland and the Irish Republic. They were quickly to learn that Sinn Féin—especially in the Irish Republic—had to offer voters more than a narrow republican agenda tied to self-imposed parliamentary exclusion.

A shift in thinking about republican politics commenced in the early 1960s. Defeated in the ballot box and with the armed conflict failing to win public support—and lacking a real sense of direction—the republican movement was forced to reassess its political and military strategies. In February 1962, all IRA units were ordered to dump arms, and the campaign itself was formally declared over later that same month. The decision to end the border campaign was very much a recognition that, lacking popular support—combined with the hardline governmental response—the IRA was not in a position to further its aims through violence.

In a statement, the IRA noted:

The decision to end the resistance campaign has been taken in view of the general situation. Foremost among the factors motivating this course of action has been the attitude of the general public whose minds have been deliberately distracted from the supreme issue facing the Irish people—the unity and freedom of Ireland.[35]

It appeared that the militant tendency in Irish republicanism had reached a final conclusion. No less a journal than the *New York Times* declared in 1962: 'The IRA belongs to history, and it belongs to better men in times that are gone. So does the Sinn Féin [*sic*]. Let us put a wreath of red roses on their grave and move on.'[36]

The sentiment may have been worthy but it was one that failed to appreciate the fundamentalist spirit that drove those who involved themselves in both the IRA and Sinn Féin. The purists may have been beaten in 1962 but the republican legacy would survive. Indeed, for the best part of the last century, hardline republicans have viewed themselves as the inheritors of the tradition and spirit of the rebels who seized the centre of Dublin at Easter 1916 and proclaimed the creation of an Irish republic. Their self-image is of a group preserving the republican tradition and refusing to accept corrupt compromises.

Despite this rigid adherence to republican principles, in the period from the 1920s onwards, remaining true to an ideological inheritance led those associated with Sinn Féin into a political ghetto. Laffan describes the party in the decades after the 1926 split as 'little more than a society of aging and quarrelsome idealists.'[37]

In effect, republican ideology was frozen in 1922 when the second Sinn Féin split over the terms of the peace settlement with Britain. The two jurisdictions and their institutions created by the Anglo-Irish Treaty were labelled as illegitimate and could not be recognised. No serious attempt was made at modernising or reshaping this doctrine to contemporary developments. But the rump republican movement that went forward after the 1926 split was well accustomed to defeat and rejection, so the situation in 1962 was not unique.

Contrary to the view of the writer in the *New York Times*, republicans were not about to disappear. In fact, only eight years later, at the outbreak of the modern conflict in 1970, republican leader Ruairí Ó Brádaigh reaffirmed the IRA/Sinn Féin inheritance: 'a republican today is one who rejects the partition statelets and gives his allegiance to and seeks to restore the 32 county republic of Easter Week.'[38]

Those eight years between the ending of the border campaign and the split, which signalled the start of the modern conflict, were marked by an attempt to redirect fundamentally the energies of the republican movement. A new younger leadership had emerged during the years of the border campaign, including Cathal Goulding who was elected IRA Chief of Staff in 1962. Goulding—along with Tomás MacGiolla, who became Sinn Féin president—had an impeccable republican pedigree. He had been interned during the Second World War and served a prison sentence in England for his involvement in an arms raid in 1953.

Goulding did not see republicans relinquishing the right to use armed action in pursuit of their aims. Indeed, military planning was authorised, but the militarist front was to exist as an option within a wider republican strategic framework that included policy development in social, economic and cultural areas. But in reality the new leadership wanted to wean the republican movement off violence. The task was to develop a policy platform beyond the traditional aspiration of removing the border, and to replace the conservative republican outlook with a leftist socioeconomic policy programme.

Sinn Féin adopted a new left-leaning economic and social position at its 1964 Ard Fheis. The programme ran contrary to the newly adopted strategy of the Irish state. The incumbent Fianna Fáil government was focused on expansion of the country's weak industrial base through the attraction of foreign investment. Goulding questioned the value of foreign involvement in the Irish economy and was extremely doubtful about the merits of Irish membership of the European Economic Community, the forerunner to the current-day European Union.

The republican movement was being transformed into a protest movement. Republicans were encouraged to join organisations in which it was possible to propagate the new message of protest—credit unions, trade unions, housing associations and any other anti-establishment groups. Republicans became actively involved in groups in their communities campaigning on issues as diverse as foreigners owning fishing rights on Irish rivers to population decline in the west of Ireland.

Few of those involved in contemporary Sinn Féin were politically active in the 1960s. Among today's leadership grouping, only Gerry Adams can refer back to the period. Adams came from a staunch republican family in Belfast. He was 17 when he left school in 1965 and went to work as a barman. But Adams was also involved in republican politics and soaked up the issues under debate. He recalled travelling by train from Belfast to Dublin to participate in protests for better living conditions for people living in the capital of the Irish Republic: ' . . . the

Dublin Housing Action Committee was a big thing, and I was on the periphery of that, you know, up and down to Dublin. The Waters Restoration Agitation campaign was also part of all of that. . . .'[39]

In addition to the policy of infiltration, at university level, Republican Clubs were established where those with republican sympathies could meet to discuss politics and policies, while more talking was done in the Wolfe Tone Societies set up in Dublin and Belfast. There was also considerable republican representation in the civil rights campaigns that grew up in Northern Ireland from the mid-1960s onwards. But republicans were active in these organisations—as well as in the campaigns and protests—as individuals, never openly representing the IRA or Sinn Féin. Not that Sinn Féin offered much hope for political advancement—the Stormont government in 1964 had once more proscribed the party.

A decision was taken to forgo electoral participation until such time as republicans had received adequate political training and Sinn Féin was sufficiently strong to contest elections successfully. The new leadership had seen the rise and collapse of the Sinn Féin vote in the 1955 to 1961 period. They were not about to let that pattern be repeated. While this education process was under way, republicans withdrew from electoral participation. Indeed, Sinn Féin stopped contesting elections in the Republic after 1965, and the following year in Northern Ireland.

The decision was also linked to an internal debate about the value of continuing with the traditional policy of parliamentary abstentionism. Goulding and his supporters argued that Sinn Féin would never benefit from the new policy programme and republican involvement in protests and campaigns while abstentionism remained in place.

Yet, despite the decision in effect to turn the republican movement into a radical left-wing protest group, the long-standing policy of parliamentary abstentionism remained in place. There was discussion at the 1965 Sinn Féin Ard Fheis about changing the policy and allowing successful candidates to take their seats in Northern Ireland, the Irish Republic and even at Westminster. The abstentionist policy effectively equated a vote for Sinn Féin with a protest vote. The Goulding clique argued that in such an environment Sinn Féin was never going to advance as a political party.

Tomás MacGiolla said at the 1966 Ard Fheis that Sinn Féin should take seats in Leinster House should the party's representatives constitute a majority of the members of parliament. The Sinn Féin president offered the ambitious but hugely unrealistic forecast that within five years his party would have a majority in Dáil Éireann.

There was considerable unease within the wider republican membership at the new direction. Ironically, one of the opponents of the Goulding strategy was Sean MacStiofain, who, like Goulding, had received a six-year prison term in England because of his involvement in an arms raid in 1953. MacStiofain had a curious background; English-born, he had been a member of the RAF in Britain and travelled to Ireland for the first time only in 1959, after his release from prison. He was 31 years old at the time.

MacStiofain argued that the leftist policy drift risked turning the IRA into 'a paper army.'[40] He later wrote of the frustration of being a member of the Sinn Féin Ard Comhairle, where meetings were 'boring and a total waste of time. Numerous projects were discussed endlessly, but very few of them ever came to anything.'[41]

There was some truth in this assessment because, by the end of the 1960s, the IRA and Sinn Féin were hardly active organisations. They had small, and largely inactive, memberships. Goulding admitted that:

> By 1967 the Movement had become dormant. It wasn't active in any political sense or in any revolutionary sense. Membership was falling off. People had gone away. Units of the IRA and the cumainn of Sinn Féin had become almost non-existent.[42]

With the outbreak of the contemporary conflict in Northern Ireland in 1968 and 1969, many believed that the IRA had failed to fulfil its traditional role as defenders of the nationalist population in Northern Ireland. The emerging conflict was the background to the split in the ranks of the IRA that occurred towards the end of 1969. Yet the sectarian violence on the streets in Northern Ireland was not the principal reason for the split, which was provoked by a move to change the abstentionist policy.

Plans were developed to end abstentionism and re-route republicans into a National Liberation Front involving other left-wing parties and groups. The 1968 Ard Fheis had mandated an internal party commission to examine the issues and report back to the membership at a subsequent Sinn Féin gathering.

In fact, the matter was considered at an Army Convention of the IRA, which took place in December 1969. The move to lift the restriction on republicans participating in elections won support from a majority of those present. The following month, on 11 January 1970, delegates at a

Sinn Féin Ard Fheis voted to abolish abstentionism. The Goulding leadership got its result but the simple majority (153 to 104) was a half-baked result, as a two-thirds majority was needed to change the Sinn Féin constitution. Sinn Féin was facing another split.

MacStiofain and his supporters had prevented the constitutional change but they were in a minority. They quickly departed to form a new organisation that would shortly come to represent the traditional republican doctrines and a majority of those within the militant republican constituency on the island.

The new movement pledged its 'allegiance to the 32-County Irish Republic proclaimed at Easter 1916, established by the first Dáil Éireann in 1919, overthrown by force of arms in 1922 and suppressed to this day by the existing British imposed Six-County and 26-County partition states.'[43] The decision to alter the abstentionist policy was repudiated.

In the aftermath of the split, the new provisional leadership turned its attention to the military campaign against British rule. There was little time for political activity. During the decade that followed, Sinn Féin acted as a mouthpiece for the IRA and functioned as a fringe anti-system protest organisation. It was more a support body than a fully fledged political party, and it certainly was not independent of its dominant partner, the Provisional IRA.

AN END TO REVOLUTIONARIES, 1969–1986

Danny Morrison arrived in the Cavan–Monaghan constituency ahead of polling day in the February 1982 general election in the Irish Republic. Morrison was a senior player in the republican movement and a close ally of Gerry Adams. As the editor of the weekly republican newspaper, *An Phoblacht*, Morrison had dispersed various writers around the country to record the last few days of the Sinn Féin election campaign. Morrison made his way to the Sinn Féin election office in Cavan town. As he saw it, he was 'hoping to collect some gems for a story on the atmosphere of the constituency. . . .'

Eight months previously, republicans had celebrated in Cavan and Monaghan when 9,121 locals cast their first preference votes for Kieran Doherty, an IRA prisoner in the Maze Prison in Northern Ireland. Doherty, who was serving an 18-year sentence, was on hunger strike at the time of his election. His victory in the June 1981 general election did little to hasten an end to the prison protests and, after less than six weeks as a member of Dáil Éireann, the new TD died. The 25-year-old from Belfast had refused food for 73 days.

Doherty's election, along with that of Paddy Agnew in Louth—and the strong vote for other prisoner candidates in other constituencies—increased expectations among many republicans that candidates contesting under the Sinn Féin banner would perform well in the February 1982 general election. The stakes had been raised ever since Bobby Sands had won a Westminster seat the previous April. Sands—who since his death on hunger strike in 1981 has attained iconic status within republicanism—was the first contemporary republican from the physical force tradition to use parliamentary means to help achieve his goals.

The Sinn Féin decision to enter electoral politics north and south of the border was tested in both jurisdictions in 1982. The general election in the Republic in February 1982 was called after the incumbent government, led by Dr Garret FitzGerald, was defeated in a parliamentary vote on its annual budget. This contest was the first time since 1961 that Sinn Féin had, in its own right, participated in a national election in the Irish Republic.

There was no ambiguity about the position of Sinn Féin candidates who, according to *An Phoblacht*, were 'complementing and reinforcing the republican fight in the North.'[1] A vote for republican candidates was very much seen as supporting the demand for British withdrawal from Northern Ireland, an end to partition and moving Ireland closer to the creation of a united socialist republic.

In republican circles, there was a strong belief that Sinn Féin would build on the prisoner vote won in June 1981. Danny Morrison had been hoping to record a republican success in Cavan–Monaghan but, without the emotive issue of the hunger strikes, the public retreated away from republican politics. They had lent their votes to Doherty and the other prisoner candidates but now they were taking them back. In a 'normal' election of February 1982, republicans were peripheral.

This was, of course, not a new experience. Sinn Féin had previously re-emerged as an electoral participant in the Irish Republic in 1957 when the party won 5.3 per cent of the national vote and took four seats. But the successes did not last. In the subsequent general election in 1961, the Sinn Féin share of the vote declined to 3.1 per cent. The four seats were all lost. It would be another two decades before republicans again entered the electoral arena under the Sinn Féin banner, and for activists like Danny Morrison who straddled both sides of the republican movement, the experience was not one to be remembered.

When Morrison arrived in the Sinn Féin office in Cavan, a coal fire glowed in the hearth while the radio was tuned to RTÉ's election special. The mood was not good: 'The election phone had been disconnected earlier that day and this heightened the sense of desolation.' The results were very disappointing—not only were seats in Cavan–Monaghan and Louth lost but the Sinn Féin share of the vote was lower than that received by the prisoner candidates only eight months previously. In fact, the republican vote had collapsed in Cavan–Monaghan, down from the dizzy heights of 9,121 (in June 1981) to 3,974 votes. A similar story was emerging elsewhere.

As results were declared around the Republic, the post-mortem was already taking place. Morrison was confronted with a piece of republican ideology as one explanation for Sinn Féin's inability to preserve the republican vote, not to mind Doherty's seat.

> A middle-aged man ruminated over the campaign . . . raising the old bogey—he said—that people would only vote for those who would take their seats. I had been previously hit up to the teeth with this by several voters who, on the one hand, looked upon armed struggle and abstentionism in the North as legitimate but, on the other hand, looked upon the Leinster House parliament as legitimate. I explained the traditional republican position—our ideology and political oppression. The shrug of the shoulders . . . indicated a not altogether subscription to our rationale.[2]

Dejected at the result, Morrison made his way back to Dublin where he met up with a colleague, Seán Crowe, for 'pints of Smithwicks' at the republican club on Blessington Street. Crowe, in his late twenties, held the position of Youth Officer in Sinn Féin. A party member in Dublin, his first sense of involvement in republican politics was joining a march to the British Embassy in Dublin in the aftermath of Bloody Sunday in Derry in early 1972. Crowe said he 'came close to joining the IRA around the time of the hunger strikes' in 1981 but opted to stay politically active in Sinn Féin.[3]

Over their drinks, Morrison and Crowe debated the electoral drubbing taken by Sinn Féin candidates and the controversial issue of fully participating in parliamentary life in the Irish Republic. Crowe was initially suspicious of talk about taking seats in Leinster House and, as such, he was in the grouping within Sinn Féin who had to be convinced about change if any debate was going to be won.

When the leadership group around Adams assessed the results of the February 1982 elections, the value of continued abstentionism from Leinster House was central to its discussions. Jim Gibney, a key Adams supporter in Belfast, was by that stage in prison, but the arguments he had been putting forward for several years lingered. Adams was familiar with the Gibney argument in favour of developing Sinn Féin not just as a vehicle for republican politics but also as an electoral force.

Individuals like Gibney and Morrison were members of a tightly knit circle of advisors around Adams. They were people of a similar generation who had been politicised by the civil rights campaign in the late 1960s and who joined the republican movement in the early 1970s.

Membership of the self-styled 'kitchen cabinet' has never been fixed; people tend to move in and out depending on their allocated role in the republican movement at any particular time. Several disappeared off the scene following their arrest and imprisonment for IRA-related offences. Gibney spent most of the 1980s in prison; Morrison was imprisoned in the early 1990s.

Almost all of the leading backroom figures in Sinn Féin have been members of the IRA—people like Adams's press advisor, Richard McAuley, and Leo Green who worked with Bairbre de Brún in the 1998–2003 period when she was a health minister in Northern Ireland. Other key personnel include Rita O'Hare who succeeded Morrison as director of publicity and was for a time the party's principal representative in Washington; Tom Hartley, a councillor in Belfast; and Ted Howell who has become one of the principal wordsmiths in Sinn Féin, drafting many of the party's policy documents and writing key leadership speeches.

This group has been pivotal in the development of Sinn Féin over the past 20 years. Aside from their republican beliefs, what they share in common is a deep sense of personal loyalty to Gerry Adams. Few of them would quibble with Morrison's description of the 'powerful charisma' of the republican leader.

This commitment to, and belief in, Adams has withstood the considerable changes in republican dogma and strategic positioning that have been made since the early 1980s. The Adams strategy has been characterised by a willingness to utilise any opportunity available to progress the republican agenda. Critics and opponents claim that the Adams leadership has been marked by acts of betrayal and treachery. He stands accused of collaboration, surrender and having accepted the partition of Ireland. Nowhere are these charges more strongly made than in relation to the debate on abstentionism.

The results of the 1982 general election in the Irish Republic confirmed to many Adams supporters that a continuation of the abstentionism policy was a significant impediment to any new strategic electoral departure. It was not just post-election pub talk between Danny Morrison and Seán Crowe. Two distinct interpretations of this policy existed in the republican movement.

For one group, it was a central component of republican ideology. These people considered abstentionism in near theological terms—the only authority they would recognise was an independent 32-county republic; anything less was a fraud. According to this viewpoint, the states and parliaments established by the 1921 Treaty were illegitimate and fraudulent. Participation in Dáil Éireann or Stormont was, therefore, not an option. Moreover, electoral participation should be minimised and utilised only at times when there were strong grounds for promoting or advancing the republican cause.

The second group—in which Adams and his supporters came to be located—preferred to see abstentionism not so much as a basic principle. Rather they viewed it as a tactic although initially they were no less enthusiastic about political involvement. Throughout the 1970s, Adams had been hinting at possible change in emphasis about electoral participation—indicating the direction in which he wanted to see the republican movement travel.

In a series of articles written while in prison, Adams provided some pointers on the future direction of the military and political side of the republican movement. Between August 1975 and February 1977, writing under the name 'Brownie', Adams appeared to indicate his acceptance of the status quo on taking seats won in elections. 'I agree completely with abstention from any . . . of the British established and orientated partitonist assemblies,' Adams wrote in October 1975. But his position did not preclude all political participation by republicans. Politics was too important—according to the Brownie articles—to be left until after military action achieved its objective: 'it must start now . . . and it's up to us to provide it.'[4]

There was no obvious dilution of support for violence but Adams feared republicans would become so focused on the military struggle that they would lose contact with the everyday concerns of their natural constituency. He recognised that many in the wider republican constituency could not relate to the rigidity of abstentionism nor could these people accept what they were being told were the apparent benefits of such ideological purity. To support and illustrate his argument, Adams wrote the following dialogue:

But sez the man in the street 'where the hell is this government?' . . . Do Republicans really believe that the ordinary people will give their allegiance to a Parliament which really doesn't exist? . . . while the SDLP and other Unionists monopolise elections I'm afraid that ordinary Nationalists will always opt for the lesser of the two evils . . . we have no way of voting Republican . . . What else do you expect people to do? . . . And that my friends, is the crux of the matter . . . We need an alternative. . . .[5]

This was the populist, pragmatic approach that would later be identified as one of the hallmarks of the Adams leadership. As early as 1975, Adams was calling for the opening up of a second front in the fight against the British presence in Northern Ireland. Political action would operate in parallel to the IRA's campaign. Adams categorised this political response as 'Active Republicanism' and 'Active Abstentionism'.

> If we are serious about our philosophy we must pose a greater threat . . . on all fronts, than we have done in the past . . . to build up our support . . . to weaken the cultural, political, military, economic or commercial hold which Britain exerts on our country . . . we must build up our support . . . and we must implement the Republican philosophy at every opportunity on as many fronts as possible. . . .[6]

Mixing politics with the physical force republicanism would take time to achieve, and in the end required a fortuitous series of events in 1981 before any real change became a credible proposition. The reality was that Sinn Féin was a weak organisation and any attempt to move republicans into political activism would have been resisted by the purists within the movement.

Adams, however, was too clever a tactician to leave room for potential opponents to undermine his nascent strategy totally. Patience has been a hallmark of his time as a senior republican leader—time and time again, he has displayed a remarkable willingness to wait for the right circumstances to occur before acting on what was his preferred course of action. This has been a feature of the republican movement's involvement in the peace process in recent times, and so it was with their initial steps into electoral politics.

The first serious—and public—attack on the status quo came at Bodenstown in the summer of 1977. One of the key dates in the republican calendar, the annual gathering at Wolfe Tone's grave in County Kildare has become a key event in recent times as the Adams leadership group has signalled changes in republican positioning. This was very much the scenario in June 1977 when veteran republican Jimmy Drumm was introduced to the crowd. The previous October, his wife Máire had been shot dead by loyalist gunmen while she was a patient in Belfast's Mater Hospital. Máire Drumm had served as vice-president of Sinn Féin from 1972 until shortly before her death in 1976.

In the circumstances, the presence of Jimmy Drumm at Bodenstown generated huge empathy from the republican crowd. But what the gathering was not to know was that Gerry Adams and Danny Morrison had drafted much of Drumm's speech. The speech picked up on the most significant theme that had featured in the Brownie articles—that is, the importance of developing a political message to co-exist alongside the military campaign.

The writers of the speech were still not confident enough to call directly for a change in the abstentionist policy. But a subtle shift in direction was suggested in the proposal that the republican movement forge links with 'workers of Ireland and radical trade unionists', to establish what Adams and Morrison called, 'an irrepressible mass movement [that] will ensure mass support for the continuing armed struggle.'[7]

The Bodenstown speech delivered by Drumm, however, went further than sketching an alternative strategy. It openly criticised the 1975 IRA ceasefire which had been called because the republican leaders believed that they could deliver a British declaration of intent to withdraw from Northern Ireland. Despite contacts between republicans and the British government, no such scenario was on offer, and the often-fragile truce was eventually ended in early 1976.

In the aftermath of the 1975 ceasefire, the mainly southern-based leadership group, centred around Ruairí Ó Brádaigh and Daithi O'Connell, was privately accused of damaging the capability and credibility of the IRA. Critics claimed the men had misread the true intentions of the British and delivered not a withdrawal but a heightened security crackdown against the IRA. The Drumm speech was, in effect, a public attack on the republican leadership that had sponsored the truce. Indeed, the first steps in a process that would isolate and marginalise leaders like Ó Brádaigh and O'Connell were taken at Bodenstown in 1977.

In the same year, Gerry Adams was released from prison, and his re-emergence into republican circles, coincided with this sidelining of the Ó Brádaigh/O'Connell leadership. In February 1978, Adams was charged with IRA membership but he was off the scene for only a short period. The case against him was dismissed due to a lack of sufficient evidence to support a conviction. Control of the IRA shortly shifted away from the veteran republicans in the Irish Republic to the northern leadership, although it was still some time before the Adams grouping was in a position to deliver the entire republican movement in its direction.

By the end of the 1970s, Adams was not only a senior member of the IRA but also someone who began to adopt a more public profile, having been elected vice-president of Sinn Féin in November 1978. He used this role to call on the republican movement to recognise that its objectives could not be secured by military means alone but would need a more active involvement in political activity. The political wing of the republican movement was about to emerge slowly from the shadows of the IRA. Over the following decade, there was greater equality in the relationship between the two linked organisations, so much so that in the period after the August 1994 IRA ceasefire, Sinn Féin became the dominant partner in the republican relationship.

But when Adams became vice-president of Sinn Féin in late 1978, Sinn Féin was not just the minor player in the republican movement but it was also a marginal organisation within the wider republican community. The party had a handful of local councillors in the Irish Republic but, as it boycotted elections in Northern Ireland, its on-the-ground presence was minimal. Few people had any real connection with Sinn Féin although the party's future prospects were assisted by two developments in the mid-to-late 1970s.

At this time, the level of non-violent republican activism increased as the number of IRA members in the prison system rose. People in the republican community started to campaign for prison rights and improved facilities for prisoners. The development of a network of Anti-H-Block groups helped Sinn Féin organisationally when the party moved back into politics and elections in the early 1980s. An organisational structure was in place for Sinn Féin to utilise, as was a constituency of new members energised by the prison campaigns.

Many republicans were scornful of the 1975 IRA ceasefire although there was one positive legacy for Sinn Féin. During the eleven-month truce, the authorities set up local incident centres in republican areas in Northern Ireland. Republicans staffed these centres, which served as information bureaus for local people. When the ceasefire ended, it was decided to keep the offices open. This network of advice centres was available to act as a framework to develop Sinn Féin, as Jim Gibney recalled:

They emerged out of the first ceasefire period. The British opened them up as centres where republicans could interface over disputed issues around the ceasefire. We held on to those and they then became the public face of what later emerged as Sinn Féin. But even at that stage there wasn't a Sinn Féin label around it . . . But there is no doubt that Sinn Féin begins to think about building a political party as Gerry Adams emerges as a public figure.[8]

One of the first public speeches given by the new Sinn Féin vice-president was at Bodenstown in June 1979. It was a significant contribution to the evolving debate within republicanism. There was a restatement of familiar objectives: an 'Ireland, free, united, socialist and Gaelic'—but there was also a language and sentiment that must have privately alarmed traditionalists: republican belief had to be 'updated if it needs be to suit today's conditions' which could include building 'a strong political alternative to so-called constitutional politics' associated 'with other sections of the working class'.[9]

By the end of the 1970s, a debate was certainly under way within republicanism. At that time, Sinn Féin participated only in the local government system in the Irish Republic, and successful candidates took their council seats. All other elections were boycotted while republicans were actively encouraged not to vote. Adams was primarily interested in developing Sinn Féin as a political voice for the republican movement. He was less clear about participation in elections and had nothing to say about overhauling the long-standing policy of abstentionism. But opening up a debate about politics was inevitably going to start a discussion about elections and taking seats.

At the Sinn Féin Ard Fheis in 1978, the previously unspeakable matter of electoral participation was debated. One motion from party members in Wexford called for a total boycott of all elections, including local government elections in the Republic. The motion was eventually deemed not in order, but not before several speakers had openly supported the universal adoption of a rigid abstentionist position.

A further motion on electoral strategy dealt with the controversial subject of nominating candidates for the local election system in Northern Ireland. Francie Molloy from Dungannon proposed that the party nominate candidates for forthcoming local elections in Northern Ireland. 'Sinn Féin members should be free to contest local government elections in the Six Counties as it [has] done in the 26,' the motion read.[10]

Most of those who spoke in the debate were opposed to the idea. But the contributions revealed a distinct fault line in Sinn Féin. Most people against the Molloy proposal were from the southern ranks of the party and were among the older group in the Republic. Northern republicans were more in favour of, at least, teasing out the implications of such a development; among them was Jim Gibney:

I was at the Ard Fheis sitting in the body of the hall when Ruairí Ó Brádaigh, who was then the Sinn Féin president, got up onto the platform and basically denounced those from the North including Francie Molloy, who wanted to stand in the North. And the force with which he argued against it—and the venom in his voice—struck me as really strange. Essentially, he said that if a motion of that nature was brought again he would personally see the removal of the person advocating it.[11]

Republicans like Gibney and Molloy were unconvinced about the status quo strategy. They were not persuaded about a policy that saw Sinn Féin boycotting all elections apart from local council elections in the Irish Republic. No adequate reason had ever been given to explain why it was acceptable for Sinn Féin to be involved in local government in the Republic but not in Northern Ireland. Gibney, Molloy and others viewed the decision to contest local elections in Northern Ireland as a natural extension of the party's position. The debate at this stage—1978—had not ventured into the territory of Sinn Féin participation in national elections in the Republic, not to mind successful candidates taking their seats.

In public at least, there was no question of republican supporters being asked to vote in elections in Northern Ireland at any level. Indeed, they were also urged to ignore elections to Dáil Éireann and the European Parliament, to which direct elections took place in Northern Ireland and the Republic for the first time in June 1979. The decision not to contest the 1979 European Parliament elections was taken only after considerable internal debate that concluded only after a single-vote victory for the abstentionists at a meeting of the Sinn Féin Ard Comhairle.

The Sinn Féin decision in relation to the 1979 European election opened the way for Bernadette Devlin to emerge as a candidate. Devlin had come to prominence as a left-wing republican radical during the civil rights campaign in the late 1960s. She successfully contested a Westminster by-election for Mid-Ulster in 1969 and held the seat until the general election in February 1974. Despite strong opposition from Sinn Féin who urged republicans to boycott the contest, Devlin used the 1979 European Parliament campaign to publicise the cause of republican prisoners in Northern Ireland. The fact that she received a credible vote was further confirmation that there was a sizeable nationalist/republican constituency in Northern Ireland just waiting to be represented by a political party other than the moderate SDLP.

During the years when the republican movement formally avoided electoral participation, Devlin was among a group of independent republican-leaning candidates who utilised the ballot box to promote republican causes along with other concerns of the wider nationalist community. Devlin was not alone; others included independent Frank Maguire who was first elected to the Westminster parliament in October 1974. A long-time republican, Maguire had been interned during the 1956–62 IRA border campaign. He was well known for his involvement in the campaign to promote the welfare of republican prisoners serving sentences in English jails. During his time as an MP, Maguire adopted a variation of the Sinn Féin abstentionist policy and, at the time of his death in 1981, he had never spoken at Westminster.

The evidence stacked up—there was a natural constituency available to republican candidates, especially in Northern Ireland. But the great unknown for Sinn Féin was how its candidates would perform given the continuation of the IRA campaign. There was no question at that time of the IRA taking second place to political involvement.

The debate moved to the floor of the 1980 Sinn Féin Ard Fheis where a motion called for the party to contest local government elections in Northern Ireland. There were several emotional contributions, with the party leadership leading the way in opposing such a radical departure from long-standing policy. Danny Morrison was among those who spoke against the proposal:

> I remember Daithi O'Connell having a very positive attitude towards contesting elections in the North. I sort of toyed with the idea, and Gerry [Adams] toyed with the idea but there was nothing firm. We hadn't set our minds on opening up an electoral front . . . I was not opposed in principle [in 1980] but I just didn't think that we had prepared the ground. When you look at the history of the republican movement, any time the movement experimented or went down that road of opening up an electoral front, it always led to inner turmoil and the whole history of the splits that occurred down the decades, including the most recent one, which was post 1969, with those who came to be known as the officials, later the Workers' Party, advocating going into both assemblies north and south with a strategy of trying to reform them. So for that reason I got up and argued against us taking part in those elections.[12]

While the 1980 motion was rejected, 'the toe in the water' strategy was under way. In a report on the Ard Fheis proceedings, it was noted in *An*

Phoblacht/Republican News that 'this was generally considered to be a tactical decision—correct at the time—rather than a principled position'.[13] There was a general sense that Sinn Féin as an organisation was not yet ready to fight elections but the pace of events quickened considerably in a way that could never have been foreseen by the republican leadership.

For several years, a war of a different kind had been ongoing between republican prisoners and the authorities in Northern Ireland. The source of the dispute was the status of republican prisoners within the prison system. Since March 1976, they had been denied any special category or political status.

In the opinion of the British authorities, they were criminals and should be treated the same as all other prisoners. The British were unwilling to concede to the demands of the prisoners, which included the right to their own clothes, the right not to do prison work and the right to have free association in their section of the prison. Conceding these demands, the authorities argued, would have amounted to the granting of political status to the republican inmates.

Republicans in the Maze Prison embarked upon a blanket and no-wash protest in a dispute over their status within the prison system. But with the issue remaining deadlocked, the prisoners in October 1980 converted their protest into a hunger strike for political status. Seven prisoners first refused food on 27 October 1980. After 53 days and with one of the hunger strikers close to death, the protest was called off. The prisoners believed that they had received concessions from the British authorities but there were differences of interpretation over what was on offer. Another hunger strike was planned for the New Year and, on 1 March 1981, Bobby Sands refused food. Twenty-seven-year-old Sands from Belfast was serving a 14-year sentence for the possession of weapons.

Over the following weeks, other republican prisoners joined Sands on the protest. The hunger strike took place against a worsening security situation in Northern Ireland, with increased IRA attacks. But the protest generated enormous support for the prison campaign although the British Prime Minister, Margaret Thatcher, was unmoved in her stance that the republican prisoners should remain categorised as criminals. By the time the strike was called off in October 1981, ten of the prisoners, including Sands, were dead. But the lasting consequences of the hunger strike period went well beyond the initial motivation for political status for republican prisoners.

On 5 March 1981, five days after Sands first refused food, Frank Maguire, the independent MP for the Fermanagh–South Tyrone constituency, died suddenly. Jim Molyneaux, the leader of the Ulster Unionist Party, moved the writ at Westminster to call a by-election. Fermanagh–South Tyrone had a natural nationalist majority but Molyneaux believed a split vote among his nationalist opponents would allow a single unionist candidate to seize the seat. The action, however, opened the door for the politicisation of the republican movement and for the eventual entry of Sinn Féin into electoral politics.

In the early speculation about the by-election in Fermanagh–South Tyrone, several names were mooted as potential candidates on the nationalist side, including Bernadette Devlin and Noel Maguire, a brother of the late MP. The SDLP was also certain to contest the by-election although there had been considerable internal difficulty caused by the party's strategy in the constituency at the previous general election.

In Sinn Féin, Jim Gibney was the first person to raise the idea of nominating a prisoner candidate. The day Maguire died, Gibney pushed the advantages of a Sands candidacy with Adams. He argued in particular that the publicity generated for a by-election contest would be hugely beneficial to the prison campaign.

At a Sinn Féin Ard Comhairle meeting two days later, it was agreed to explore the option with local republicans in the constituency, although it was made clear that 'nothing firm has yet been decided.'[14] The main reason for the hesitation was conveyed to Danny Morrison by a republican veteran, who told Morrison, 'Sands is going to be beaten because our people won't come out and vote.'[15]

The risks of running Sands were considerable. Should Sands be nominated but fail to win, there was no telling the damage the result would do not only to the prison campaign but also to morale in the wider republican movement. It was against this backdrop that Adams and Gibney travelled to the constituency to meet local republicans, many of whom had been active in Frank Maguire's successful Westminster campaigns.

Gibney was confronted by an argument similar to that heard by Morrison in Belfast: 'The reality was the republicans in that area didn't want Bobby to stand. They were afraid of him standing and not being elected. But they were quite happy to allow someone else other than Bobby. . . .'[16]

The Adams grouping had for some time been weighing up the merits of increased political and electoral involvement. Martin McGuinness now argues that irrespective of the developments in Fermanagh–South Tyrone in 1981, Sinn Féin candidates 'would have contested the elections' to the proposed new Assembly in Northern Ireland in November 1982.[17] Whether such a radical departure would have come so quickly from internal developments is uncertain.

The decision to push the candidacy of Bobby Sands undoubtedly hastened the politicisation of the republican movement and confirmed, not for the last time, the ability of the Adams leadership to make significant shifts in internal positioning in response to unplanned external developments. Seeing the opportunity to accelerate the move into electoral activism, Adams and his supporters pursued the risky strategy of pushing for Sands to contest the by-election. Opposition was overcome, although it took two meetings with local republicans before they agreed that Sands should be the candidate.

Owen Carron was privy to the decision-making process. From County Fermanagh, Carron was a teacher by profession, having trained in England. He grew up during the civil rights era but his family background was not a republican one. The prisoners' campaign for political status drew him into republican politics: 'I helped form a local support group in Fermanagh and we campaigned in our local area . . . informing people . . . there were marches and candle-light processions saying the rosary and so on.'[18]

The death of Frank Maguire drew Carron even further into the prisoner campaign, so much so that he would come to play a very prominent part in the dramatic events that ensued throughout 1981. Along with other prominent prisoner campaigners, Carron was asked to come to a meeting in Monaghan town where the issue of Sands's candidacy was discussed. Leading republicans including Adams and Ó Brádaigh were present, as Carron recalls:

> There was a vote taken which decided not to put forward Bobby Sands. A small group of us went to Gerry Adams, Jim Gibney and Daithí O'Connell, and said we still thought it would be a good strategy to put Bobby forward. So it was from that that the idea started to gather a bit of speed. There was a second meeting . . . and at that a vote was taken and the idea was pushed through. But it was by no means a majority. There was a majority vote but it was by no means by popular acclaim. People were very afraid. There was an understandable fear that a prisoner candidate would get a small vote and would be demolished.[19]

There was understandably considerable support for Noel Maguire who was put under enormous pressure not to stand in the event of Sands being nominated. Another potential candidate was Austin Currie who had been beaten by Frank Maguire in the 1979 general election when he stood as an Independent SDLP candidate.

Currie was selected to run by the SDLP on 27 March 1981, but two days later, the party's executive decided to withdraw his nomination. The SDLP was faced with an acute dilemma of either taking the blame for defeating a hunger striker who then went on to die, or garnering fewer votes than the same prisoner candidate. Noel Maguire eventually decided not to contest the vacancy, so, when the nominations closed, there was a straight fight between Bobby Sands and Harry West, a political veteran who had led the Ulster Unionist Party from 1974 to 1979.

For many republicans, the by-election campaign was a totally new experience. This was especially so for many Belfast republicans more associated with the IRA than with Sinn Féin. The previous decade had been dominated by the campaign of violence to end British rule in Northern Ireland. Canvassing for votes was an unknown skill for many republicans who had long been encouraged not even to cast their own vote, as the ultimate expression of the abstentionism policy. Republicans came from all over to help with the election effort and, as Jim Gibney recalls, many were initially ill equipped:

> We hadn't a clue. I hadn't fought an election in my life. Anybody who came in from Belfast was the same. We didn't know how to fight elections but in Fermanagh–South Tyrone there were loads of republicans who knew because they were the people that put Frank Maguire in. So we were coming from Belfast into an area where people knew the game and what we brought to the campaign was this incredible enthusiasm, a raw energy. The clock was ticking on Bobby's life, so that meant everything was put to one side while we poured all our energies into getting him elected. But to find our way around the election scene you had to go along with people who knew it. And that was really in many ways a baptism of fire, I suppose. A steep learning curve for us.[20]

Danny Morrison was also surprised at the number of republicans in the area who were familiar with the business of elections. He was impressed with their expertise in ensuring that everyone of voting age was registered to vote and also that the sick or those abroad were registered for postal votes. First-hand experience in electioneering was being learned by those who, within a few short years, would move republicans into full-time political activity. But in Fermanagh–South Tyrone in 1981, naivety was on open display, as Morrison later recalled:

> I remember a group of Belfast women returned to the election office in Dungannon totally despondent about Bobby's chances after they got an extremely cold reception outside a church on the Ballygawley Road. Francie Molloy asked them to describe where they had made the speeches. It turned out they had been addressing and leafleting parishioners leaving a Church of Ireland service![21]

Owen Carron had been nominated as Sands's election agent. In the run-up to polling day, he visited Sands in prison; it was the first time the two men met:

> I had to go to get him to sign his nomination papers. I didn't know what to expect and no more than today there was a fair bit of demonisation going on, talk about criminality and so on. I expected to find a bit of a gurrier when I went in but was surprised to find an individual who could have passed for a university student. We talked about the situation. He didn't have high hopes of being elected. He believed he would die and the next man would die. I think he believed that if the first two hunger strikers died that would have led to a major shift.[22]

Polling day was set for 9 April. The turnout reached almost 87 per cent. When the votes were counted, Sands received 30,492 votes to the 29,046 won by West. The implications of the Sands victory went well beyond the huge international attention it attracted for the hunger strike and the campaign for political status. The rules of the electoral game in Irish politics were fundamentally rewritten as Adams and his colleagues seized on the result to move their organisation on its first tentative steps into the democratic mainstream.

The Sands election, momentous as it was, has tended to overshadow the electoral successes of republican candidates in the local government elections in Northern Ireland which took place in May 1981. The legislation governing these elections differed from that which applied to the Westminster parliament, as convicted prisoners were precluded from contesting local elections in Northern Ireland. Moreover, because of the decision taken at the 1980 Sinn Féin Ard Fheis there were no Sinn Féin candidates on the ballot papers. Many nationalist candidates, however, chose to associate themselves with the prison crisis.

Voting in these elections was set against the backdrop of the death of Sands and another hunger striker, Francis Hughes. The community in Northern Ireland was engulfed in a cycle of protests, killings and violence. Nevertheless, nationalist voters across Northern Ireland followed those in Fermanagh–South Tyrone in backing candidates who supported the prisoners and their demands. Many of these candidates had no link to the republican movement but their success was further confirmation that a constituency existed which wanted to use the ballot box to endorse republican-type causes.

Adams and his supporters would undoubtedly have shared the sentiment of an article in a post-election issue of *An Phoblacht/Republican News* which asked if the decision at the 1980 Ard Fheis to avoid the local elections had been a 'miscalculation and a lost opportunity to secure more permanent gains from the hunger strike given the clear militant shift in nationalist opinion.'23

With the death of Bobby Sands, the voters in Fermanagh–South Tyrone were back to the polls in August 1981. The British government altered the electoral rules in the aftermath of the Sands victory to prevent convicted prisoners from standing for Westminster elections. With the exclusion of prisoner candidates, republicans nominated Owen Carron, as a 'proxy prisoner candidate'. Four months earlier, he had been Sands's election agent.

Carron contested the August by-election on a prisoner platform but more importantly his candidacy also marked a break point with republican electoral tradition. He promised that once the H-Block campaign was concluded, he would continue to fulfil his duties as an elected representative although obviously he would not take his seat at Westminster. Carron pledged to 'transfer to being a republican MP, fighting the national, social, economic and cultural battles of our people.'24 With his election—increasing the majority received by Sands earlier in the year—Carron became the first Sinn Féin politician to enact the 'Active Abstentionism' strategy proposed by Adams.

At the following Westminster election in 1983, with a split in the nationalist vote, Carron lost his seat. Two years later, he was arrested in Northern Ireland on terrorist charges. The security forces stopped the car he was travelling in. Another man in the car was found to be in possession of a gun. Having been released on bail, Carron fled south of the border. Attempts to extradite him were eventually dismissed by the courts in Dublin although a warrant for his arrest is still active in Northern Ireland. During the failed political talks in 2003 and 2004, the issue of the so-called 'On-The-Runs' was discussed but unresolved.

Carron, who today lives in County Leitrim, has no involvement with Sinn Féin but remains committed to his republican beliefs:

> There is peace at the moment. There is no war going on and that is good. But the constitutional matters haven't changed and there is no power-sharing. I think maybe that unionism is incapable of change. But having said that the nationalist people have made tremendous strides over the last few years. And I think that the sacrifice of the hunger strike and the prison struggle has helped the nationalists stand up on their own two feet more than anything else.[25]

The election of Owen Carron in August 1981 most certainly also played a role in the birth of the peace process. His victory on the back of the success of the prisoner candidates earlier in 1981 challenged the republican status quo and encouraged Adams to sponsor further debate on the subject of electoral participation at the 1981 Sinn Féin Ard Fheis.

The leadership grouping around Adams shifted its position from twelve months earlier when the leaders had signalled their opposition to Sinn Féin contesting local elections in Northern Ireland. At that time, the view was that Sinn Féin was not quite ready to embark upon electoral activism even at a local level north of the border. But the hunger strike shifted the debate into a different arena. A political agenda was now insufficient. Republican candidates would have to sell their agenda at the ballot box. Moreover, the 1981 local elections presented a scenario that if Sinn Féin did not step forward to represent the republican constituency, the vacuum would be filled by others.

Now the Adams grouping wanted republican candidates on ballot papers and, more significantly, wanted them to run as Sinn Féin candidates, a classification not used by either Sands or Carron in Fermanagh–South Tyrone or the other republicans who contested the Republic's general election in June 1981.

Danny Morrison took to the platform at the 1981 Ard Fheis and asked delegates: 'Who here really believes we can win the war through the ballot box? But will anyone here object if, with a ballot paper in one hand and the Armalite in the other, we take power in Ireland?'[26]

Morrison now says he was 'playing to the gallery' but his intervention formally signalled the commencement of a new phase in the contemporary republican struggle—the 1970s were about the IRA and its military campaign; the 1980s would see Sinn Féin's political activism increasingly match the IRA's violence.

The delegates passed a motion authorising a more positive electoral policy; Sinn Féin candidates could now contest elections in the local government system in Northern Ireland and, if elected, they would be allowed to take their seats. Moreover, Sinn Féin candidates could also contest national elections in the Republic and elections to any new assembly in Northern Ireland although no successful candidates would take their seats. This truly was the start of the 'Armalite and the Ballot Box' strategy.

The Sinn Féin Ard Comhairle was entrusted with making the decision about contesting future elections in Dáil Éireann and any assembly in Northern Ireland. That decision, it was said, would be 'considered in a positive light—in contrast to previous policy.' Moreover, the party leadership was to study republican attitudes to future elections to the European Parliament, 'to which Sinn Féin's abstentionist policy does not apply.'[27]

There was considerable internal unease about this new electoral departure. Ruairí Ó Brádaigh, who supported limited electoral participation, had cautioned about an outright embrace of elections. Ó Brádaigh, who was still the president of Sinn Féin, preferred to keep open the option of dipping in and out of the system as the public mood and other circumstances best suited the republican cause. But the Adams group, which was moving to cement its control over the republican movement, ignored his warning.

The 1981 Ard Fheis witnessed the effective demise of the Ó Brádaigh leadership although those in that grouping would soldier on in the same organisation as Adams until the end of 1986. The old guard was undermined not only on attitudes to electoralism but also on the Sinn Féin policy on federalism. Interestingly, the Adams group was confident enough to take on the Ó Brádaigh wing only on the issue of federalism. Even at that stage it was clear that any direct challenge to abstentionism would lead to a bitter—and, possibly bloody—internal split in the republican ranks. Adams could carry the necessary two-thirds majority to change the Sinn Féin constitution but he first and foremost wanted to avoid a damaging split. He moved with caution, a defining characteristic of his leadership style.

Ó Brádaigh was closely associated with the Éire Nua policy, Sinn Féin's federal solution to the problems in Ireland. As a political programme, Éire Nua proposed a four-province federal model with the creation of an All-Ireland democratic socialist republic. The policy had been written largely by Ó Brádaigh and was used to counter republican critics who argued that they were interested only in violence.

Given this background, the decision to delete the word 'federal' from the Sinn Féin constitution was a huge personal humiliation for Ó Brádaigh who was still party president. The Adams group argued that federalism could be seen as a sop to loyalists whose voice would be guaranteed in Éire Nua's nine-county Ulster sub-federal assembly. Morrison told the Ard Fheis 'an Ulster parliament would perpetuate the loyalist bloc and would preserve its power and influence, instead of breaking it up.'[28]

As the proposal meant a change to the party constitution, a two-thirds majority was required before it could be accepted. The vote was actually taken twice. On the first occasion, an exact two-thirds majority of voting delegates backed the move to delete 'federal' from the party constitution. A recount was requested and in the second ballot those supporting the new policy fell short of the crucial two-thirds threshold. If ever there was a warning to Adams to proceed with caution, it was delivered on this vote. He was in a strengthened position within the republican movement but as yet he had not reached a position of overwhelming dominance.

A further motion at the 1981 Ard Fheis called for the federal solution to be dropped as a Sinn Féin policy. As there were no constitutional implications, a simple majority of delegates was all that was needed and the Ard Fheis duly obliged. The decision, however, left Sinn Féin out of step with the IRA over its attitude to federalism. Nevertheless, *An Phoblacht* confidentially predicted, 'the anomaly can be expected to be resolved next year. . . .'[29]

Twelve months later, when delegates next met, a motion was duly passed confirming that federalism was no part of republican policy or a constitutional objective. The decision was not taken, however, without considerable debate—the session on federalism was the longest of the conference—another indication that the Adams leadership had to move carefully as it cemented control over the entire republican movement.

But Sinn Féin was changing—the morbid organisation of the post-1969 period was no more; in its place was emerging an active party with a stronger membership base. One of the consequences of the prisoner campaigns in the late 1970s and the heightened atmosphere during the hunger strikes in 1981 was an influx of people into republican politics. The Relatives' Action Committees and the H-Block Committees in effect bequeathed Sinn Féin a new generation of members.

Aengus Ó Snodaigh, a future Sinn Féin Dáil deputy, was a teenager at the time of the hunger strikes. 'There was a huge anger amongst a lot of young people but also a desire to do something about it,' he recalled.[30] An attempt to set up a H-Block/Armagh committee in his secondary school in Dublin was frowned upon but Ó Snodaigh did join in numerous protest marches.

He had enjoyed a middle-class upbringing in Sandymount in Dublin. His father was a librarian, his mother an artist. The family was nationalistic in outlook and very active in the Irish language movement. The hunger-strike marches were not Ó Snodaigh's first political involvement. In the mid-1970s he had delivered leaflets for Labour politician Ruairí Quinn as part of a campaign to protect Sandymount Strand against development. While a student at University College Dublin, Ó Snodaigh decided to join Sinn Féin, and by the mid-1980s he found himself active in party politics and working for *An Phoblacht*. His story is not unique.

Another person drawn into republican ranks at the time of the prison campaign was bank official Caoimhghín Ó Caoláin who served as Director of Elections for the Kieran Doherty campaign in June 1981. He had a family connection to the republican movement's border campaign in the 1950s but by 1981 there was no direct Sinn Féin or IRA link to his family. Indeed, Ó Caoláin's mother was a member of Fianna Fáil and his late father had been a 'staunch supporter' of the same party.

The experience of Ó Caoláin was not unusual in the 1981/82 period:

> From the ending of the hunger strike [in October 1981] through into 1982 I agonised as to what I would do. I was still single, and so in the late summer of 1982 I tendered my resignation from the bank, pulled the branch door after me on a Friday and walked in as General Manager of *An Phoblacht* on the following Monday morning. And since November 1982, almost a quarter of a century later, I have been a full-time Sinn Féin activist.[31]

Ó Caoláin was first elected to Monaghan County Council in 1985 and during that campaign found himself a candidate in an election in which his Fianna Fáil supporting mother was backing a rival candidate. After three failed campaigns, Ó Caoláin became a Dáil Deputy for the Cavan–Monaghan constituency in 1997.

The year 1982 was probably not the best time for the Ó Caoláin decision to sign up for employment with Sinn Féin. Republicans were forced to put a brave face on the 1982 election result in the Irish Republic. Matters had not been helped by the arrest just before the election of Jim Gibney, who was the Sinn Féin National Organiser. By the time Gibney was released from prison in 1988, Sinn Féin had been transformed. That process started days after the February 1982 general election as Sinn Féin sought to learn the lessons of its very poor showing at the polls.

The lack of success was put down to a failure to appeal to a wider constituency outside its core republican base, along with a general lack of organisational preparedness. One post-mortem account in *An Phoblacht* noted 'each of the seven results can be described as a sound base for the future.' But there was acceptance of the challenges facing the party in achieving genuine political success. Sinn Féin, the same writer acknowledged, was 'faced with the serious task of soberly, and intelligently, assessing its structures, strategy and policy . . . The other main issue raised by the election is, of course, the taboo republican one of abstentionism. It was a question raised by voters and it is not a question to shy away from.'[32]

Abstentionism was also raised in a comprehensive assessment provided at the first post-election meeting of the Sinn Féin Ard Comhairle. The party leadership accepted that it faced the 'difficulty of selling in a two to three week campaign the idea of an abstentionist— albeit a working—TD.'[33]

There was an acknowledgement that Sinn Féin's message got lost in what in effect had become a 'bread and butter' national election. The lack of an issue to capture the public's imagination—like the hunger strikes the previous year—squeezed Sinn Féin out of the election debate. The party also accepted that it needed to broaden its range of interests and membership base in the Republic: 'There is a need for a more disciplined and ideologically committed membership rather than a membership of some who consider themselves in a "Brits Out" role.'[34]

The Adams leadership did not consider abstentionism a core principle. Indeed, by the early 1980s this grouping considered abstentionism a tactic that had outlived its usefulness. There was particular concern that the policy was hindering the development of Sinn Féin in the Republic where the electorate was unwilling to turn to a party whose candidates refused to participate fully in the political system. While Adams had initially argued for a stronger political message to accompany the IRA campaign, the elections of 1981 and 1982 indicated that electoral participation was also needed. Now Sinn Féin's involvement in elections was opening up the issue of successful party candidates taking their seats, most specifically in Dáil Éireann in Dublin.

The poor results in the February 1982 general election in the Irish Republic led to caution about contesting a second election called later that same year. The party leadership concluded that no election would be contested unless the case had been proven that 'the necessary groundwork essential to victory had been carried out.'[35] There was, however, a more practical reason for ignoring the contest in the Republic —elections were scheduled for a new assembly in Northern Ireland and Sinn Féin decided that it was best to concentrate resources in an area where the party could achieve some success.

Plans for a new elected assembly in Northern Ireland were included in a political initiative sponsored by Jim Prior who had been appointed Northern Ireland Secretary in September 1981. Prior proposed a cross-community assembly that would receive increased responsibility as its members showed a willingness to work constructively together. There were 78 seats on offer in the new Assembly. Elections were scheduled for October 1982 and the presence of Sinn Féin candidates was a new development.

Sinn Féin nominated 12 candidates in seven of the 12 constituencies and the party contested on an abstentionist platform. The decision to nominate senior republicans like Adams, McGuinness and Morrison sent out a clear signal about the seriousness of republican participation. Nevertheless, the IRA was still the dominant partner in the Sinn Féin–IRA relationship. A motion passed at the 1982 Sinn Féin Ard Fheis had determined that 'all candidates in national and local elections, and all campaign material, be unambivalent in support of the armed struggle.'[36]

Sinn Féin may have been new to electoral involvement in Northern Ireland but the party was no slouch in identifying its main threat. The moderate, constitutional nationalist SDLP—and its 'collaborationist leadership'—was in the direct firing line of Sinn Féin's attack. The SDLP leader, John Hume, was described as 'a dangerous collaborator . . . not to be trusted . . . [who was] . . . concerned more with lining his pockets than with defending nationalist interests.'[37] The charge was utterly unfair on Hume but the level of republican vitriol displayed an early vote-getting ruthlessness on the part of the long-time electoral isolationists in Sinn Féin. The personalised nature of the attacks did not, however, prevent the SDLP leader from identifying—and seizing—a few short years later, the possibilities of dialogue with Gerry Adams, dialogue which eventually led to the 1994 IRA ceasefire.

Sinn Féin emerged out of the election with five seats and over 10 per cent of the total first-preference votes. With new competition within nationalism it was no surprise that the SDLP lost ground, but the scale of the Sinn Féin breakthrough was notable. The results confirmed that there was an electoral market for the Sinn Féin demand for British withdrawal, and that a significant section of the nationalist vote was not put off by the IRA's military campaign. Following on from the disappointment in the Republic's general election the previous February, the Assembly election in Northern Ireland gave the Adams camp an incredible boost to its strategy to add a political dimension to physical force republicanism.

Further electoral success followed in Northern Ireland when Adams was elected on an abstentionist platform to the Westminster parliament in June 1983. Sinn Féin edged closer to the SDLP, taking 13.4 per cent of the vote against 17.9 per cent for the latter party. The results confirmed Sinn Féin as the party on the march. There was disappointment, with Owen Carron being defeated in Fermanagh–South Tyrone, although the result was not unsurprising given that the nationalist vote—although greater than the total unionist vote—was split between Sinn Féin and the SDLP. A similar situation prevailed in the Mid-Ulster constituency where the combined Sinn Féin/SDLP vote was 2,399 more than all the votes cast for all other candidates. But the split nationalist vote allowed the Democratic Unionist Party to take the seat, albeit by the narrowest of margins. Sinn Féin's Danny Morrison missed out on a seat by a mere 78 votes.

Sinn Féin quickly established a strong political and electoral presence in Northern Ireland. Those voting for republican candidates were less perturbed by their links to the IRA than were voters in the Irish Republic. Moreover, the policy of abstentionism was not an issue north of the border as a significant section of the Catholic community empathised with not giving allegiance or loyalty to institutions that derived their authority from Britain.

But south of the border it was obvious that a radical response was needed if Sinn Féin's electoral standing were to be improved. Once more, Adams used the occasion of the annual Bodenstown commemoration to indicate the need to alter long-established republican strategy.

In June 1983—just weeks after his success in being elected to the Westminster parliament on an abstentionist ticket—Adams observed that republicans would have to accept that a majority of people in the Republic:

Electoral success: Éamon de Valera speaking in Ennis after his victory in the East Clare by-election, 1917. (© *Hulton/Getty Images*)

Victory procession: Sinn Féin supporters, including Countess Markievicz in a white coat, are led by pipes as they parade through Ennis, 1917. (*Courtesy of the National Gallery of Ireland*)

Mansion House, 1 February 1919. The first Dáil meets. (© *Topfoto*)

Leading Sinn Féin figures in 1919, including (in the front row) Count Plunkett (far left) and Éamon de Valera (centre front). Fr Michael O'Flanagan is pictured on the left in the back row alongside Arthur Griffith. (© *Bettmann/Corbis*)

Women protest at the execution of Sinn Féin prisoners in 1921. (© *Hulton-Deutsch Collection/Corbis*)

The Sinn Féin delegation to the Treaty talks in 1921, including Arthur Griffith on the far left and Michael Collins seated in the centre. (© *Mary Evans Picture Library*)

Splits: The divisions in Sinn Féin after the Treaty were illustrated by the pro De Valera poster which was placed over an anti De Valera poster during the 1923 general election. (© *Mary Evans Picture Library*)

New departures: Seán MacBride speaking at a Clann na Poblachta meeting in 1948. The political failure of Sinn Féin led many republicans to support parties like the Clann. (© *TLP/Getty Images*)

On the margins of political life: Sinn Féin supporters march through Belfast in protest against a visit to Northern Ireland by members of the British Royal family, June 1951. (© *Topfoto*)

Keeping the flame flickering: a republican protest meeting in London in August 1955. (© *Hulton/Getty Images*)

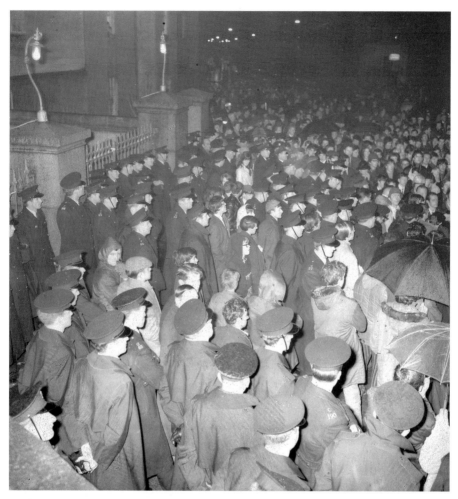

With Sinn Féin only a marginal influence in the 1960s, many republicans joined in demonstrations like this one organised by the Dublin Action Housing Committee. (*Courtesy of the Irish Times*)

Tomás MacGiolla, President of Sinn Féin, photographed in 1966 as republicans predicted they would soon be a majority in Dáil Éireann. (© *TLP/Getty Images*)

Leading republicans, 1972. Martin McGuinness is on the far left, alongside Daithi Ó Connell, Seán MacStiofain and Séamus Twomey. (© *Camera Press Ireland*)

Ruairí Ó Bradaigh, Sinn Féin President until 1983 when he was forced out of the position by Gerry Adams and his supporters. (© *Camera Press Ireland*)

Máire Drumm who was Vice-President of Sinn Féin when she was shot dead in 1976 by loyalist gunmen while she was a patient in Belfast's Mater Hospital. (© *Camera Press Ireland*)

Daithi Ó Connell, a leading member of Sinn Féin and the IRA, addresses a meeting outside the GPO in Dublin in 1976. (© *Camera Press Ireland*)

IRA volunteers form a guard of honour at a Sinn Féin rally in Belfast's Casement Park in 1979. (© *Camera Press Ireland*)

Gerry Adams and his close confidante, Danny Morrison, in 1982. (© *Topfoto*)

Joe Cahill and Daithi Ó Connell at the 1982 Sinn Féin Ard Fheis. (© *Photocall Ireland*)

Republican icon: Gerry Adams alongside a Belfast mural of IRA hunger striker Bobby Sands. (© *Topfoto*)

Dual strategies: Martin Ferris was convicted of IRA gun running in the 1980s, but elected to Dáil Éireann for the Kerry North constituency in 2002. (© *Photocall Ireland*)

Southern leaders: Mary Lou McDonald was elected to the European parliament in 2004, and Caoimhghín Ó Caoláin, TD for Cavan-Monaghan since 1997. (© *Photocall Ireland*)

Connecting history: Gerry Adams, with a copy of the 1916 Proclamation in the background. (© *Camera Press Ireland*)

Gerry Adams and Martin McGuinness. (© *Alan Lewis/Corbis*)

The Sinn Féin delegation that met British Prime Minister Tony Blair at Downing Street in December 1997. Martin Ferris (far left), Martin McGuinness and Gerry Adams were all believed to have been members of the IRA Army Council. (© *Photocall Ireland*)

... accept the Free State institutions as legitimate. To ignore this political reality is to ... undermine the development of our struggle ... A firm foothold and a relevant organisation in Southern politics is vital. We must apply ourselves to that objective ... we must ... develop our republicanism so that it meets today's political conditions.

The assessment of the situation was very clearly defined: 'Armed struggle, a necessary and morally correct form of resistance in the six counties ... has no part to play in the development of our republican struggle within the twenty-six counties.'

Adams commenced what was soon to become the dual Sinn Féin strategy process of attacking the British presence for an audience in Northern Ireland, while attacking the mainstream political parties in the Irish Republic for a southern electorate. 'Leinster House with its patronage, double standards and corruption has become the Tammany Hall of what passes for Irish politics,' he concluded.[38]

Abstentionism was written into the constitutions of the IRA and Sinn Féin. Any move to amend the relevant sections of the respective constitutions required the support of a two-thirds majority at an IRA Convention and at a Sinn Féin Ard Fheis. For several years, Adams had moved with what was to become a customary caution; the pattern would become familiar—first allowing a debate to ferment at grassroots levels about the status of abstentionism—was it a core principle or an adaptable tactic?—and then, with a majority in sight, formally indicating the direction favoured.

In the aftermath of the hunger strikes—and, particularly, with Sinn Féin's disappointing 1982 Dáil Éireann election results—Adams and his leadership group started to prepare their movement for an ideological change of historical proportions. Just a few short years earlier, the project had been to develop a political agenda to complement the IRA campaign, then electoral participation had been sanctioned, and now the possibility was being opened up that successful Sinn Féin general election candidates would take their seats in Leinster House.

For several years, Adams had been shifting the internal debate in the direction of this significant u-turn. While Adams and his supporters viewed changes to abstentionism as a pragmatic response, there were many who had a theological-like attachment to abstentionism. They believed that it embodied republican opposition to those institutions created out of the 1921 Treaty arrangements.

As this debate intensified, the Ruairí Ó Brádaigh wing of the party continued to be undermined. Ó Brádaigh did not seek re-election as Sinn Féin president at the 1983 Ard Fheis. His position as party president had, in fact, been untenable since the debate on federalism in 1982. The Roscommon man accepted as much when he admitted that his 'credibility was serious[ly] impaired with the defeat of policies which I wholeheartedly believed in and had publicly espoused over a long period of time.'[39]

Throughout 1983, Ó Brádaigh lost several arguments on policy matters at the party's Ard Comhairle. The most obvious defeat was over the decision to allow Sinn Féin candidates to participate in European Parliament elections planned for 1984 and also to take their seats should they be successful. Ó Brádaigh believed this position was contrary to the abstentionism spirit and that entering the European Parliament would only weaken the party's opposition to what it saw as a capitalist power bloc. A sub-committee of the Ard Comhairle had also rejected a position paper on Sinn Féin's political strategy, prepared by Ó Brádaigh. He had been president of Provisional Sinn Féin since it had emerged out of the 1969–70 republican split. Now, twelve years later, he was in receipt of a blunt message about where power rested within Sinn Féin.

Despite the isolation of Ó Brádaigh and his supporters, the Adams wing still did not have the ability to get acceptance for all the policies it favoured. But the group was prepared to move slowly to achieve its objectives eventually. So a ban on discussing abstentionism was reaffirmed at the 1983 Ard Fheis. Ó Brádaigh took a swipe at his opponents: 'Discussing going into Leinster House, Stormont or Westminster is as foreign and as alien as that the IRA would sit down and discuss surrender of arms.'[40] In the mid-1980s, Ó Brádaigh may not have guessed at how accurate his crystal-ball gazing would be. But just over a decade later, Sinn Féin would indeed take its seats in all but the Westminster parliament, while the IRA would sanction two acts of decommissioning before ordering an end to its armed campaign, in July 2005.

In his final speech as Sinn Féin president in 1983, Ó Brádaigh remarked: 'We hand over the great Sinn Féin organisation to a new generation, more vigorous and more successful at the polls than at any time since 1918.' But there was a warning to the Adams wing. The Ó Brádaigh leadership had prevented serious internal dissent because it followed the orthodox republican line: 'there were no splits or splinters—long may it remain so, as it will, provided we stick by our basic principles.'[41]

Ó Brádaigh had been humiliated in public and in private by the Adams leadership. His exit also coincided with the departure of Daithi O'Connell. Indeed, as soon as Ó Brádaigh left the podium, O'Connell was the next speaker to the microphone to confirm that he would not be standing for re-election as party vice-president. O'Connell also identified the abandonment of the federal aspect in the Sinn Féin policy, while also challenging the Northern-based leadership surrounding Gerry Adams:

> The calculated result of last year's Ard Fheis resulted in a leadership which, in my view, was not representative or reflective of the organisation as a whole. I have no reason to believe that it will be different this year and I firmly hold that without representative leadership of a geographical national character, the organisation will not develop, in either structural or policy terms, along national lines.[42]

Adams was elected Sinn Féin president at the 1983 Ard Fheis. His election moved the centre of gravity within the organisation away from Dublin and towards Belfast. The Northern-based leadership now controlled both wings of the republican movement.

In his first presidential address, Adams touched upon the pragmatism, which has come to define his leadership of the republican movement over the subsequent two decades:

> The rapid developments since the prisoner candidates performed so well in 1981 had led to numerous inconsistencies in the republican attitude to abstentionism. Nowhere was this more obvious than in relation to the recognition of courts in Northern Ireland and the Republic. The traditional practice had been for republicans to simply refuse to recognise the authority of the courts. This stance was manifest by IRA members declining to challenge charges brought against them. The policy, however, was strained in the nineteen seventies with so many IRA members before the courts. In many cases republicans alleged abuse by the police authorities. But where no defence case was mounted republicans were unable to formally raise their allegation and the courts were simply finding them guilty of the changes entered. Pragmatism won over and the policy was modified to allow republicans defend themselves, a move, which by its very nature involved recognition of the legal system.[43]

In a rare early public signal of his pragmatic leadership traits, Adams signalled approval for republicans to use the legal system. Diluting existing abstentionist policies was the objective of the Adams leadership; it was not driven by a desire to extend any isolationist tendencies. At the 1982 Ard Fheis, two motions were proposed, calling for the party's constitution to be changed to prevent republicans from taking civil actions of a political nature in the courts of either Northern Ireland or the Irish Republic—described as 'partitionist states' in the motion.

Those favouring the change argued that rejection would bring the morality of the republican movement into question. But Adams moved to end support for the idea. He referred to a slander case being taken at that time by two Sinn Féin members against Merlyn Rees who had been Secretary of State in Northern Ireland until September 1976. Playing to the crowds, Adams asked: 'If we can make Rees pay our election expenses —shall we do it?' The question was met by a resounding 'yes' from the conference delegates.[44]

Regardless of the attitudes to the courts, there was no question but that a confused and ambiguous Sinn Féin attitude to electoral abstentionism had been allowed to develop. National elections were contested but any seats won were not taken, as republicans refused to recognise the legitimacy of the institutions to which they sought election. Sinn Féin sat out the 1983 abortion referendum campaign in the Irish Republic, citing as a reason the party's non-recognition of the 1937 Constitution.

This lack of clarity was one outcome from the slow cautious movement pursued by Adams as he inched towards transforming republican attitudes to the Irish Republic. He was still not confident enough of his ability to get all the party to back his strategy. The situation was made even more ambiguous at the Ard Fheis in 1983 when it was agreed that Sinn Féin's involvement in future constitutional debates would be determined solely by the aims of the given campaign.

The issue of abstentionism was dealt with during a one-hour debate on the Sunday afternoon of the 1985 Sinn Féin Ard Fheis. There was no move to directly amend or abandon the policy. The main motion on the topic sought a recommitment of Sinn Féin's policy on abstentionism, while another proposed that abstentionism be regarded as a tactic rather than a principle. The latter would have allowed scope for flexibility, especially in relation to republican attitudes to participation in Leinster House.

Adams declined to give a clear public direction on the matter. But in his presidential address a preference was signalled in placing the debate in a historical context. 'Since then [the 1920s], this country has undergone many changes and in terms of social composition and policies Sinn Féin is a different party.'[45]

Adams also moved to counter any allegations that a policy change in relation to political participation might have a negative bearing on the IRA's military campaign. His speech contained the usual expressions of sympathy for IRA members who had died during the previous twelve months, along with condolences for their families. The traditional message of support for IRA prisoners drew an enthusiastic response from those attending the Ard Fheis.

The Sinn Féin president was also uncompromising in his defence of the two wings of the republican movement, although the attention to the political wing was a further sign that the dual strategy would be open to development. 'Sinn Féin isn't a party of violence. Sinn Féin isn't a party of poverty and Sinn Féin isn't a party of exploitation. I have no trouble repudiating terrorism—the only terrorists in this country are the British gunmen and gunwomen.'

There was also an attempt to pre-empt criticisms of Sinn Féin's association with the IRA: If Sinn Féin took the 'unprecedented and unimaginable step of repudiating the legitimate armed struggle of the IRA, you would be looking for another president . . . The IRA are not terrorists—they are freedom fighters.'[46]

The premier position of the IRA within the republican family was reaffirmed but the military organisation could not have been immune to the pressures for changes in Sinn Féin. Pat Doherty from Donegal opened the 1985 Ard Fheis session on abstentionism. Doherty who was born in Glasgow was another one of the Adams circle. He had stood unsuccessfully in local elections in Donegal in the 1970s and since 1979 had been an influential republican figure. His brother, Hughie, was serving time for his involvement in an IRA bombing campaign in Britain in the mid-1970s.

There was little standing room in the Mansion House when Pat Doherty rose to speak. He was Director of Elections for Sinn Féin at the time and observed that while republicans may have been latecomers to 'the mechanics of electioneering', they were learning the political game: 'seeing and hearing on the doorsteps the day-to-day problems of the people of Ireland.' The implication was clear—Leinster House was the next logical step to advance this understanding of electioneering and concerns of the people of Ireland. But Doherty warned that moving closer to Leinster House did not mean republicans would not boycott any new Northern Ireland assembly.

Further words of comfort were offered by Danny Morrison who spoke on behalf of the Ard Comhairle. Morrison expressed support for the two motions as a restatement of Sinn Féin policy, while offering the reassurance that the IRA campaign would not be run down and that the military side of the movement supported the development of an electoral strategy. Morrison's contribution was about setting the boundaries for the debate over the following months. Republicans were told to 'debate freely and debate honestly' but there was a warning—they should avoid 'parading the republican dead'.[47]

Those opposed to any change feared the party was on a 'slippery slope'. One opponent of change asked: 'How can we claim to be a revolutionary organisation if we take part in the institutions of the State which we oppose?'[48]

Support for exploring the Leinster House option came mainly from Northerners associated with Adams and McGuinness as well as from a new generation of republicans from the Republic of Ireland. Among the latter group was Seán Crowe, a future Dáil Deputy but in 1985 a member of the party's Ard Comhairle who had been won over by the arguments in favour of change. In his contribution, Crowe countered the view that to enter Leinster House would be to follow in the path of Fianna Fáil, among others. Those parties, Crowe argued, 'were not republicans, they weren't separatists, secular, nationalists or socialists.' The implication was that Sinn Féin was all of those things.

The motion restating Sinn Féin's commitment to abstentionism was passed by an overwhelming majority of the delegates including the party leadership. But another motion defining abstentionism as a policy rather than a tactic was lost by 20 votes. With this result, the motion that defined abstentionism as a principle was 'deemed passed'. The decision reached at the 1985 Ard Fheis was described by The Irish Times as a 'defeat of the leadership line'. But the Adams leadership had used 1985 as a dry run.

The formal decision on the policy was eventually taken in November 1986 but Adams and his supporters had spent the preceding months ensuring that there would be only one result. The most important message that Adams had to get out to the Sinn Féin membership concerned the activities of the IRA. That the decision to enter Leinster House would not compromise the IRA campaign was the firm line. The opening moments of 1986 confirmed as much.

The near-permanent tension arising from the conflict in Northern Ireland meant that even New Year's Eve was less a celebration than in many other parts of the world. And yet there were revellers out in Armagh as the city's cathedral bells rang out to welcome in the New Year —1986. Armagh was home to the Catholic and Protestant archbishops and had long had a name as the Irish ecclesiastical capital. St Patrick had come here when selecting a site to represent the Christian tradition on the island.

There was plenty of noise and singing as the old year closed and a new one was welcomed. But when the bells started to ring there was no jubilation in one house just off the main city-centre area. Earlier that evening—at about seven o'clock—three masked men had forced their way into the house. The family was held hostage as the three IRA men waited patiently. Their target: RUC officers on foot patrol in the centre of the town.

Constable James McCandless had joined the RUC four years earlier. He had said goodbye to his wife and two children at home earlier that evening. Michael Williams was 24—he was also married, although the couple had not yet started a family. Williams was a member only of the part-time police reserve. Along with another police officer, McCandless and Williams were doing their rounds in the centre of Armagh city. A small group of revellers wished the RUC men 'Happy New Year'. Constable McCandless acknowledged the greeting. As the police officers passed a litter-bin, there was a massive bang.

The three IRA men holed up in the nearby house had detonated by remote control their 5lb bomb. Dust and smoke clouded the street. James McCandless and Michael Williams were left dead. The third officer on the foot patrol was injured in the explosion. It was just one minute past midnight when the IRA had detonated their bomb—the first killings of 1986 in Northern Ireland.

The brutal action of the IRA carried a chilling resonance—1986 would be no different from the year that had gone before. As *An Phoblacht* reported: 'The New Year opened with a loud and clear message from the IRA that there will be no peace in Ireland in 1986, nor indeed can there be peace so long as the British government and its military wing deny freedom to the Irish people.'[49]

An IRA spokesman, in a New Year interview in the same newspaper, reaffirmed the republican strategy: 'The vast majority of the Irish people are sympathetic to our struggle in the six counties because they understand it in essence is a just liberation struggle. They equally perceive the gardaí and the Free State army as their legitimate forces. . . .'[50]

The IRA campaign of violence would continue alongside moves to change republican ideology radically. In May 1986, more than 300 republican activists attended an internal conference in Ballyfermot in Dublin. The gathering was in effect a forum to allow republicans to air their views on the future direction of Sinn Féin. From the perspective of the republican leadership, the gathering was an invaluable exercise in setting out its strategy; it was also a useful listening forum. The leadership did not want to move too far ahead of the general membership. Adams was prepared to sanction the necessary constitutional changes only when he was guaranteed grassroot backing and had minimised the possibility of a damaging split.

The Ballyfermot conference was a private event with no media attention sought by republicans. Even in the pages of An Phoblacht there was no reporting of the contributions made. The in-house republican newspaper noted that the main theme of the conference 'was the necessity to harness all the forces in the struggle for national independence.' Those familiar with An Phoblacht would have taken this to signal a debate over the increasing politicisation and electoralism of the republican movement. The conference report did acknowledge— without giving an indication of the direction the debate had taken—that 'abortion and abstentionism were the last subjects covered . . . but both of those controversial issues were debated in a calm and reasonable manner.'[51]

Among those who spoke at the two-day gathering were Seán Crowe and Aengus Ó Snodaigh; both were full-time Sinn Féin activists living on subsistence from the party, various part-time jobs and state-provided social welfare assistance. Sixteen years later, both men would enter Dáil Éireann together as Sinn Féin TDs. But in the summer months of 1986, the possibility of Crowe or Ó Snodaigh—or indeed, any other Sinn Féin public representative—walking the corridors of Leinster House was going to be determined by a bitter battle for the ideological soul of the republican movement.

Interestingly, however, Crowe and Ó Snodaigh approached the subject with a considerable degree of pragmatism. Crowe's initial scepticism about the value of entering Leinster House had waned, and by 1986 he was supporting the idea. Ó Snodaigh, on the other hand, argued that the party was not ready for such a development: 'the organisation wasn't there, the professionalism wasn't there and the work on the ground hadn't been done.'[52]

At the Wolfe Tone Commemoration in June 1986, Martin McGuinness signalled his support for the 'era of pragmatism'. He told republicans at Bodenstown that 'as people who preach revolution we should begin with examining ourselves . . . Every time we refuse to consider new options . . . we betray reality.'[53]

Over the following months, other meetings were organised around Ireland as the ground was laid for the changes to come. The Adams leadership was on the verge of jettisoning 60 years of ideological purity in favour of the possibility of electoral advancement. There were repeated private and public reassurances that increased political activity —and an end to abstentionism in the Republic—would not dilute the commitment to the IRA campaign.

In early August 1986, Danny Morrison told a meeting of 200 republican activists in Newry that the 'IRA cannot be defeated'.[54] A week later, at an internment anniversary rally in Belfast, Gerry Adams offered more words of comfort to the doubters: 'We will see an end to foreign rule in our country. Your strength and the cutting edge of the IRA are our guarantee of that.'[55]

The pages of An Phoblacht were filled with correspondence on the controversial proposal. Prisoners wrote letters, mainly in support of the proposed change. Hughie Doherty—one of the Balcombe Street Gang —wrote from Wakefield Prison in England, 'It is time that we grasped the nettle of taking seats in Leinster House.' There was also backing from John McCombe in Long Lartin Prison in England who had opposed discussion of abstentionism at a previous Ard Fheis: 'After much inner conflict over a long period of time I have some to the view that we should when elected take our seats and take the struggle to the opposition.'[56]

Twice in October 1986, the pages of An Phoblacht carried correspondence from senior IRA man Gerry Kelly who had been involved in the Maze Prison escape in September 1983. Kelly had been arrested in the Netherlands in January 1986. Writing from Amsterdam Jail, Kelly described the abstentionist debate as the single most important issue affecting the republican movement at that time:

We must fight the enemy on many fronts. When we participated in the 1981 elections in the Six Counties, we shook the British establishment to its core. We overturned years of propaganda and myths and we put them on the defensive, both internally and internationally . . . Setting aside the abstentionist policy will open up another battlefront equally devastating to the British and Free State establishment. Perhaps it will not be as immediately dramatic, but it will be even more effective in bringing British withdrawal much closer.[57]

Not all republican prisoners were as positive. Dave Minto wrote from Birmingham that increased electoral involvement would be a waste of energy and resources: 'Remember how, in 1926, when Dan Breen exchanged his gun for a seat in Leinster House his effectiveness was nullified.'[58]

Opponents of the move believed that the reformists were tinkering with a fundamental truth and engaging in heresy. Liam Ó Ceallacháin from County Cork declared: 'by entering Dáil Éireann, Sinn Féin would be betraying all those who died for a 32-county republic since December 1921 when the ill-fated Treaty was accepted by renegade Irishmen.'[59]

The IRA formally intervened in the debate in early October 1986, issuing a statement that confirmed the passing of two resolutions at a recent Army Convention: 'The first removed the ban on a Volunteer discussing or advocating the taking of paramilitary seats. The second removed the ban on supporting successful republican candidates who take their seats in Leinster House.'[60] It also reminded the movement that under IRA rules offensives against the administration of the '26 Counties' and its forces were prohibited.

The IRA Army Convention is believed to have taken place in September in County Meath, alongside a Sinn Féin conference at which over 100 people contributed to a debate, reported as concentrating on 'Sinn Féin's task of becoming relevant to the people of the twenty-six counties and the major topic was the abstentionism issue.'[61] An Phoblacht reported Gerry Adams as saying that 'revolution would not happen overnight' and that 'Sinn Féin members in the twenty-six counties must take the struggle more seriously than they do at present.'[62]

Despite the IRA's endorsement of the new republican electoral strategy, talk of a split in the movement dominated in the weeks preceding the November 1986 Sinn Féin Ard Fheis. Adams spoke with many in the Ó Brádaigh camp. They were warned about the consequences of challenging the leadership. 'I am firmly convinced that anyone who leaves us over this issue will regret their decision in the years ahead,' Adams predicted.[63]

But Ruairí Ó Brádaigh stood firm. The Adams grouping had eroded his authority in the republican movement—after his resignation as party president in 1983, he had returned to teaching in Roscommon—but Ó

Brádaigh was driven to oppose changes that challenged the very core of the republican ideology. 'This thing is not acceptable to us. It would mean that for the first time since the foundation of the Fenians, that there wouldn't be a revolutionary movement to resist the status quo in all of Ireland.'[64]

Ó Brádaigh argued that ending abstentionism was like 'riding a horse going in two opposite directions', and he took the argument to Adams, challenging the Sinn Féin president with republican history and pointing out the incompatibility of constitutionalism in a revolutionary party:

> The armed struggle and sitting in parliaments are mutually exclusive. One is about absolute demands. Parliament is the world of compromise; the art of what is possible. The two cannot exist side by side, in the same house. Accept an end to abstentionism and the balance will have been tipped decisively in the direction of purely political campaigns that wind up in establishment parliaments. [...] These people will be shaped by the decisions they take, and by the people they will then work. Their careers will be linked to that system. They will be signing their own extinctions as revolutionaries not because they want to but because it cannot be otherwise. [...] This is the greatest struggle of the republican movement. If it is carried I won't accept it. I didn't get this far, and to this age, to be made a Free Stater of, at this stage of my life.[65]

On the morning of Sunday, 3 November 1986 Sinn Féin members gathered in the Mansion House in Dublin. The Round Room was hot and stuffy. There was hardly standing room as the aisles and the gallery quickly filled. Outside, members of the Garda Special Branch kept a watchful eye on movements in and out of the building. The overlap in membership between Sinn Féin and the IRA meant that many senior republicans were in attendance.

The debate on abstentionism started at half past eleven. As a reporter for *An Phoblacht* wrote: 'At 11:32 and 25 seconds, Gerry Adams lit his pipe. That was the signal that we were really down to business.'[66]

Adams was joined on the platform by Danny Morrison—decked out in a pink necktie—and an Aran-jumper-wearing Martin McGuinness. Another Adams loyalist, Seán McManus from Sligo, chaired the debate. A long line of delegates gathered to speak on motion 162, which was proposed by the party's Ard Comhairle. The resolution called for an end to Sinn Féin's abstentionist attitude to Leinster House, with elected party representatives taking their seats. There would be no change to the party's stance in relation to Westminster or any new assembly in Northern Ireland.

Pat Doherty opened the debate, admitting that, whatever the republican view of the parliament of the Irish Republic, the reality was '95% of the people accept Leinster House as being their government.' In effect, pragmatism was driving the constitutional change. Doherty succinctly described the favoured strategy: 'Armed struggle in the Six Counties, in pursuance of British withdrawal, and political struggle throughout the whole 32 counties in pursuance of the Republic. . . .'[67]

In all, 54 delegates spoke on motion 162 in a debate which lasted for over four hours. Veteran republicans John Joe McGirl and Joe Cahill argued that comparisons with the bitter debate that split the republican movement in late 1969 and early 1970 were unfair and inaccurate. McGirl said that he had changed his position on abstentionism, opposing change in 1969–70 but now viewing the boycott of Leinster House as a 'millstone' and a 'handicap' to the development of the republican agenda in the Republic. Cahill appealed for unity in the movement with an emotional contribution that traced his involvement in the IRA and Sinn Féin: 'The dedication and commitment which brought me to the foot of the scaffold in 1942 is the same in my heart today as it was then. The only thing that has changed is that my age is against me.'[68]

There was a standing ovation for the movement's former leader when Ó Brádaigh reached the speaking podium on the top platform. This was followed by an obviously uncomfortable exchange of pleasantries when Adams left his top-table seat and approached Ó Brádaigh.

As he reached into Irish history, Ó Brádaigh delivered a succinct analysis of the abstentionist doctrine so central to the militant strand of Irish republicanism:

> A chara, I put it to you this way, we have not been wrong for 65 years . . . we have been right and we should continue to be right . . . [but now those who oppose us can say] . . . 'Ah, it took 65 years but we have them at last,' and those in Leinster House who have done everything, the firing squads, the prison cells, the internment camps, the hunger strike and weren't able to break this movement; they can say at last 'We have them toeing the line. It took us 65 years but they have come in from the wilderness and we have them now.' Never that's what I say to you—never.[69]

If Adams was intent on presenting himself as a conciliator, Martin

McGuinness was content to play the role of hardline opponent. McGuinness launched the bitterest attack on Ó Brádaigh and his supporters, referring back to their role in the 1974–75 IRA ceasefire: 'The reality is that the former leadership of this Movement has never been able to come to terms with this leadership's criticisms of the disgraceful attitude adopted by them during the disastrous 18-month ceasefire in the mid-1970s. . . .'[70]

In dredging up the recent past, McGuinness was clearly signalling that the fault lines in the republican movement went well beyond the immediate matter of amending the abstentionist policy. The Northern-based leadership had emerged after the 1975 ceasefire ended and quickly forged a distinct identity for itself within the movement, to the detriment of those in the Ó Brádaigh grouping who were perceived as traditionalists from the IRA's border campaign in the 1950s. Moreover, in abandoning Sinn Féin's Éire Nua policy, figures likes Adams, McGuinness and Morrison were not just signalling a change of policy direction but were also publicly sidelining the old guard and all their associations.

'Shame, shame, shame,' McGuinness spat out as he rounded on those who favoured the status quo. There was also a warning delivered by someone who obviously spoke with a certain confident knowledge of how the IRA Army Council would actually behave: 'The IRA will not split. They will not walk away from the armed struggle. They are the real revolutionaries. If you allow yourselves to be led out of this hall today, the only place you will be going is home.' The leadership of the IRA had spoken, and the majority of the delegates present were willing to back the new strategy.

When the vote was called, some 628 delegates expressed a preference, with 429 voting to amend the abstentionist policy that had been in place for over 60 years, and 161 rejecting the proposal. The necessary two-thirds majority had been achieved.

As the vote was read out, Ó Brádaigh, who was sitting near the back of the hall, readied himself to depart. He was joined by a small group of supporters. There was cheering outside the Mansion House where a woman dressed in uniform carried a four-provinces flag. Those who walked out numbered fewer than 100 people. They went on to form Republican Sinn Féin, which has remained a small grouping linked to the paramilitary organisation, the Continuity IRA. The Ó Brádaigh-led splinter group remains opposed to the direction taken by Gerry Adams, including signing up to the Belfast Agreement in 1998.

The November 1986 vote sealed the complete takeover of the republican movement by the Adams–McGuinness faction. They now had complete control of Sinn Féin and the IRA. Ironically, many of the predictions made by Ó Brádaigh ahead of the 1986 Ard Fheis have come to pass, including an end to the Provisional IRA's military campaign and increased Sinn Féin participation in constitutional politics, on both sides of the border.

There were nervous responses in the Republic to the 1986 Ard Fheis decision. The then Taoiseach, Garret FitzGerald, noted that, 'For the first time a party which is engaged actively in a brutal campaign of violence, and which requires from all its elected representatives a specific commitment to support this murderous campaign, has committed itself to seeking, and, if elected taking seats in Dáil Éireann.'[71]

Republicans might have decided to open up the possibility of entering Leinster House but they still had little regard for the parliament of the Irish Republic or the institutions of that state, as an editorial in *An Phoblacht* made very plain:

> Leinster House *does* corrupt. It corrupts corruptible people, just as any parliament, even a 32-County parliament, would corrupt the weak and the vain, the insincere and the gombeen. It cannot corrupt a revolutionary. [. . .] Our position on Leinster House is that it is not at the head of a sovereign nation as envisaged in the 1916 Proclamation. It is a partitionist institution, and we say that. The Garda and the Free State Army are the constituted force of this institution and we wish them no harm. If there is, by some unforeseen chance, a clash between them and the IRA, our public position in Leinster House on such a clash would be the same public position had we never crossed the floor.[72]

In no uncertain terms the message had been delivered to the republican grassroots and the wider political establishment—successful Sinn Féin candidates would now take their seats but they would not give loyalty, not to mind allegiance, to the Republic's parliament.

Indeed, in the opinion of Sinn Féin and the IRA, the Irish Republic is not a republic at all; it is a sham creation derived from the flawed 1921 settlement. The same attitude has prevailed in relation to the institutions of the Irish state, including the army and the police force, although electoral pragmatism necessitated no direct confrontation with these bodies as the IRA continued its campaign of violence in Northern Ireland.

This position was laced with considerable inconsistency and deep hypocrisy. In an interview with the author in early 2002, Gerry Adams advanced the republican position somewhat publicly, stating for the first time that Sinn Féin recognised the Defence Forces as the only legitimate army in the Irish state: 'We are very, very clear in terms of our recognition and acceptance and support for the Garda Síochána as the only legitimate policing service in the State and also in terms of the legitimacy of the Defence Forces as the only legitimate force.'[73]

This statement in 2002 was a serious development in Sinn Féin's attitude to the Irish Republic and its institutions. After all, at the 1986 Sinn Féin Ard Fheis, Adams's close colleague, Pat Doherty, had remarked, 'Leinster House is a partitionist institution pretending to be a national parliament.'[74]

What Adams left unsaid in 2002 was the attitude of the IRA towards the legitimacy of the Irish state. As noted previously, republican theology is rooted in the IRA's self-proclaimed position as the legitimate government of all-Ireland, with an authority handed on by the anti-Treaty republican faction in the mid-1930s. The divided loyalty of republican politicians and militarists became evident in the aftermath of the shooting dead of Detective Garda Jerry McCabe in County Clare in 1996.

The IRA initially dissociated itself from the attack but when it became clear that its members were responsible, the republican movement threw the cloak of solidarity around them. The early release of those who shot Garda McCabe dead even became a deal breaker for the Sinn Féin leadership in negotiations on a political settlement in 2003 and 2004. The allegiance and loyalties of republicans were still rooted in the sentiments expressed by the editorial writer in *An Phoblacht* back in 1986: 'If there is, by some unforeseen chance, a clash between them [the Garda Síochána] and the IRA, our public position in Leinster House on such a clash would be the same public position had we never crossed the floor.'[75]

Sinn Féin members who have taken their seats in Leinster House in recent times still have to deal with their divided allegiances and loyalties. Arthur Morgan, who was elected for the Louth constituency at the 2002 general election, succinctly describes the very mixed attitudes within his party to the parliament of the Irish Republic:

I might as well have been walking into Long Kesh when I walked in Leinster House [after his election in 2002]. It wasn't an institution that I was going to offer loyalty to. I don't offer particular loyalty to it now because it doesn't represent all the people of this island . . . The parliament is legitimate; I wouldn't deny that for one moment. It organises the business of the twenty-six County State, so to that extent of course it is legitimate but loyalty is a different story in my view. I don't have a particular loyalty with Leinster House.[76]

While such divided loyalties still exist for republicans, it did appear that the debate over abstentionism was concluded at the 1986 Ard Fheis. The election performances of Sinn Féin in the Republic in subsequent years were, however, hugely disappointing. Adams had promised a two-election strategy before any Sinn Féin successes would materialise. This was to prove a highly ambitious forecast as is discussed in the next chapter. Indeed, the first Sinn Féin member to sit in Leinster House since the 1920s took his seat only in 1997. A little over a year after that historic event, the republican movement would return to abstentionism, but this time in relation to taking seats in a new Northern Ireland assembly located in the old Stormont building outside Belfast.

In September 1982, *An Phoblacht* baldly stated:

Sinn Féin candidates will never attend the new Stormont and have never attended the old one. Republicans have consistently opposed the six-county state since its inception. We have a clear record in this regard. We stand on this record.[77]

At the 1986 Ard Fheis, the Adams leadership declared that ending abstentionism in relation to Leinster House set no precedent for republicans taking seats at Stormont or at Westminster. Indeed, Martin McGuinness told the delegates that he was giving 'a commitment on behalf of the leadership that we have absolutely no intention of going to Westminster or Stormont'.

But such certainties were not guaranteed as pragmatism again came to the fore in determining republican strategic thinking on political advancement. In the aftermath of the signing of the 1998 Belfast Agreement, Sinn Féin once more considered its tactical use of the abstentionism policy, this time in relation to taking seats in a new Stormont assembly in Northern Ireland. The Belfast Agreement allowed for the establishment of a cross-community, power-sharing assembly and, with the IRA on ceasefire, Sinn Féin was intent on playing its role in the new institutional arrangement.

Just as in 1986, the Sinn Féin constitution had to be amended—a process that again required a two-thirds majority. And just like in 1986, ideological purity was downgraded in the face of potential political and electoral advancement. Pragmatism was the central rationale advanced by the Adams–McGuinness leadership for modifying this once core value.

Pat Doherty, who proposed the 1986 motion that sanctioned Sinn Féin TDs taking their seats in Leinster House, once more advocated change. Arguing that republicans should take their seats in the new Stormont Assembly, Doherty now observed:

> We always knew the path to freedom was never going to be simple or straightforward. What is essential is that we are prepared to adapt our tactical positions without ever losing sight of our ultimate objectives ... Tactics are there to be adapted and changed when the need arises but principles are there to be achieved ... we will deliver Irish unity and independence.[78]

The change passed with minimal rancour and nothing like the divisions that were evident at the 1986 Ard Fheis. Successful Sinn Féin candidates subsequently took their seats at Stormont, and when it came to participation in the power-sharing governmental arrangement in Northern Ireland, the party nominated two of its Assembly members to hold ministerial office. The task of publicly announcing those names fell to party president Gerry Adams. There was considerable surprise when Martin McGuinness joined Bairbre de Brún as one of the Sinn Féin nominees. McGuinness was, for many unionists, the public personification of the organic link between Sinn Féin and the IRA. The Derry man, long reported as a member of the IRA Army Council, was nominated as Education Minister in the Executive arising out of the Belfast Agreement.

Previous promises about avoiding Stormont were forgotten. For Adams, the ending of abstentionism in relation to a devolved assembly in Northern Ireland was made less difficult by the 1986 decision concerning Leinster House:

> I think 1998 was probably an easier decision [than 1986] ... I didn't have any great difficulty about actually being in the place ... Myself and Martin McGuinness had been up at a meeting with the British Government, in one of the other buildings on the estate; and one guy, the chief caretaker, showed us the place. I felt as I think anti-apartheid activists must have felt in South Africa. When we came to being in the

Assembly, there were big decisions that people had to face up to—
would we vote for David Trimble, as the first minister; and then when
it came to nominating our own ministers and people looked at the
Pledge of Office, and it said, 'Northern Ireland'. Strange as it may
sound, these were the things that when it actually came down to it, as
opposed to being in the building or being about the place.[79]

In taking their seats in the Northern Ireland Assembly, Adams sponsored
a second fundamental rewriting of the script of contemporary
republicanism. It was a departure no previous republican leader had
endorsed. Not even de Valera when he departed Sinn Féin in 1926 argued
that republicans should end abstentionism in the context of
parliamentary representation in Northern Ireland. The so-called
compromisers in 1926, who re-emerged as Fianna Fáil, and those in the
post-1970 Official movement who evolved into the Workers' Party, broke
ranks with republican dogma purely in the context of taking seats in Dáil
Éireann. The idea of republican representatives sitting in an assembly of
a partitioned Northern Ireland was never an issue. In effect, with the 1998
decision, Adams moved his Sinn Féin organisation even further away
from the party that called itself Sinn Féin after the 1921 Treaty split.
Indeed, over the changing course of republicanism's attitude towards
abstentionism, one of the main themes associated with the Adams era
has undoubtedly been the way in which pragmatism has come to
dominate republican politics. The objective of a united Ireland might
have remained in place but the self-styled revolutionaries had, over a 20-
year period, displayed, time and time again, a real grasp of the 'politics of
pragmatism'.

THE BUSINESS OF
ELECTIONS, 1981–2005

C hristy Burke comes from a working-class background in Dublin.
He has memories of his mother singing republican songs and
recalls having a sense of excitement at hearing stories associated
with the Easter 1916 Rising. When the modern conflict started in
Northern Ireland in the summer of 1969, Burke was working in the coal
yards in the docklands area in Dublin. Up to that time, his involvement
in republican politics had been confined to selling the movement's
weekly newspaper and attending meetings. It was after a protest march
on O'Connell Street that Burke decided to attach himself firmly to the
republican movement. Volunteers were sought and a bus was leaving that
same evening from Dublin:

> I will never forget it. The bus was parked in Parnell Square and
> anyone who wanted to go to the border could board that bus. I never
> told my wife or my mother as off I went to Dundalk where we were
> helping refugees who were coming from Belfast; these people had
> been burnt out of their homes by loyalists.[1]

The Dubliner then travelled to Derry where nationalists in the Bogside
area were involved in running battles with the police and loyalists. A
lifelong commitment to the republican movement had started and this
involvement continued when Burke eventually returned home. 'I began
to organise people in Dublin to go north and also to get help, be it
financial or providing billets for people who were on the run.'[2]

There was an influx of members into the republican movement in the
early 1970s and the security forces on both sides of the border were
monitoring as best they could the activities of these individuals. The

Provisional IRA had emerged as a dangerous armed organisation, pursuing an offensive military agenda to end British rule in Northern Ireland. Bombings and shooting became regular occurrences, as did killings and injuries, with civilians bearing the worst of the violence. Alongside the IRA's campaign, republicans organised protest marches against the British government's policy of internment without trial. Support networks for prisoners and their families were established. A whole organisational infrastructure was being put in place, although Sinn Féin was still very much the lesser participant in the so-called republican struggle.

Like its counterpart in Northern Ireland, the Garda Síochána in Dublin was keeping a close watch on people who were known to have republican associations. Burke was included in that group and, in 1973, he was arrested in a Garda raid on a house in Ranelagh in south Dublin. He was charged with possession of explosives and firearms, as well as IRA membership.

There was—and still is—membership overlap between the two strands of the republican movement. Many Sinn Féin figures have had associations with the IRA. In the Republic, Sinn Féin figures such as Martin Ferris and Arthur Morgan have served time for IRA activities, as have numerous elected representatives in Northern Ireland. Gerry Adams is almost unique in not admitting to an IRA past. Senior republicans like Martin McGuinness and Danny Morrison have in recent years openly stated that they were members of the IRA, although they refuse to reveal any detail about the nature of their IRA involvement.

Many members of Sinn Féin were not—and are not—members of the IRA. But to be a member of Sinn Féin involves a commitment to the modus operandi of the IRA. 'I never opposed the IRA,' Aengus Ó Snodaigh admits, adding, 'I canvassed on doorsteps where I was asked about the IRA and I would have had to defend it.'[3]

The inclusion of Sinn Féin and the IRA under the same organisational heading meant Sinn Féin acceptance that political objectives could be pursued through violent methods. 'There can be no doubt where we stand,' Caoimhghín Ó Caoláin quipped in his party's Monaghan election office in early 1982 as he nodded to a plaque on the wall that read, 'Join the People's Army—the Provisionals.'[4]

Nevertheless, Ó Caoláin says that when deciding in 1982 to resign his banking job to devote his energies to full-time republican activism, he never considered joining the IRA:

I never did. The proposition was never put to me. I don't know that it was something I would have been able to deal with, or whatever, I can only say that the best utilisation of my skills and talents was in terms of organisation, the business of building the party and political development. . . .[5]

The hunger-strike era drew many people into Sinn Féin. People like Ó Caoláin and Owen Carron became involved in the committees set up to lobby for the demands of the republican prisoners. In the aftermath of the hunger strikes, they remained active in republican politics. Many of those who became actively involved have tended to devote themselves full-time to their cause. Life-long activism is not unique as the lines between personal and professional lives blur. Senior figures like Adams and McGuinness have spent their entire adult lives working full-time for the republican movement.

Many of those who hold internal party positions have had no other employment. Numerous potential Sinn Féin public representatives operate as full-time politicians long before they are elected to local or national office. Few Sinn Féin politicians have had a career outside the republican movement and those who had tended to scale back their involvement early in their working lives. Christy Burke recalled his own situation: 'I was getting £20 [from Sinn Féin] for doing my political work and, of course, I had the dole [social welfare] because I was always available for work but nobody would employ me because I was a Sinn Féin activist.'[6]

Other party members tell a similar story. When Aengus Ó Snodaigh left University College Dublin in the mid-1980s he pondered the choice of becoming a full-time republican activist:

It was a huge decision. In 1985 I started my HDip [teaching diploma] so I was working for *An Phoblacht* while teaching in Sion Hill in Blackrock. By going full-time [with *An Phoblacht*] I was basically saying, 'I will live on the dole and a sub of about twenty pounds a week for the foreseeable future.' But at the time I wasn't married and had no kids, and it was eleven years before I left *An Phoblacht*.[7]

Ó Snodaigh supplemented his income with a variety of part-time evening jobs, including bar and cleaning work. As his personal situation changed after his marriage in 1992, he found the balancing act increasingly difficult and eventually took a full-time job with Bord na Gaeilge.

The republican movement had long had an ability to find internal positions for prospective electoral candidates. For example, Caoimhghín Ó Caoláin left his job as a banking official in the early 1980s to become general manager of *An Phoblacht* newspaper, before returning to his native Monaghan to establish a political base. Seán Crowe held a variety of internal party positions, including post-1994 servicing the Sinn Féin delegation at the Forum for Peace and Reconciliation in Dublin.

Throughout the 1980s and 1990s, dozens of republican activists survived on a weekly sub of about £20 (€25) from Sinn Féin, social welfare payments and income from a variety of part-time jobs, invariably in the black economy. In more recent times, Sinn Féin has used official monies from its parliamentary presence in Leinster House, Stormont and Westminster to fund its organisational structure.

The party's elected representatives receive a sum equivalent to the average industrial wage, with the remainder of their income being transferred to Sinn Féin head office. Mary Lou McDonald acknowledges that public representatives like herself as a member of the European Parliament see this arrangement as 're-investing in the party. It is a vital stream of revenue.'[8]

The ability of a small political party to fund such an operation has led to questions about the sources of Sinn Féin monies, a topic discussed in Chapter 8. Indeed, the party has never been short of resources and even in the 1970s, as a very marginal political operation, it owned a number of properties in Dublin and Belfast. One of these was in Blessington Street in Dublin's north inner city. After his release from prison in 1974, Christy Burke ran the newly opened republican advice centre from the Blessington Street property. Initially the centre acted as a meeting place for republicans as they organised protests and raised funds. At that time, republicans like Burke did not see themselves as community activists or politicians in the making. Their task was to further the republican cause. The prison protests in Northern Ireland, however, produced a fundamental reorientation in their attitudes to electoral politics.

I was in Blessington Street one day in 1981 having a cup of tea when there was a bang on the front door. When I opened the door, there were about 20 women and children outside. They said they had been evicted for squatting and they wanted someone to help them. I told them they were in the wrong place, that the Workers' Party was over in Gardiner Place. But they said no, they had been told to come to Blessington Street.[9]

The women and children were brought in off the street but despite protests from Burke that he was not involved in politics, they refused to leave. Chips were ordered from the local takeaway and eventually Burke agreed to go with his visitors to make representations with housing officials at Dublin Corporation. But the former squatters were not prepared to be fobbed off with promises of housing in the near future, and Burke was not about to ease himself away from their plight. A three-day sit-in at the council offices followed: 'They all got houses, and it was in the newspaper so as a result everyone who was squatting or had been evicted was coming to Christy Burke to get them a house.'[10]

The decision to contest elections in 1981—even with prisoner candidates and with the aim of generating publicity for the prison protests—had numerous unforeseen consequences for the republican movement. In several areas, a republican constituency had long existed and these voters liked the idea of having republican candidates to support. In other areas, particularly economically deprived areas, people wanted a voice to represent their interests which were often neglected by the mainstream parties. In both cases, Sinn Féin came to fill that political and electoral void.

Republicans like Christy Burke began to increase their level of community activism, resulting in increased recognition for the Sinn Féin name. The decision in early 1982 to contest elections under the Sinn Féin banner was a natural progression, although the timing was very much influenced by the dramatic events associated with the previous year's hunger strike. 'I wasn't elected to anything but I was running advice centres on Wednesday and Friday nights in Blessington Street and they would be jammed with people,' Burke recalled.[11]

Burke was elected to Dublin Corporation at the 1985 local elections. For several years, there had been some limited Sinn Féin representation on local government councils in the Irish Republic. But the symbolic breakthrough in the Irish capital was politically significant. Burke was the sole Sinn Féin representative on Dublin Corporation. The reaction he received was a good indication of the political pariah status afforded to Sinn Féin in the 1980s by the vast majority of politicians and, indeed, media commentators. The IRA's campaign of violence meant that Sinn Féin members were the 'unwashed' in political terms.

I was excluded from virtually everything on Dublin Corporation. The leaders of some left-wing parties instructed their councillors not even to have tea with me, not to mind speaking to me. When I stood up to

speak on a motion if Tony Gregory [independent councillor] wasn't
in the chamber, the motion would fall as I wouldn't be able to get
someone to second it. I used to feel like an orphan because when I'd
speak there'd be comments from Labour and Fine Gael that the IRA
representative is now speaking.[12]

Interestingly, in light of his subsequent pivotal role in the peace process,
Bertie Ahern adopted a different approach to the sole Sinn Féin
representative. 'Bertie Ahern was leader of the Fianna Fáil group on the
council. He got me onto the housing committee. I have to say he was fair
to me and always courteous,' Burke said.[13] The fact that the two men
shared a similar geographical electoral area may also have influenced
Ahern's stance.

Burke's breakthrough in the local elections in 1985 was matched by the
appearance on the political scene in Monaghan of Caoimhghín Ó
Caoláin. These local success stories did not, however, detract from the
problems Sinn Féin faced in building a political base in the Irish
Republic. The disappointing results in the February 1982 general election
in the Republic provided clear evidence that there would be no early
electoral victory for Sinn Féin in national politics. The party did not
contest the second set of Dáil Éireann elections later in 1982, preferring
to concentrate republican efforts on the more profitable Assembly
contest in Northern Ireland. But the message on the doorsteps in the
Republic clearly indicated that an early breakthrough would require
republicans to tackle a core ideological belief—taking seats in Leinster
House, as Christy Burke was bluntly told:

> I remember one woman saying to me, 'Christy, you're a nice fellow
> and you're hard working, and I know all your family but if you get
> elected to the Dáil and there's a vote on VAT on children's shoes—
> what good would you be to me if you weren't in there?' I pointed out
> to her that I could be vocal outside the chamber but she wasn't buying
> it. She said, 'That's fine Christy but you wouldn't be there for the
> vote.'[14]

As discussed in the previous chapter, Burke was not the only republican
taking this viewpoint to the leadership of the organisation. At the time of
the crucial 1986 Ard Fheis, Gerry Adams predicted that it would take two
elections for Sinn Féin to develop to an organisational base in the
Republic capable of winning seats in Leinster House. This assessment

provided some space for the party as it entered the 1987 general election—the first national election in the Republic contested by contemporary Sinn Féin on a platform of taking any seat won by the party.

Whatever about the election strategy professed to, Adams and his colleagues must have seen the 1987 campaign as an opportune time to test the electoral possibilities for Sinn Féin in the Republic. There were clear policy demarcations between the mainstream parties, especially on the issues of Northern Ireland and the economy. Sinn Féin, having registered in the Republic as a political party for the first time, was offering a very distinct alternative. The party leadership had expectations in urban Ireland of attracting some of the working-class vote alienated from the Labour Party following its involvement in the outgoing government but not sufficiently turned on by the left-wing Workers' Party.

A considerable volume of research material indicates that electoral support for the left has always been remarkably low in Ireland, rarely reaching even 20 per cent of the vote, whereas in Western Europe the average share of vote won by left-wing parties was in the region of 30 per cent, and in some countries reached as high as 40 per cent. This contrast between Ireland and other European countries is manifested in terms of government formation where the left vote in many other jurisdictions is enough to make forming a left government on its own a realistic possibility. This has never been the case in the Irish Republic.

If Sinn Féin was hoping to tap into the smallish left-wing and protest constituency, it also had expectations about winning over voters motivated by the national question. The party was positioned as hardline republican, with only Fianna Fáil among the mainstream parties sharing any similar policy ground, although Fianna Fáil was a totally constitutional party that rejected the use of violence to advance the nationalist cause in Northern Ireland. Fianna Fáil was unequivocal in its support for Irish unity but by 1987 the party was at best offering mild opposition to the Anglo-Irish Agreement. There was much less enthusiasm for territorial unity among the other parties, all of which had endorsed the document agreed between Margaret Thatcher and Garret FitzGerald in 1985.

Sinn Féin nominated candidates in 24 constituencies at the 1987 general election, including Aengus Ó Snodaigh who ran in his home area of Dublin South-East, generally a middle-class constituency with some working-class areas.

There was a great buzz but I knew there wasn't a hope in hell that I was getting elected. The majority of us [Sinn Féin candidates] realised that. Most people were polite. They'd say no and close the door. But we were testing the waters. To be honest we hadn't a proper concept of how to run an election campaign. The expertise we have today has taken 20 years to develop.[15]

In truth, Sinn Féin was on the very margins of the campaign debate in 1987. The party was, after all, entering the electoral process as a small fringe organisation which at best was going to find it difficult to get its message heard in any national contest. But Sinn Féin faced a unique additional barrier that would hamper its participation in the election campaign—its support for IRA violence. This endorsement of the IRA meant that the controversial Section 31 broadcasting ban was applied to Sinn Féin candidates.

Throughout a quarter of a century, a deliberate government policy was pursued to push republicans to the margins of Irish life. The policy crossed into broadcasting censorship, as well as a deliberate attempt at political isolation. Successive administrations in the Irish Republic persisted with a broadcasting ban, the main effect of which was to prevent broadcasters from directly reporting the political views of the republican movement.

The outbreak of the contemporary conflict in Northern Ireland in 1969 was the first time the new television service in the Irish Republic was faced with the issue of reporting on the IRA in a systematic fashion. RTÉ television had started only on New Year's Eve, 1961, while challenging current affairs output in the long-established radio service was a recent innovation.

The initial period after 1969 was complicated by—as Professor John Horgan has observed—'the fact that although paramilitary activity was illegal, political activity by organisations which supported paramilitary action was not.'[16] So, republicans were initially interviewed in their capacity as Sinn Féin representatives, even when they were known, or believed, to have also been key players in the IRA. The situation led to phone calls from the government to the Chairman of the RTÉ Authority about the frequency with which Sinn Féin figures were appearing on television and radio programmes.

A pressure point was reached in September 1971 when the Irish government reacted furiously to the presence of a republican representative on RTÉ commenting on a meeting that had just taken place between Taoiseach Jack Lynch and his British counterpart, Ted Heath. The government in Dublin saw a challenge to its authority and responded by issuing a directive under Section 31 of the Broadcasting Act of 1961.

The infamous Section 31 stated: 'The Minister may direct the Authority in writing to refrain from broadcasting any particular matter, or matter of any particular class, and the Authority shall comply with the direction.' The directive issued under Section 31 in September 1971 was incredibly vague, prohibiting RTÉ from broadcasting 'any material that could be calculated to promote the aims and activities of any organisation which engages in, promotes, encourages or advocates the attaining of any particular objective by violent means.'

For over a quarter of a century, RTÉ adopted a highly rigid interpretation of the directive that permitted journalists to report on Sinn Féin and IRA statements and activities but prevented sound broadcast of members of either organisation. The policy presented journalists with considerable difficulties in reporting on matters relating to Northern Ireland. Moreover, the situation was made even more problematic with the emergence of Sinn Féin as an electoral participant in the aftermath of the 1981 hunger strikes.

Garret FitzGerald was one of those who supported the ban. FitzGerald was a minister in the 1973–77 Fine Gael–Labour coalition. He argues that Section 31 was introduced and maintained so as to protect the 'security of the state' in the face of the 'ineffectiveness of interviewers ever interviewing extremists successfully'. His argument centres on the view that with the Irish state broadcaster giving a voice to the IRA, there was an increased possibility of loyalists being provoked into attacking nationalist communities in Northern Ireland. In addition, FitzGerald argues that giving republicans access to the national airwaves had the potential to create difficulties in the Irish government's relationship with its British counterpart.[17]

Whatever the motivations and objectives underpinning Section 31, the ban resulted in republicans being kept off the airwaves in Ireland for a quarter of a century. It meant that republicans were able to avoid having to defend IRA actions on Irish radio and television. But the fact that, by the late 1980s, over half of the population had access to British television stations exposed Irish censorship to some ridicule. Moreover, RTÉ extended the ban to all members of Sinn Féin, no matter what topic they were discussing, even when the subject had nothing to do with politics or the conflict in Northern Ireland. In 1990, a trade union representative representing workers in an industrial dispute at a bakery in Dublin was banned from RTÉ under Section 31. The union official—Larry O'Toole—was denied access to the airwaves because he was a Sinn Féin activist.

The voice of Martin McGuinness was, however, heard in an RTÉ radio report in March 1988. The short segment featured in a report on the cortège with the bodies of three IRA members shot dead by the SAS in Gibraltar. McGuinness was not interviewed but his voice was heard explaining that the RUC would not allow the coffins across the border because they were draped with the Irish national flag. The ensuing controversy resulted in the reporter Jenny McGeever having her contract terminated, although none of her supervisors was ever disciplined.

The impact of Section 31—which was ended as a so-called 'confidence building measure' prior to the 1994 IRA ceasefire—still rankles with Sinn Féin members. 'It crippled Sinn Féin candidates,' Christy Burke claims. 'May I just remind you that the three elections that I lost were all against the backdrop of Section 31 censorship, where I didn't even have access to local radio. So with the ban gone, the election in 1997 was the first election that I fought that we had an informed electorate,' Caoimhghín Ó Caoláin asserted.[18]

There were, however, always ways to counter the ban. Indeed, even in the absence of an official television outlet, Sinn Féin still made party political broadcasts. These short advertisements for Sinn Féin were shown in pubs sympathetic to the party. The pirate radio sector was less rigorous in its attitude to Sinn Féin, with several pirate stations broadcasting interviews with republican representatives. Moreover, on some occasions, republicans reacted to their lack of access to the airwaves by simply operating their own stations. In 1982, in the Sligo–Leitrim constituency, Sinn Féin set up a pirate radio station that played republican ballads and pre-recorded broadcasts favourable to Sinn Féin candidates.

But these were just small gestures of defiance, as throughout the 1980s Sinn Féin found itself at the receiving end of a deliberate policy of marginalisation. This policy was most forcefully pursued by the Fine Gael–Labour coalition government, which came to power in late 1982. For example, in February 1984, Eddie Fullerton, a Sinn Féin councillor in Donegal, was refused a meeting with the Minister for the Environment while, later that same month, the Minister for Labour declined to meet with members of Gorey Town Commission, as their chairperson was a member of Sinn Féin. The policy, which was a direct response to the electoral emergence of Sinn Féin, was aimed at isolating republicans. Taoiseach Garret FitzGerald and a Labour minister, Barry Desmond, even went as far as resigning from the Irish branch of the Anti-Apartheid movement because of its affiliation with Sinn Féin.

At another level, the party was denied use of state-owned property. 'I remember in the 1980s when we were barred from holding the Ard Fheis in the Mansion House where Sinn Féin always had its Ard Fheis. We ended up having the conference out in Tallaght [in the basketball arena],' Seán Crowe recalled. 'But that was no problem as the locals opened up their homes and over one hundred delegates were put up by local people.'[19]

Whatever about a warm welcome from some people in Tallaght, the fact remained that Sinn Féin was an electoral disaster zone in the Irish Republic. In the 1987 general election, Sinn Féin won 2 per cent of the national vote. The result was twice the party's performance in the February 1982 general election, but lower than the vote received by the prisoner candidates in the June 1981 contest. On a strictly proportional allocation of the seats, the vote won by Sinn Féin would have given the party three of the 166 seats in Leinster House. This would have been the historic breakthrough promised by the supporters of ending abstentionism. But with candidates in only a handful of constituencies and poor transfer patterns from other parties, an under-representation of small party representatives is not unusual in Irish elections.

The electoral system hurt Sinn Féin more than the larger parties but this reality could not have been used to distract from what was a distinctly poor performance. In all, 24 of the 27 Sinn Féin candidates failed to win the minimum number of votes necessary to get their deposits refunded. Trinity College academic Michael Gallagher concluded, 'there was little in its [1987] performance to suggest that dropping the abstentionist policy will bring about any change in its fortunes.'[20]

Nevertheless, the 1987 result provided some indication of where Sinn Féin had a natural support base, a constituency which was not obviously put off by the party's backing for the IRA campaign of violence. In a sense, this was the core Sinn Féin vote that could be relied upon to back the party, irrespective of most external events.

At that time, Sinn Féin was strongest in the border constituencies—it won 8 per cent in Donegal North-East, 7 per cent in Cavan–Monaghan and 6 per cent in both Sligo–Leitrim and Louth, respectively. These were heartland areas with a traditional republican vote evident in the 1981

H-block campaign when prisoner candidates won seats in Louth and Cavan–Monaghan, while polling well in the other border constituencies.

The best Sinn Féin performance in the capital at the 1987 general election was in Dublin Central—5 per cent of the first preference vote. Gallagher speculated that, 'this probably represents its best prospect of winning a seat at some stage in the not very imminent future.'[21]

The 1987 general election result confirmed that there would be no early breakthrough for Sinn Féin in the Republic—the expectation that the outcome of the 1986 Ard Fheis would reposition republican candidates in electoral terms was not realised. Indeed, the end of abstentionism had simply bypassed most voters who were more clearly knowledgeable about the party's links to the Provisional IRA. The broadcasting ban undoubtedly hampered efforts by Sinn Féin candidates to convey their message to the electorate, but links with a private illegal army engaged in a campaign of violence was most likely the number one impediment to the electoral development of the republican vote in the Irish Republic.

Looking back, Caoimhghín Ó Caoláin admitted as much:

It was a part of it, I have no doubt, in terms of the marketability of Sinn Féin as a political force in mainstream political life. There is no doubt that it [IRA violence] was there in the backdrop. But that said, I think the people still needed to have more time to evaluate our abilities, how we would deliver. . . .'[22]

The Sinn Féin progress in Cavan–Monaghan was somewhat better than in many other constituencies but the party's electoral base was so low that the results in 1987 appeared to consign republicans to the very margins of electoral participation. The Sinn Féin leadership was not unprepared for the outcome. As mentioned previously, Adams had signalled on numerous occasions before the 1987 poll that the real test of his party's prospects in the Republic would be not at that election but at the following one. So, when a general election was called in the Republic for June 1989, there was an opportunity to test the Adams hypothesis.

There were 13 fewer Sinn Féin candidates in 1989 than two years previously. But there was one outcome shared between the two elections —the Sinn Féin candidates polled poorly and again most lost their election deposits. Of the 14 candidates who contested, all but two lost their deposits.

In all, Sinn Féin lost a third of the votes it had received in 1987. If

Michael Gallagher had been bleak in his assessment of the Sinn Féin performance in 1987, his conclusion after the 1989 general election was damning. Sinn Féin's support, Gallagher wrote, 'means that it is scarcely more popular among the southern electorate than it is among northern Protestants, and the "long road" to success on which its activists say it is embarked in the south looks more like a cul-de-sac.'[23] The TCD political scientist forecast that the 1.2 per cent vote share won by Sinn Féin in 1989 gave the party 'little future in the south'.[24]

After two tests of its post-abstentionist policy, Sinn Féin could not but draw the obvious conclusion—Northern Ireland was not a burning issue for the vast majority of voters in the Irish Republic. Moreover, there was little support for a political party that was linked to an illegal paramilitary organisation.

The IRA campaign stunted the development of Sinn Féin south of the border, while north of the border, by the end of the 1980s, the images of bombings, shootings, death and injuries prevented the development of the party beyond about 10 per cent of the overall vote. Sinn Féin members grew used to taking the blame for IRA activities, with criticism from their political opponents, the media and the general public. 'You would go, "Oh fuck, not again, how am I going to defend this?" It didn't make you think twice but you knew you were going to be insulted by people,' Aengus Ó Snodaigh recalled.[25]

Voting in the general election in June 1989 was held on the same day as the elections to the European Parliament. Sinn Féin was in a strong position to offer an alternative perspective, in that all the mainstream parties had reached a consensus on membership of the European Economic Community, as the European Union was then known. Sinn Féin did marginally better in the 1989 European Parliament elections than in the general election which was held on the same day—obviously because the party was contesting only a limited number of Dáil constituencies, there were potential Sinn Féin voters elsewhere who availed of the European contest to indicate their preference for the party. But once more, the Sinn Féin share of the vote was poor even if the party could take some limited comfort from its 5 per cent showing in Connaught–Ulster where the republican vote was more attracted to Neil Blaney, the Independent Fianna Fáil standard-bearer, who won a seat.

In the late 1980s and early 1990s, the political agenda in the Republic was dominated by issues such as unemployment, emigration and the state of the health services. Opinion polls indicated that most left voters (Labour and Workers' Party) ranked unemployment as the most important issue and they placed less emphasis on tax reform than did supporters of the other main parties represented in Dáil Éireann.[26]

If Sinn Féin were to compete seriously for votes, it was going to have to address more closely the issues that the public considered important. Gerry Adams had long preached this mantra. But life was always going to be difficult for a small fringe party attempting to make an electoral breakthrough. The other parties on the left were already dominating the political space that opposed the expenditure-reduction policies supported to varying degrees by Fianna Fáil, Fine Gael and the Progressive Democrats. Moreover, the IRA's violence was far less acceptable to voters south of the border, as the Sinn Féin electoral development after the 1994 ceasefire confirmed.

There was greater focus on social and economic policies in the Sinn Féin manifesto for the 1992 general election, but again the party's agenda was more concerned with Northern Ireland and traditional republican issues. On this occasion, Sinn Féin nominated 41 candidates but in reality this meant only that there were more people to share in the indignity of electoral defeat. The party won 8,000 more first preferences than at the previous general election in 1989. But this marginal increase could not even be attributed to increased support for Sinn Féin as the party ran three times as many candidates as at the previous election—41 in 37 constituencies in 1992, against 14 in 12 in the previous contest.

An analysis of the Sinn Féin support did not make for good reading: of its 41 candidates, 35 received fewer than 1,000 first preferences. Their average vote was a mere 678 first preferences. By comparison, Democratic Left candidates won an average vote of 2,397, Green Party 1,269, Pro-Life candidates 901, Independents 968. Only candidates from the Workers' Party (641)—which had been torn apart by an internal split earlier that year—won a lower average vote than Sinn Féin candidates.

There were several similarities between the first three post-abstentionist elections contested by Sinn Féin in the Republic—little electoral support and loss of deposits. In 1992, none of the Sinn Féin candidates, with the exception of Caoimhghín Ó Caoláin in Cavan–Monaghan, secured the minimum number of votes required to hold onto their deposit of £300 (€381). This fact led Michael Gallagher of TCD to observe that Sinn Féin's participation resulted in the party's 'contributing £12,000 towards the cost of running the election'.[27]

The succession of poor results in Dáil Éireann elections was not good for party morale. Gerry Adams, however, was keeping his eye on a bigger picture, as he recalled: 'I think that was more of a burden for the grassroot activists on the ground because remember we were highly busy at national leadership level with the peace process.'[28]

Seán Crowe in Dublin South-West was one of the party's three-time losers, facing electoral defeat in 1987, 1989 and 1992. 'I remember I was hitting the bar at around 1,000 votes and I said, "there's no point in me running again unless we can increase the vote." I remember saying, "I'll fight the next election but if we don't make a breakthrough, then it will be time for someone else."'[29] In fact, Crowe's vote increased significantly at the 1997 general election and he won a seat five years later. The long-time Sinn Féin activist entered Leinster House on the same day in 2002 as his party colleague, Arthur Morgan, who also shared a similar electoral history marked by initial disappointing results.

Morgan joined the IRA in 1971 and was later convicted of smuggling guns. He spent seven and a half years in prison in Northern Ireland before being released in late 1984. 'I immediately went back into Sinn Féin and nine months later I contested the local elections. I contested a three-seat area in North Louth where I topped the poll, about one hundred votes ahead of my nearest rival. But I got pipped for a seat by eleven votes. We got no transfers, so that was a bit of a setback,' Morgan admitted.[30]

The results of subsequent general elections (1987, 1989 and 1992) in Louth were also relatively disappointing but perseverance won out: 'They were particularly difficult elections. There was nothing to encourage you. But we knew we had a job to do so we simply buckled down and got on with it. There was a sense of duty to those who were in prison or who had relatives killed to build an alternative political struggle,' Morgan said.[31]

The 1992 general election result was a blow for those republicans who predicted a significant constituency for Sinn Féin in the Republic. A bleak outlook was hard to avoid. In 1992, Sinn Féin won fewer votes than it had in 1987—and to add to the pessimistic assessments offered after the contests in 1987 and 1989, TCD's Michael Gallagher noted that with its 1992 performance, the party's 'future in southern politics is not bright.'[32] But politics is not a static business. The dynamic of the nascent peace process was not a factor which Gallagher or other political observers could have contemplated in the early 1990s.

By the time the Irish electorate would again go to the polls in a general election, there would have been a fundamental transformation of the political landscape as far as Sinn Féin was concerned. The declaration of the IRA ceasefire in August 1994 removed the single biggest impediment to Sinn Féin's electoral prospects in the Irish Republic. In the absence of violence, many voters who otherwise would never have supported the party would possibly be more open to voting for Sinn Féin candidates.

In Northern Ireland, Sinn Féin made maximum gain out of a mantra: 'a vote for Sinn Féin is a vote for peace'. With the August 1994 ceasefire in place, the party openly canvassed nationalists to 'lend' them their vote. Those who had long cast their preference for John Hume's SDLP were asked to switch allegiances.

A bitter rivalry exists between the two parties in Northern Ireland. The emergence of Sinn Féin into electoral politics in the aftermath of the 1981 hunger strikes ended the near monopoly on the Catholic vote that the SDLP had long enjoyed. Sinn Féin candidates won five of the 78 seats on offer in the 1982 Assembly elections, taking 10 per cent of the vote— almost 119,000 first preferences—in what was, in effect, the party's first electoral outing for any sort of local parliamentary institution in Northern Ireland. The party was contesting on an abstentionist ticket but the result confirmed that there was, indeed, a constituency for Sinn Féin, irrespective of the IRA campaign.

Republicans, however, faced a steep learning curve. Several of those nominated to contest the 1982 Assembly elections in Northern Ireland were not even registered to vote. Danny Morrison had rectified this omission by the time he was a candidate in the Mid-Ulster constituency in the 1983 Westminster elections. Adams emerged victorious in West Belfast while Morrison lost out by a mere 78 votes to the Democratic Unionist Party in Mid-Ulster. Like many of his colleagues, Morrison was rapidly acquiring the skills of electoral activism, while also experiencing at first hand the nascent Sinn Féin–SDLP rivalry:

Each candidate went around the polling stations and thanked the person who was sitting doing personation for them. So I went into this polling station; I think it was in a place called the Loop in South Derry and there were tables to the right, to the left and to the middle. The table in the middle was for the presiding officer and another official, the table on the right was for the Sinn Féin representative and an SDLP representative, while the unionists were at the other table. I went over and shook hands with Sheila O'Neill who was representing me. She was having tea with this other man, so I also shook hands with him. Then I went up and shook hands with the presiding officer and then went over to the other unionist table. I put my hand out to the man who I thought was the unionist but he turned his head away but actually limply shook my hand. I then put my hand out to the other guy at the same table who told me to 'Fuck off', that there was no way he was shaking a hand with me as I belonged to a 'murdering organisation'. I went back over to Sheila O'Neill and the guy beside her, and said, 'Did you hear that old bastard from the DUP?' And the guy with Sheila turned to me and said, 'I'm actually the one from the DUP, that other man is from the SDLP.' I had to apologise profusely. I just assumed that he was representing the DUP.

Morrison may have made an honest mistake but the bitterness between his party and the SDLP was considerable. This was reflected in *An Phoblacht* where references to John Hume in particular bordered on contemptuous. As mentioned earlier, the SDLP leader was considered 'a dangerous collaborator . . . not to be trusted . . . [who was] . . . concerned more with lining his pockets than with defending nationalist interests.'[33]

Despite this hostility, John Hume can be credited with bringing Gerry Adams and his supporters in from the political cold. Hume's efforts in the 1980s and early 1990s, matched only by the work of Fr Alex Reid and Martin Mansergh, succeeded in building the peace process from which Sinn Féin has profited so much in electoral terms.

The peace process in Northern Ireland, as discussed in Chapter 7, probably would not have developed at the time it did without Sinn Féin's entry into political life. The fact that the republican movement established a credible political voice was crucial in allowing other parties to open even secret contacts with what was, in effect, the political arm of the IRA.

Once the decision was made to try to build on the 1981 prisoner candidate successes, Sinn Féin quickly established a presence on the electoral landscape, especially in Northern Ireland. Whereas politics in the Irish Republic was a real struggle, the party received immediate support north of the border. The untapped constituency that Adams had suspected existed turned out in its thousands to back republican candidates.

The presence of republican heavyweights such as Adams, Morrison and McGuinness on the Sinn Féin ticket for Assembly elections in Northern Ireland in late 1982 was in part a signal to the grassroots that the new electoral strategy had IRA backing. McGuinness was a senior IRA figure, and his involvement was an obvious sign that the military wing approved of the political wing's electoral development. *An Phoblacht* placed considerable stress on McGuinness's decision to contest the elections. McGuinness was described in *An Phoblacht* as a 'well known militant republican' who was 'one of the driving forces behind the radicalisation of the republican movement.'[34]

Throughout the 1980s and early 1990s, Sinn Féin managed to take hold of about 35 per cent of the nationalist vote in Northern Ireland. But the IRA campaign appeared to have inserted a ceiling to Sinn Féin's progression, with the party repeatedly receiving in or around 10 per cent of the total vote. While the violence continued, many Catholics could not bring themselves to support Sinn Féin candidates. The peace process years were to release these voters as Sinn Féin came to dominate nationalist politics in Northern Ireland.

But before that point was reached, there were disappointments to rank alongside the party's electoral progression. For one, the SDLP was not about to stand aside and meekly watch an onward Sinn Féin march. In 1992, Joe Hendron of the SDLP returned to fight Adams for the third time for the West Belfast seat. Tactical voting by unionists in part gave the SDLP man a boost in the poll, and this allowed him to overtake Adams.

Jim Gibney was a key member of the Sinn Féin election team. He was with a group of Sinn Féin members at Belfast City Hall at nine o'clock on the morning of the 1992 election count. The early mood among the Sinn Féin strategists left Gibney concerned:

> These were the people who knew the game inside out. They could read ballot boxes and trends. I knew looking at their faces that we were in trouble. I remember sitting beside Gerry and we could see his pile of votes and the SDLP pile going up and down. He was overtaking Joe and then Joe would overtake him, then he would overtake Joe again, and Joe would overtake him again. That was the way it went, and then it settled down. I looked at Gerry and I just asked, 'Have we lost this seat here?' My heart just sank, just sank, because we had lost the seat . . . There was massive disappointment. That particular election, I think, was probably the low point of Sinn Féin's electoral strategy. . . .[35]

The 1992 West Belfast defeat was a bitter blow for Sinn Féin. It was a personal loss for Adams. But there was no reassessment of the Sinn Féin electoral strategy or the party's commitment to political activism. The result was seen internally as a temporary set-back as Adams explained:

'We lost the seat because we underestimated the ability of unionists to think flexibly and to actually vote for a non-Unionist candidate. But we started to fight that election the evening we lost it.'[36] Indeed, the sight of a motorcade of black taxis driving through west Belfast with Adams thanking people for their support, despite the loss, was very early confirmation that Sinn Féin was committed to its electoral project.

The peace process undoubtedly provided a significant boost to the Sinn Féin vote. The party gained handsomely in the period after the August 1994 IRA ceasefire. In an environment of peace, many Catholics had less difficulty in voting for republicans, despite the continued presence of the IRA. In a series of elections since 1994, Sinn Féin has moved ahead of the SDLP as the dominant force in nationalist politics in Northern Ireland.

The Sinn Féin eclipse of the SDLP is clearly evident from the results of European Parliament elections in Northern Ireland over the past 20 years. The two parties first went head-to-head in 1984 when John Hume won a seat with 22.1 per cent of the vote against the 13.3 per cent secured by Sinn Féin's Danny Morrison. Five years later, Hume again took the nationalist seat, increasing his share of the vote to 25.5 per cent, while Morrison, again the unsuccessful Sinn Féin candidate, won 9.1 per cent of the vote. Sinn Féin nominated three candidates for the 1994 European Parliament elections but the combined efforts of Martin McGuinness, Francie Molloy and Tom Hartley produced only a marginal increase in the Sinn Féin vote to 9.9 per cent, whereas Hume again romped home, increasing the SDLP share of the first preference vote to 28.9 per cent.

In a peace process environment more receptive to Sinn Féin, in 1999, Mitchel McLaughlin won just over 17 per cent of the vote, but even the improved Sinn Féin performance could not take from the dominance of John Hume who won 28.06 per cent, a slight decrease on the previous European Parliament elections. The dependency of the SDLP on the persona of John Hume, and his ability to stave off Sinn Féin, was confirmed in 2004 when voters in Northern Ireland went to the polls to elect their three representatives to the European Parliament.

With the retirement of Hume, the SDLP share of the vote fell significantly to just under 16 per cent, while Bairbre de Brún was elected for Sinn Féin with 26.31 per cent of the first preference vote. The two nationalist parties in Northern Ireland had, over a two-decade period, engaged in a process of role reversal. In the 1984 European Parliament elections, when Sinn Féin and the SDLP first went head-to-head for the single nationalist seat in Northern Ireland, there was a considerable vote gap between the two parties. This vote gap favoured the SDLP. But 20 years later, the gap, while still existing, had moved in favour of Sinn Féin.

In fact, the Sinn Féin bandwagon moved ahead of the SDLP for the first time at the 2001 Westminster elections. Four Sinn Féin MPs were returned in Northern Ireland, with the party securing 21.71 per cent of the vote, against the 20.96 per cent and three seats won by the SDLP. There may have been only 6,000 votes between the two parties but Sinn Féin was the party with momentum. Whereas once there had been a battle between the two parties in West Belfast, now Sinn Féin emerged triumphant, with Gerry Adams taking over 66 per cent of the vote, to the mere 19 per cent secured by the SDLP. Adams and Martin McGuinness were elected, along with Michelle Gildernew and Pat Doherty. Gildernew won in the old constituency of Bobby Sands and Owen Carron, although her majority in Fermanagh–South Tyrone was a mere 53 votes.

But four years later, Gildernew consolidated her hold on the Westminster seat with her majority in the constituency increasing to over 4,500 votes. Like her party colleagues, Gildernew argues that Sinn Féin's dominance over the SDLP is now a permanent feature of the political scene in Northern Ireland. 'I don't believe our vote is borrowed from anyone. It's based on our work rate and how we represent people locally and nationally. There's less and less of our votes that are being borrowed but we still have to go out and ask for them,' Gildernew said.[37]

The 2005 Westminster contest provided further evidence of the strength of the Sinn Féin vote in Northern Ireland. The party won a record fifth seat, with Conor Murphy in Newry–Armagh filling the vacancy created by the retirement of Séamus Mallon of the SDLP. Murphy had served a prison term for IRA-related offences in the 1980s, but in the peace process period became a familiar face in the Sinn Féin negotiating team. His election to Westminster helped the overall Sinn Féin vote rise to 24.3 per cent, while the SDLP vote—even with the party holding off its nationalist rivals in the Foyle constituency—fell by 3.5 per cent to 17.5 per cent.

The republican success did not, however, seem to alter the only part of the Sinn Féin abstentionism policy left in place by the Adams-led concessions. Sinn Féin representatives dropped their ideological attitudes to Leinster House in 1986 and Stormont in 1998 but the policy was still preserved in relation to Westminster. 'I don't believe as an Irish republican there is any advantage in me sitting in Westminster. After all, I have access to Tony Blair at 10 Downing Street,' Gildernew said.[38]

The outcome in the 2005 Westminster contest had actually been foretold two years previously when voters in Northern Ireland went to the polls in the elections for the cross-community power-sharing assembly established under the Belfast Agreement. The 1998–2003 period had been marked by the stop–start nature of the institutional arrangements and the inability of Sinn Féin to reach a lasting agreement with David Trimble's Ulster Unionist Party. Nevertheless, the majority of Catholic voters sided with Sinn Féin candidates in elections in November 2003. The party won six seats more than the SDLP as it consolidated its newly established position as the dominant nationalist party in Northern Ireland.

The party's development on the other side of the border has been somewhat different. For one, Sinn Féin in the Irish Republic is a minor electoral presence, although the party has shown an ability to make decent gains from its small base. Again, the peace process and the positive public response to the 1994 IRA ceasefire have benefited Sinn Féin. Moreover, when a general election was called in the Republic in 1997, the long-standing broadcasting ban had been ended. Over the previous three years, republican leaders like Adams and McGuinness had become very familiar figures on the airwaves—and the public could hear them articulate their political agenda against the backdrop of the peace process.

The first IRA ceasefire had ended in early 1996 but there had been only a limited return to republican violence, although further lives were lost. Nevertheless, going into the June 1997 general election in the Republic there was an expectation that the IRA ceasefire would be restored. The previous month at Westminster elections in Northern Ireland, Sinn Féin had capitalised on its strategy of 'a vote for Sinn Féin is a vote for peace'.

The party's electoral strategy was more focused than in 1992— Michael Gallagher of TCD described it as 'more sophisticated'—and it was evident that the party was getting better at the business of electoral participation. Whereas in 1992 Sinn Féin contested nearly every constituency, the party adopted a more selective approach in 1997, nominating only 15 candidates. The strategy was to focus efforts on the areas where there was a tradition of republican support, such as Kerry North and Cavan–Monaghan, alongside the development of the party as the voice of alienated communities in urban areas such as Dublin South-West and Dublin Central.

Without doubt, the beginning of the Sinn Féin electoral advance in the Republic is evident in the 1997 election results. The average candidate's vote increased to 3,041 (compared to 678 votes in 1992) while

12 of the party's 15 candidates held their deposits. Small advances but advances nonetheless. More importantly, several Sinn Féin candidates polled strongly and the party won its first post-abstentionist seat in Leinster House.

Caoimhghín Ó Caoláin topped the poll in Cavan–Monaghan. He was the first Sinn Féin TD to be elected to Dáil Éireann since 1957 but, 40 years on, the important difference was that Ó Caoláin would take his seat in Leinster House. The electoral breakthrough hoped for at the 1986 Ard Fheis had finally been achieved, as Ó Caoláin recalled:

> People are more accustomed now to the flag-waving and air-punching reaction of the Sinn Féin team when success is delivered. It was quite a unique moment and everybody was clearly euphoric. I wasn't able to join in that celebration quite the way that everybody else was. All I could think of, from the moment of the announcement, [was] that eventually I would have to go through the gates of Leinster House . . . and I knew at that point I would be on my own, and I have to say that was a very uncomfortable thought and I was very conscious of what lay before me.[39]

Alongside the election of Ó Caoláin in 1997, there were other positive signs for Sinn Féin—Martin Ferris polled strongly in Kerry North, while Seán Crowe secured almost 4,000 first preferences in Dublin South-West. But there were obvious reasons to caution about a Sinn Féin advance on the back of the party's performance. As Michael Gallagher observed, 'the context of the 1997 election was unique in that some of the votes for Sinn Féin could be interpreted as encouragement for the IRA to call a ceasefire, a factor that will (presumably) not obtain at future elections. This might suggest that the party will find it difficult to repeat its 1997 performance at future elections. . . .'[40]

Despite this conclusion, Gallagher was, like other observers, aware of other advantages available to Sinn Féin that might work in the party's favour:

> The party is noted for its youthful and committed constituency organisations and in areas of discontent is able to mobilise support that owes more to local feelings of alienation from the state and the established parties, especially over the issue of drugs than to any great interest in what is happening north of the border; so it believes that it may make future gains.[41]

One notable feature of the 1997 general election was Sinn Féin's ability to expand its support base. This is very clear from an analysis of voter behaviour data contained in an exit poll compiled for RTÉ by Lansdowne Market Research. The poll indicated the Sinn Féin success in retaining its 1992 vote—some 71 per cent of those who voted for the party in the 1992 general election also backed Sinn Féin candidates five years later.

This was a very positive outcome for the party, given the considerable number of concessions and compromises agreed in the 1992–97 period by the leadership of the republican movement. Moreover, the retained loyalty figure for Sinn Féin compares very well with that for the other parties—in 1997, Fianna Fáil held 81 per cent of its 1992 voters, Fine Gael 76 per cent, Labour 59 per cent, the PDS 63 per cent, Democratic Left 56 per cent and the Greens 61 per cent.

These loyal voters, however, made up only 40 per cent of the Sinn Féin vote in 1997. The expansion of the party's vote between 1992 and 1997 came from a variety of sources. The poll data indicates that 8 per cent of those who voted for Fianna Fáil in 1992 switched to Sinn Féin in 1997; the figure for former Fine Gael voters was 2 per cent. Sinn Féin also attracted 9 per cent of its new support from 1992 Labour supporters, while there was no movement from either the PD or Green voters in 1992 to Sinn Féin in 1997.

But by far the biggest source for new Sinn Féin support in 1997 came from those who indicated in the Lansdowne exit poll that they had not voted in 1992—either new voters or abstainers in 1992. Almost 30 per cent of the Sinn Féin vote in 1997 came from new voters or 1992 abstainers. This Sinn Féin figure for new voters was almost twice that obtained by Fianna Fáil, Fine Gael and Labour.

The 1997 general election proved that there was a pool of potential voters available for Sinn Féin to tap to increase its electoral presence. 'Getting the vote out' was going to be central to the party's advancement strategy. So, why were voters attracted to Sinn Féin? Again, an examination of the RTÉ/Lansdowne exit poll led Marsh and Sinnott to conclude that people were more likely to vote for Sinn Féin based on local issues rather than on strength of the party's candidates, a fact which they noted 'underlines the party's unwillingness to emphasise personalities.'[42]

However, voters were turning to Sinn Féin for more reasons than its political activity on the ground. A series of factors increased the likelihood of someone supporting Sinn Féin—obviously an interest in Northern Ireland, but also being male, living in an urban area, coming from a working-class background and holding views that could be classified as from a left-wing orientation.

In terms of policy having an impact on the direction of a person's vote in 1997, the analysis undertaken by Marsh and Sinnott indicated that taxation—a major issue of the campaign in 1997—was not a factor in supporting Sinn Féin. It would seem that national policy issues and Sinn Féin were not yet considered as co-existing, a situation which may have pertained because most people—even, perhaps, Sinn Féin voters—did not yet see the party as a party of government.

Sinn Féin continued, however, with its policy that it was travelling on a long road to success. The 'long electoral campaign' pursued by Sinn Féin increasingly appeared to be replacing the IRA's 'long military campaign'. The 1999 local elections in the Republic allowed the party to consolidate and build on its electoral position across the country. The party trebled its representation, winning 21 seats across 10 of the 34 councils, with an important showing in Dublin where several of its new councillors looked like potential Dáil winners.

The emergence of Sinn Féin was signalled in the opinion polls undertaken during the life of the 28th Dáil. After the 1997 general election, Sinn Féin had a poll rating of 2 per cent but by the time the last *Irish Times*/MRBI poll was undertaken prior to the calling of the 2002 general election, that figure had risen to 8 per cent.

Facing into the 2002 general election in the Republic, Sinn Féin could take heart from its performance in the 1999 local elections in which many potential Dáil candidates had won seats on local authorities. Moreover, the practical electoral benefit from that trebling of Sinn Féin's council seats in the Republic of Ireland was matched by the psychological boost of overtaking the SDLP as the largest nationalist party in Northern Ireland in the 2001 Westminster elections.

On the back of that notable success, Sinn Féin prepared for a general election south of the border in the first half of the following year. The party concentrated on a number of target constituencies, with Sinn Féin officials believing that three to four seats could be added to the Cavan–Monaghan seat first won in 1997. As in previous elections since the ending of the abstentionist policy, Sinn Féin had two key constituencies that it tapped for support—people living in poorer urban communities who had not benefited from the economic boom, and people living mainly in rural areas where there was a traditional republican vote. The strategy—while limited to a handful of constituencies—paid handsome dividends.

So, when voters went to the polls in the May 2002 Irish general election, memories of candidates forfeiting their deposits—so much a feature of the 1987, 1989 and 1992 general elections—were left aside as Sinn Féin made further electoral advances. The party doubled its national vote and increased its Dáil representation from one to five seats. As well as making gains in Dublin, the party retained its seat in Cavan–Monaghan and increased its presence in rural constituencies with a republican tradition.

The party's appeal spread to younger voters who had little living memory of the campaign of violence waged by the IRA. Many first-time voters in 2002 were only ten years old when the IRA called its first ceasefire, and their impression of the republican movement would obviously be just as influenced by the media presence of Adams and other republican leaders arguing their peace process agenda.

After four failed attempts, Seán Crowe took a Dáil seat in Dublin South-West. Aengus Ó Snodaigh was another winner. He had had several unproductive elections in Dublin South-East, a most unlikely constituency for Sinn Féin. 'I ran in the Pembroke area in the locals in 1991 which was a disaster but we knew that. I think I got 211 votes. We had paper candidates in some areas [to maintain a Sinn Féin presence] and I was a paper candidate in Pembroke—we literally put up posters and that was it.'[43] Ó Snodaigh moved to Ballyfermot in 1994 and set about establishing a political base in the Dublin South-Central constituency. His work paid dividends in 2002.

Two of those elected had had very public careers in the IRA, Arthur Morgan in Louth and Martin Ferris in Kerry North. Both men had served prison sentences for IRA-related offences. The British Army had apprehended Morgan as he attempted to smuggle guns across Carlingford Lough. One of those who worked on his campaign in Louth was Paddy Agnew, the prison candidate who had won a Dáil seat in the same constituency back in 1981.

Ferris had been a minor footballer for Kerry but gained greater notoriety when, in September 1984, he was arrested on board the *Marita Ann*, a fishing trawler, off the coast of Kerry. The *Marita Ann* was said to have left Fenit for a meeting outside Irish territorial waters with an American trawler. Seven tonnes of guns and ammunition were offloaded from the American trawler to the *Marita Ann*. But unknown to Ferris and the others on board, the Irish authorities had been tipped off about the IRA's weapons-smuggling operation. The Irish Navy swooped and, as an officer boarded the *Marita Ann*, Ferris is said to have shouted, 'We haven't got any salmon on board here.'

But the Navy was looking for more than an illegal fishing catch. What they discovered were pistols, submachine guns, flak jackets, rockets and hand grenades. Ferris spent the following decade in prison. After his release in 1994, he embarked on a political career with Sinn Féin, establishing a base in his native Kerry. He polled well in the Munster constituency in the 1999 European Parliament elections but was more successful in getting elected to Kerry County Council in local elections in the same year.

Like republicans elsewhere, Ferris and his supporters were active in the local anti-drugs movement, although they rejected allegations that they used intimidation and vigilante tactics against local drug dealers and others involved in anti-social behaviour. Stolen property was, however, returned from burglars after the intervention of republicans. Republicans have long operated a type of local policing service in heartland areas in Northern Ireland, often with local support where long-standing hostility exists towards the police force.

In a few limited areas south of the border, republicans were known to have taken upon themselves small-scale 'policing' work. Sinn Féin representatives were actively involved in organising marches against drug dealers in parts of Dublin in the 1980s and mid-1990s. It was well known that requests were made to criminals involved in drug dealing, car theft and burglaries, to leave local communities. Sinn Féin denied that it had taken this type of 'policing' work upon itself but republicans with Sinn Féin and IRA backgrounds were known to issue these requests which were, more often than not, delivered as threats. In May 1996, a small-time drug dealer was beaten to death in Dublin. Republicans were blamed but Sinn Féin denied any involvement.

In the run-up to the 2002 general election, allegations of vigilante behaviour were made against leading republicans in Kerry. Marches were organised to the houses of alleged drug dealers, with public identifications of those involved in the drug trade. In late 2001, a man who it was alleged was selling drugs in Castleisland was attacked. Ferris was questioned by the Garda Síochána as were other leading republicans in the area, although all were released without charge.

Sinn Féin claimed that the arrests were politically motivated, although given what would emerge in subsequent years, the incidents in Kerry were an early warning to the party that there could be no ambiguity about its commitment to democratic principles. But at that time, the problem issues were localised, and hoped by many to be passing, as the peace process delivered further normalisation on the island.

In the Irish Republic, the pattern of the Sinn Féin vote at the 2002 general election, combined with the party's strong showing in the 2004 local elections, points to further electoral gains in the years ahead. Looking at the unsuccessful Dáil candidates in 2002, several lost out with more than half a quota of the first preference vote. So, with increased local government representation and continued constituency activism, it would be expected that this group would be good prospects to win at the future Dáil elections. A further expansion of the Sinn Féin vote could see wins in Dublin North-East, Dublin North-West, Dublin Central, Meath West, Donegal South-West, Donegal North-East and in Waterford.

Despite all the hype associated with Sinn Féin, it is worth recalling that in the Irish Republic the party is coming from a very low voter base. In 1997, there was a single Sinn Féin TD in Dáil Éireann, four more were elected in 2002. Further growth may see the party with still less than a dozen seats. Moreover, there may well be a ceiling on Sinn Féin's immediate growth south of the border. Michael Gallagher has noted that the party's candidates 'cannot expect to be swept into the Dáil on a national tide; they need to build up a strong local support base first.'[44] On average, each of the five Sinn Féin TDs elected in 2002 had contested two general elections before being elected to the Dáil. Moreover, with the exception of Aengus Ó Snodaigh, all had used the local council route to entering national political life.

There may be another impediment to the growth of Sinn Féin in the Republic where a proportional representation (PR) system is used in national elections. Transfers are vital to the political parties in a PR system if they are to maximise the number of seats they can win. The evidence from the 2002 general election indicates that many voters are still unwilling to give lower preference votes to Sinn Féin candidates. Even with an end to the IRA, the revelations about republican links to criminality may place a cap on the expansion of the Sinn Féin vote, the end result of which may cost Sinn Féin in terms of the number of Dáil seats the party can win. In effect, being for so long in the shadow of gunmen may act as a self-inflicted drag on the growth in the Irish Republic of the political wing of the republican movement.

The fall-out from the Northern Bank heist revelations and allegations of IRA links to criminality have reduced in the short-term any prospect of a governmental role for Sinn Féin in the Republic. All parties need to participate in government to survive, especially small parties whose membership base can become demoralised without the prospect of holding power and implementing policies. But Sinn Féin may well be an exception to this rule. The party may be able to grow significantly while on the opposition benches in Leinster House, although this growth will be coming from a very small base.

The traditional Sinn Féin image has evolved during the peace process years. For almost two decades, Sinn Féin tended to nominate candidates who had backgrounds in the IRA. For example, in the 2002 general election in the Irish Republic, many party candidates had served prison sentences before embarking on political careers. Nicky Kehoe who narrowly lost out on a Dáil seat in 2002 in Dublin Central—the constituency of Taoiseach Bertie Ahern—had served time for IRA offences. Dessie Ellis in Dublin North-West faced explosives charges relating to the London bombing campaign in the early 1980s. The party's candidate in Mayo, Vincent Woods, benefited from the early release programme in the Belfast Agreement. Woods had served five years of a 17-year sentence for storing semtex explosives for the IRA.

A similar pattern was evident in elections in Northern Ireland where the influence of the IRA over Sinn Féin campaigns was evident in the selection of party candidates. Ahead of the 'rolling devolution' Assembly elections in late 1982, all the candidates profiled in *An Phoblacht* had roots in the conflict and, even if they were not directly associated with the IRA, they had strong indirect connections. For example, Sean Begley's sister-in-law was married to a republican prisoner, while Francis Hurson was a brother of a dead hunger striker. Readers of the weekly republican newspaper were informed that Benedict McElwee had served five and a half years in prison, four 'on the blanket', while Alex Maskey's wife, Liz McKee, was the first woman interned in Northern Ireland.

These traditional Sinn Féin candidates appeal strongly to the core republican base. But as the party has sought to grow its support base, a new breed of election candidates has been pushed forward. Many of these newcomers have had no direct or indirect association with the IRA campaign, although that does not mean they would condemn the violence perpetrated by the IRA since 1969. The presence of this group at top-table platforms has been noticeable at recent Sinn Féin conferences. Many of the new recruits, like Michelle Gildernew in Fermanagh–South Tyrone, Pearse Doherty in Donegal and David Cullinane in Waterford, are, in effect, post-ceasefire republicans.

The new Sinn Féin membership is not rooted in the IRA. These are people without a personal republican history. They have no experience of paramilitary activity, prisons or protests. But they are vital to the Adams strategy to develop his party into a dominant political force, north and south of the border. They help to broaden the party's electoral base, while also making it somewhat easier for supporters of other parties to give transfer votes to Sinn Féin.

The ability of Sinn Féin to win support beyond its core constituency was exemplified by the successful campaign run by Mary Lou McDonald in the June 2004 European Parliament elections. Like so many other Sinn Féin figures, McDonald was a full-time party employee as she set out to build an electoral base. A strong but ultimately unsuccessful outing in the 2002 general election was followed by a dramatic victory in the Dublin constituency in the 2004 European elections.

McDonald took over 14 per cent of the vote in Dublin, indicating that there was support for Sinn Féin beyond its traditional constituency. She was a different type of candidate for the party. In her mid-thirties, McDonald had enjoyed a middle-class upbringing with private schooling and academic qualifications from third-level institutions, including Trinity College, Dublin.

McDonald says that her republicanism was awakened by the images from the hunger strikes in 1981. While her first political attachment was to Fianna Fáil, she left to join Sinn Féin towards the end of 1999. 'Sinn Féin is the unique blend of a politics that's of the left and also that's very solid around the national questions. All that appeals to me,' the Dublin MEP said.[45]

The Mary Lou McDonalds of the Sinn Féin world are very different political animals from those who emerged during the years of the conflict in Northern Ireland. McDonald studied English literature, whereas the vast majority of her future colleagues in the republican movement graduated from the university of life on the streets of Northern Ireland. The influx of these new members will undoubtedly alter the internal dynamic within Sinn Féin.

Senior republicans acknowledge this new development, although they do so without any indication of potential for future internal conflict. 'I don't think that people of my generation and people in the leadership should be threatened or feel afraid of the young Turks. I think we should welcome them,' Adams remarked.[46]

The Adams leadership emerged out of the conflict in Northern Ireland and consolidated its authority within the republican movement from a base north of the border. The peace process has allowed a new strengthened southern membership to emerge into leadership positions.

'There's this notion that there's an all-seeing and all-knowing northern leadership and a naive rump in the south. That's a complete misunderstanding of the dynamic of the party . . . What we have within the party is huge diversity,' Mary Lou McDonald acknowledged. She rejected the idea that she herself and her southern colleagues play a lesser role. 'There is still in the public consciousness that Sinn Féin is a party that's led from the north. But increasingly, south of the border you have people coming through the ranks, and the southern voice and the southern dimension of our politics is coming to the fore.'[47]

One of the architects and long-time backers of the Adams strategy accepted the focus of republicans may be moving south of the border. 'I think it is inevitable that at some stage the president of Sinn Féin will not be Gerry Adams and will be from the South,' Danny Morrison said.[48] Morrison predicts that the new membership will result in a significant change within Sinn Féin:

I remember being astonished talking to a group of young people about two years ago who actually asked what actually happened during the hunger strike. I just assumed everybody knows about the hunger strike. But when you consider it, it would have been like me asking my mother and father about the Second World War in 1945 which was eight years before I was born . . . So I think it is inevitable that as young people come in, the sense of history they are going to have is having either listened to us or read it somewhere, and it isn't the same thing obviously because they weren't involved, they weren't there. So they don't have the raw material to draw from but they are going to have different material that maybe I don't have. . . .[49]

There would seem to be no need for Sinn Féin activists to have lived through the conflict to identify and associate with the republican comprehension of those years. When veteran republican Joe Cahill was buried in Belfast in the summer of 2004, the party's new Dublin MEP did not hesitate to step forward to take her turn in bearing the coffin. Cahill had had a long IRA and Sinn Féin career, stretching back over 60 years; on the other hand, McDonald was never a member of the IRA and was a Sinn Féin member of only four years' standing. 'I was puzzled by criticism although it came from the usual quarters. I knew Joe. I worked with him. I was privileged to carry his coffin,' McDonald said. In this way, the new post-1994 ceasefire members can subscribe to, and share in, the ideology that defines their brand of republicanism.

No more than any other organisation, Sinn Féin is made up of different component factions with different priorities and positions. But the party membership and its elected representatives have an uncanny ability to agree to, and stick to, a common message. 'People come from different perspectives but we're very good at agreeing positions and then staying within those positions. There's a certain discipline,' McDonald said.[50]

The objective of securing a united Ireland is the glue that keeps these disparate groups together. They also share in a common republican thinking and worldview. This connection was evident when McDonald declared in her first address to the European Parliament that, 'As Irish republicans, following in the tradition of Bobby Sands MP, we are committed to the politics of equality, justice and freedom.'[51]

Making reference to the dead hunger striker and cloaking current political positioning with his iconic status is one thing but it is another altogether when considered against republican beliefs that have been dramatically modified in the period since the death of Sands in 1981. This record remains a contentious matter for Adams, his supporters and his critics. The changes and concessions sponsored by the Adams faction have assisted in the electoral development of Sinn Féin but they have also left a serious question mark over the real successes of the republican movement, especially in light of the long-time Sinn Féin and IRA objective of British withdrawal and the creation of a united Ireland.

GETTING OUT HONOURABLY: PEACE PROCESS POLITICS

When the contemporary conflict started in Northern Ireland, members of the Roman Catholic Church's Redemptorist Order found themselves on the frontline of sectarian violence. The priests and brothers witnessed at first hand the causes and consequences of the conflict. More specifically, through their location on the peace line in Belfast, and through their pastoral activity in republican areas, the Redemptorists came to know the personnel in the republican movement.

Given their involvement with the local community and the level of local knowledge available to them, the Redemptorists knew just who to talk with when the time came to start a peace process. One of the leading individuals involved in Redemptorist peace work, Fr Alex Reid, said, 'When there is a battle outside your door, you couldn't but get involved. We became a ministry to the Troubles, if you like. And then through dealing with the local situation . . . you get involved in the bigger picture.'[1]

Alphonsus Liguori founded the Redemptorists, or the Congregation of the Most Holy Redeemer, in Scala, a village south of Naples in Italy, in the 1730s. Missions, spiritual exercises and renewals drove the work of the Congregation. The first Redemptorists to work in Ireland came to conduct a mission in Limerick in 1851. The first Belfast residence was established in 1896 in the Springfield area, located on what one writer labelled 'that ethnic frontier zone between Protestant and Catholic enclaves of west Belfast.'[2]

In his autobiography, Gerry Adams recounts a childhood memory of the Redemptorist Monastery at Clonard off the Falls Road in Belfast: 'To me Clonard was a wondrous place with high, high ceilings and a huge high altar. The altar boys wore long, red soutanes and white gowns. The priest's incense spiralled upwards through the shafts of sunlight which came slanting down from stained-glass windows at the very top.'[3]

Clonard would come to play an important role in the Irish peace process. Inside the Redemptorist buildings, Adams would meet key political figures as the transition of the republican movement into the democratic fold was undertaken. One individual played a hugely significant role in convincing Adams that there was merit in political activism. Indeed, from the 1970s onwards, Fr Alex Reid was a close confidant of Gerry Adams. 'I put to him [Reid] my view that armed struggle occurs in the absence of an alternative way to bring about conditions of justice and equality. The focus, therefore, of those wishing to see an end to armed struggle had to be on building this alternative,' Adams wrote.[4]

Fr Alex Reid was born in County Tipperary but had been based at Clonard since the start of the contemporary conflict. His role in the Northern Ireland peace process can be traced back to the start of the Troubles. As a member of the Redemptorist Order, Reid saw himself as a mediator but he was to become an active participant in the peace process, arguably the key person in starting the process. Moreover, he was more than a peace facilitator. He became an active participant in what became the peace process.

When the IRA announced its first ceasefire in August 1994, Albert Reynolds acknowledged the role played by Reid: 'That priest was absolutely vital in trying to bring about peace. He never gave up in going back and forth. He was at all times absolutely reliable in conveying what the various views were.'[5]

Reid had over many years built a reputation of trustworthiness with leading members of the republican movement. This had been earned through his involvement with known republicans in Belfast who used Clonard as a type of 'safe house' in which differences could be resolved. For example, Reid played a mediating role between rival republican groups—the Irish National Liberation Army and the Official IRA—in the mid-1970s. In 1977, Adams asked the Redemptorists to intervene to calm tensions between the Official IRA and the Provisional IRA. The former accused the latter of bombing its Easter parade although loyalists were later identified as being responsible.

This type of mediating intervention continued over many years—for example, in March 1987, a statement confirming the end to an internal feud in the INLA was issued in the name of Redemptorist priests, Gerry Reynolds and Alex Reid. The statement noted the intention of those involved 'to terminate all hostilities forthwith to resolve matters without further loss of life.'[6]

Reid had also built his credibility with republicans through an involvement with prisoners. In the late 1970s, Reid, along with another priest, Des Wilson, met two Sinn Féin leaders in the company of Tomás Ó Fiaich to discuss the situation in the prisons. This role continued during the hunger strikes in 1980 and 1981. Reid was a frequent visitor at the Maze Prison and a conduit for messages between the different sides.

Reid has always sought to maintain a low-key background role. However, in March 1988, he found himself involved in a huge international event related to Northern Ireland. Two British soldiers, Derek Woods and David Howes, had been murdered in horrific circumstances after they drove into an IRA funeral on the Falls Road. The two men were dragged from their car, beaten and driven away by IRA members. The two soldiers were found a short distance away, lying on a patch of waste ground. They had been stripped to their underpants and socks before being shot. Reid arrived on the scene. In photographs reproduced the following day on newspaper front pages across the world, he was seen kneeling beside the almost naked bodies of the two men. As the dying soldiers lay on the ground, Reid said to journalist Mary Holland: 'This one is still breathing, do you know how to give the kiss of life?'[7]

Reid's belief was that the Church had a responsibility wider than just condemnation of Adams and his colleagues. From his earliest contacts with senior republicans in Belfast—at a time when church condemnation of their actions was vocally strongest—Reid identified a constituency prepared to examine actively the feasibility of a political alternative to the military campaign.

Reid explained: 'One of the things I discovered very quickly was that the people who most wanted peace were the IRA. Who wants to live that kind of life, always on the run? These were young men in their early twenties, with wives and young children, caught up in nightmare stuff. They wanted some way of getting out of that honourably.'[8]

But the conflict that broke out after 1969 positioned the Catholic Church in a struggle with the republican movement for the allegiance of the local Catholic community. In the first instance, the hierarchy was confronted with a position that the bishops were denouncing the use of violence that was initially used to defend the Catholic community from loyalist attacks. However, this period was short-lived as IRA actions went well beyond purely defensive activities.

The Northern bishops issued a statement in May 1970, noting that an individual or group seeking to 'deliberately provoke violence' would be acting in a manner that was a 'betrayal of the Catholic community—a stab in the back.' During the initial stages of the post-1969 conflict, the Church advocated reform within Northern Ireland. There was support for an internal solution to—it was hoped—improve the political position of the Catholic community in a reformed Stormont-type arrangement. Moreover, at that time, the Church hierarchy, led by Cardinal William Conway, was also conscious that its statements must not provoke loyalist violence against members of the Catholic community.

The Church stance was in line with the policy of political participation advocated by the SDLP, the voice of constitutional nationalism. It was not just the hierarchy that was close to the SDLP way of thinking. A 1986 survey of clerical attitudes found that 87.9 per cent were inclined to vote for the SDLP while only 3.9 per cent said that they would be 'most likely' to vote for Sinn Féin candidates.[9]

The response of the Catholic Church to physical force republicanism came in a variety of ways. In the first instance, there was repeated condemnation of the actions of the IRA and other paramilitary groups, although republicans paid little heed to this criticism, clearly distinguishing between the Church as their religion and the Church as an institution. 'It's my Church as well as Cahal Daly's,' Adams observed.[10]

There was also the threatened imposition of theological sanctions on IRA members in the form of excommunication and withdrawal of Catholic burials for paramilitaries. The issue of how republican funerals were conducted was frequently highlighted by the tricolour on the coffin and presence of balaclava- and black-beret-wearing IRA members in the graveyard, readying for the gun salute.

But IRA activity continued for three decades. The threat—and imposition—of official church sanction had little impact. The bishops gained little from their repeated denunciations of the IRA campaign. Interestingly, there were few public interventions by the Redemptorist Order or by its members, despite—as discussed—the crucial involvement they played in ending the conflict.

There were considerable degrees of difference in attitude within the Church hierarchy towards issues associated with the Troubles. Cardinal Tomás Ó Fiaich was more sympathetic than most clergy and members of the hierarchy to nationalist aspirations. Shortly after succeeding Cardinal Conway as Archbishop of Armagh in late 1977, Ó Fiaich explained his political positioning in an interview with the *Irish Press* newspaper:

> I think the British should withdraw from Ireland. I believe in a
> declaration of intent. I know it's a coloured phrase but I think it's the
> only thing which will get things moving . . . I don't see any long-term
> solution for the Northern Ireland problem save in an all-Ireland
> context. We are only putting off that day.[11]

Despite Ó Fiaich's intervention, cognisance must be taken of the fact that
these were personal views and not an official Church position. Under
Canon Law, each bishop has a considerable degree of ecclesiastical
autonomy. Ó Fiaich was not issuing a collective viewpoint. Nevertheless,
the subtleties of Canon Law were not appreciated by many reading Ó
Fiaich's interview. Given the position he held, most people equated his
comments with official Church thinking. Ian Paisley dubbed Ó Fiaich—
'the IRA bishop from Crossmaglen'.

Bishop Cahal Daly of Down and Connor articulated an alternative
and more hardline attitude to the republican movement; on one
occasion, he described the IRA as 'an evil and barbaric organisation'.[12]
Not unsurprisingly given his view of the republican movement, Daly did
not accept the traditional nationalist analysis of the Northern problem,
observing: 'There can be no imposed unity within Northern Ireland,
within Northern Ireland as its now stands . . . In both cases we have the
need for consent.'[13]

Nevertheless, while the Church engaged in 'incessant condemnation
of republican violence', there was also a parallel strategy of engagement
with republican leaders.[14] This latter strategy was primarily pursued
through the Redemptorist Order in Belfast where there existed a belief
that the Catholic Church had a responsibility wider than just
condemnation of Adams and his organisations.

A private paper prepared by the Redemptorist Peace Ministry (RPM)
in 1988 sought to explain the pastoral mission that motivated its response
to the ongoing conflict: 'The daily, tragic consequences of the conflict in
Northern Ireland—bloodshed, imprisonment, widespread suffering and
general despair of any just and democratic solution—are a constant
source of anguish to the Christian heart and demand a compassionate
and effective response from it.'[15]

The RPM was located in Belfast. It facilitated contact between the
various participants in the peace process and drafted a number of
documents on the subject, most of which were private publications,

including those referred to in this chapter. A mission statement for the peace work of the Redemptorist Order was drawn up in 1988 at the suggestion of Cardinal Ó Fiaich. The statement was, in fact, a blueprint for the ministry, which endorsed the idea of direct face-to-face dialogue with representatives of the IRA.[16] The old Gaelic term '*tearmann*' was used to reflect the desire for the Clonard Monastery to be seen, according to Fr Reid, 'as a space or sanctuary where politicians could come under the auspices or invitation of the Church in order to find some way of making peace.'[17]

There has been considerable debate about the genesis of the Northern Ireland peace process. Several journalists and academics have sought to date the start of the process and also to link that date to the involvement of particular individuals. Initially, the peace process was acknowledged as having started with the private discussions between Gerry Adams and John Hume in the mid-1980s. However, as more details of the clandestine contacts between the various participants have emerged, the role of the Redemptorist Order in establishing political contacts and developing political ideas has been accorded much greater prominence.

Members of the Redemptorist Order have been active in peacemaking since the first day the Troubles began. Indeed, from the mid-1970s onwards, Redemptorist priests have been involved in attempts to produce an IRA ceasefire. They believed that they had a pastoral responsibility to intervene directly in the conflict. Their objective was clear: 'seeking to channel the course of events away from the road of armed and violent confrontation . . . and on to the road of political communication and dialogue which is marked out by the principles of justice and charity and characterised by the democratic use of political diplomatic persuasion.'[18]

It was against this backdrop that the RPM operated. 'The Church has a missionary and pastoral duty to intervene directly and to do all she can to bring its violent dimensions and their tragic consequences to an end.'[19] What was meant by direct intervention was unambiguous and clearly established in the mission statement—'to use her resources, her influence and her lines of communication to encourage, promote and, when necessary, even to facilitate it'.[20] This was not a priest-led initiative, rather approval was forthcoming from the official Church in the guise of Cardinal Ó Fiaich 'who fully supported and indeed participated in the ministry.'[21]

The Clonard Monastery was, however, located in the Diocese of Down and Connor where Bishop Cahal Daly was not prepared to meet republican representatives, even in a pastoral capacity. But under Church rules, the Redemptorists were not directly answerable to their local bishop. The position and authority of the Provincial Superior of the Redemptorist Order in relation to the priests and brothers in his Order are similar to those of a bishop in relation to the clergy in his diocese.

The peace ministry had the approval of the Provincial Superior of the Redemptorist Order. This allowed Reid to tell those he was meeting that his activities were being undertaken 'under the authority of the official church'.[22] There could, therefore, be direct and formal contact with Adams. At that time, it was clear that there were two significant ingredients required to kick-start a peace process. Firstly, republicans needed a political wing—talking with political representatives was always going to be easier for politicians in Northern Ireland and the Republic, even when the lines between republican politics and IRA military action were blurred. The one positive outcome from the 1981 hunger strikes was the emergence of Sinn Féin. The election of Bobby Sands to Westminster and the electoral success of two other prisoners in the general election in the Republic in June 1981 clearly demonstrated a previously untapped constituency for republican political activity.

Secondly, with an alternative to armed struggle opening up to republicans, they needed the credibility of talks with constitutional nationalists in Northern Ireland and, more importantly, with those in the Republic. The latter was a major stumbling block to progress. The idea of a ceasefire was strongly resisted within the republican movement. A memory of the internally debilitating ceasefire in 1975 still remained with republicans like Adams and McGuinness.

Reid was repeatedly told, 'there is nothing as bad as a ceasefire that doesn't work'.[23] But he was also told that political movement could come through the creation of a united nationalist position, involving Sinn Féin, the SDLP and the main political parties in Dublin. 'And if they could come together and agree on a common democratic strategy, that would provide an alternative strategy that could credibly be sold to the IRA,' Reid recalled.[24]

There was little prospect of this thinking winning over the Garret FitzGerald-led Fine Gael–Labour coalition government that was in power in Dublin between November 1982 and February 1987. As Taoiseach, FitzGerald's principal motivation in the aftermath of the 1981 hunger strikes was to prevent a resurgent Sinn Féin supplanting the SDLP as the main nationalist party in Northern Ireland.

The IRA campaign continued, but in Reid's interpretation of what

Adams was telling him, a historic breakthrough was possible. The republican leadership, if offered the possibility of an alternative, purely political, route for achieving its objective was open to persuasion if a strategy involving nationalist parties in Northern Ireland and the Republic could be built. Reid recalls: 'So the problem then was, the Sinn Féin leadership could do nothing about developing such a strategy unless they were able to talk directly to the other parties. And the other parties at that time wouldn't speak to them unless the IRA stopped.'[25]

In effect, the peace process started with the Redemptorist priest. Numerous attempts were made to get the SDLP and senior politicians in the Republic to talk with Sinn Féin. But for a variety of reasons, none of these attempts was successful in establishing the first contact. The process was stillborn until 1986 when Reid himself seized the initiative.

The Clonard-based priest put pen to paper: 'I decided this was the last throw of the dice, that I would put it all on paper so that the opportunity that was there to end the armed struggle would be known and on paper. . . .'[26] The 15-page typed letter was sent to John Hume in May 1986 and to Charles Haughey in November of the same year.

Reid subsequently held separate meetings with the two senior politicians. He argued that the Adams-led republican leadership could be convinced to lay down arms but that the only way this could come about was through face-to-face discussion. Talks had to be aimed, in the first instance, at ending the isolation of the republican movement. Adams and his supporters had to be shown that a broad constitutional and nationalist family existed which they could join to pursue the objective of a united Ireland. But this would happen only when the IRA no longer felt that it was out on its own.

John Hume was prepared to listen to what Reid had to say. The SDLP leader had debated with Adams on radio in 1985 and had given some consideration to the Sinn Féin leader's call, at the time, for talks between the two parties. But with deep suspicions about the intentions of the republican leadership, no movement was recorded.

Despite the abstentionism decision in 1986, there was little public evidence that Adams was serious about advancing a political strategy. Electoral success was moving alongside the IRA campaign. Sinn Féin published *Scenario for Peace* in 1987—a document that covered traditional republican concerns and included familiar demands, including calls for British withdrawal and the unconditional release of prisoners.

But Adams was serious about finding a 'scenario for peace' that would end the IRA's 'long war'. The Hume–Adams dialogue, which Reid facilitated, opened in January 1988. Close confidants, Tom Hartley, Danny Morrison and Mitchell McLaughlin, accompanied Adams to the early meetings. For the first time, Adams found himself challenged to defend the republican assessment of the situation in Northern Ireland. Hume argued that Adams was wrong in viewing the British presence as the primary source of the problems. The starting point for progress, Hume argued, was an end to military violence.

Alongside debating with the SDLP leader, Adams was also being forced to defend his strategic outlook at another set of meetings. Alex Reid's correspondence had opened up another channel of communication, this time with Charles Haughey in Dublin. Haughey was interested in Reid's assessment. He listened but his instinct was not to meet Adams while the IRA campaign continued. However, the Fianna Fáil leader introduced Reid to his party's Head of Research, Martin Mansergh.[27]

The Mansergh–Reid–Adams connection was another crucial aspect to the development of the Irish peace process. The Redemptorist priest facilitated communications between Adams and Mansergh. After Albert Reynolds replaced Haughey and the process entered deeper negotiation in the 1992–94 period, Reid would become a regular figure in Dublin.

Reid would type up the contents of these discussions and pass the documents on to the other side, generally with some personal commentary about positions and possibilities. The Irish government was given documents with significant republican fingerprints, as Mansergh admits:

> The IRA were kept informed of the state of the dialogue, though it was not always clear if a particular written message had come from the IRA or Sinn Féin, as from time to time we received both, or indeed whether it always strictly mattered. My working assumption was that one was always dealing with the one movement, in which people had different roles at particular times.[28]

It was a slow process. As each new version of what emerged as a joint position paper was exchanged, Adams continued to argue with Reid that face-to-face dialogue would speed up the entire process. When Fianna Fáil returned to power in 1987, direct contact was made with Sinn Féin. Mansergh—along with two Fianna Fáil colleagues—met with Adams and two other senior republicans—Pat Doherty and Mitchell McLaughlin—in Dundalk. There was some unease in the Fianna Fáil delegation about the contacts, especially as republican violence continued. It was only a few months since the Enniskillen bombing on Remembrance Day in November 1987, when IRA actions had left eleven people dead and more than 60 injured.

The first meeting took place at the Redemptorist monastery in Dundalk. Reid made the introductions. He said: 'I'll be leaving you in a minute but I'd just like you to pause a moment for a short prayer to help you in your deliberations.' The meeting lasted for two hours. The atmosphere was cordial and business-like. The first tentative steps, which would lead to the August 1994 IRA ceasefire, were being taken.

The first face-to-face meetings were hugely significant for Adams and his colleagues, as Reid explains:

> It was a big thing for Sinn Féin to say they had met representatives of Fianna Fáil, in brackets the Irish Government. That created credibility with the military side of their movement, that they were actually being taken seriously and engaging at the highest level. . . .[29]

While these early contacts served to tease out definitions of key concepts such as self-determination and consent, the discussions ended without any apparent movement. The Fianna Fáil delegation concluded that the IRA was not yet prepared to call a ceasefire. It was clear to those involved that the main republican objective with the dialogue was to win political credibility and to end their isolation. North of the border, John Hume was also reaching the same conclusion from his Reid-sponsored talks with Adams.

Both sets of face-to-face contacts concluded before the end of 1988, although Reid kept channels of communication open. A position paper, written in 1989 by the Redemptorist priest, sought to explain the clandestine 'dialogue of peace' that was under way. The document—originally intended for public consumption but unpublished—was prepared to help forward the cause of a just and lasting peace.'[30]

The 1988 mission statement of the RPM was incorporated into the 1989 paper by way of explaining the pastoral considerations motivating the Redemptorists. However, the significant material in the 1989 document concerned the contemporaneous account given of the state of the peace process at that time and the active role being played by the Redemptorist Order.

The document clearly set the origins of what became known in the early 1990s as the Northern Ireland peace process.

Here we wish to concentrate on the pastoral efforts we have been making, particularly over the past four or five years to persuade the Republican Movement, namely the I.R.A. and the Sinn Féin Party to end the use of armed force in the pursuit of their aims and to change over completely to the use of political and diplomatic forces. . . .[31]

The 1989 document was prepared against 'a state of impasse' in the dialogue. The Redemptorists noted that they had been involved in 'a long process of dialogue with the leadership of the Sinn Féin Party during which formulas and proposals aimed at defining and implementing "a political alternative to the armed struggle" were considered and discussed in terms of the democratic principles that must govern a just resolution to the conflict.'[32]

The document pointed towards progress in the discussions with the republican leadership.

We managed to define 'a democratic over-all political and diplomatic strategy for justice, peace and reconciliation' which, in terms, at least, of its broad thrust, the Sinn Féin leadership were prepared to recommend as a credible, political 'alternative' to the armed struggle of the I.R.A. provided they were satisfied before they recommended it that, if the I.R.A. were to accept it as such, it would, in fact be implemented by the Irish Government and other relevant parties on the nationalist side of the conflict.[33]

There was a considerable distance to travel in terms of dealing with unrepentant republican dogma but Adams had already displayed a strong streak of pragmatism over taking seats won in Leinster House. The early contacts—Hume–Adams and Mansergh–Adams—helped to tease out definitions of key concepts such as self-determination and consent. Much of the peace process was about finding a common language that could accommodate the objectives of various participants. Traditional republicanism was about to undergo a radical transformation that ultimately removed all justification for the existence of the IRA and its campaign of violence.

The Anglo-Irish Agreement had provided the republican movement with both linguistic and theoretical challenges. The agreement showed that the British government was prepared to acknowledge the legitimacy of Irish nationalism. Both Mansergh and Hume argued that the British were now neutral participants in the Irish question.

But republicans like Adams were still using a language encumbered by history. They talked about the partitionist parliament at Leinster House, about British imperialism and about the necessity for a fixed timetable for British withdrawal. Mitchell McLaughlin from Derry recalled the language learning curve faced by the republican movement: 'That was a challenge particularly for Sinn Féin. One of the early benefits was the advice we were being given . . . about how certain words and language was charged in a very political way.'[34]

The dialogue with Adams spawned almost six years of debate on these fundamental principles. The ideological issues underlying the conflict were for the first time directly debated alongside the conditions under which Irish unity could be achieved in the future.

Despite the apparent progress achieved in the Redemptorists' dialogue with the republican leadership, a major difficulty remained. Adams wanted talks without an end to the IRA campaign. However, the Irish government was unwilling to discuss what the RPM described as 'proposals for peace' unless 'the IRA ends that campaign or, at least calls a cease-fire.'

The latter distinction is highly significant in light of the controversy which developed over the usage, or lack of usage, of the word 'permanent' in the August 1994 IRA ceasefire statement. It would appear that in 1989 consideration of a 'cease-fire' by the republican movement was not in terms of a permanent end to violence but, rather, as a prelude to political discussion, with the option of a return to conflict left open.

The Redemptorists noted the information being supplied by the republican leadership who 'could not prudently or realistically advocate or support any proposals for "a political alternative to armed struggle" or any new formulas for defining and applying the democratic principles which, in theory at least, should govern the exercise of political self-determination as it relates to the present conflict, unless and until they could discuss them directly and without pre-conditions (in particular, the pre-condition that the I.R.A. should first end its armed campaign) with the Government or Governments and other political parties whose co-operation would be necessary to implement them or, at least, to facilitate their implementation.'[35]

This was not a viable option for the Irish government. Private contacts facilitated by Reid were one thing but opening face-to-face contacts with Adams while the IRA campaign continued was not a scenario that could be sold publicly with any confidence. The impatience of the RPM is evident in the 1989 document.

This impasse, we believe, is holding up the opportunity of a real break-through on the road to a just and lasting peace . . . We are convinced, from our knowledge of the possibilities, that it could be satisfactorily and even quickly resolved by means of a special pastoral intervention. . . .[36]

The Redemptorists proposed a 'communication sanctuary' under their auspices to end the impasse. This sanctuary—described as a mission of the Church—'could be set up and maintained without loss of face or compromise of principle by any of the parties concerned provided all of them accepted the intervention as an authentic exercise of the Church's mission in the present conflict and were prepared to co-operate with it.'[37]

The arrival of Peter Brooke as Northern Ireland Secretary in July 1989 would turn out to be a significant development in the nascent peace process. Brooke's declaration that the IRA could not be defeated by military means left Adams and his colleagues intrigued. Within the republican leadership, a debate was under way about the morality of continuing the IRA campaign when neither defeat nor victory was a likely conclusion. Then Brooke trumped the republican view of Britain as a colonial aggressor when he declared that the British had no 'selfish strategic or economic interest' in Northern Ireland and would support Irish unity if that was the wish of a majority of people in Northern Ireland.

A significant shift in Sinn Féin political thinking was revealed when the party published *Towards a Lasting Peace in Ireland*, a discussion document that failed to include for the first time the long-time republican call for a British withdrawal. Moreover, the party made far more accommodating references to unionism than in any previous policy document on the constitutional issue.

The secret discussions, including contacts with the British, continued, but the IRA campaign continued at a relentless pace, especially in 1993 as the speed of political events quickened. The death toll in October 1993 was the highest in any month since October 1976. Twenty-seven people lost their lives in October 1993. Ten people were left dead, and another 57 injured, when an IRA bomb exploded in a fish shop on the Shankill Road in Belfast. The IRA said that the attack was intended to kill members of the Ulster Defence Association who, they claimed, were meeting in a room above the shop.

The bombing was recalled in the book, *Lost Lives*: 'The attack caused widespread horror, particularly since two children and four women were among the casualties of the explosion, which took place when the Shankill Road was thronged with shoppers on a Saturday afternoon.'[38] Moreover, there was widespread condemnation of Adams when he helped to carry the coffin of Thomas Begley, the IRA activist who had died in the Shankill bomb explosion.

The first tangible outcome from the discussions between Adams and Hume on the one hand and between Adams and Mansergh on the other emerged in December 1993 when the Irish and British agreed a Joint Declaration at Downing Street. The Downing Street Declaration was a blueprint for an end to violence. The document was based on the twin principles of self-determination and consent. These were the twin issues that had consumed so much of the time in the contacts over the previous years.

Adams had started from a simple majoritarian theory of national determination but came to accept a more sophisticated definition. In a key section, the Downing Street Declaration noted: 'It is for the people of the island of Ireland alone, by agreement between the two parts respectively, to exercise their right of self-determination on the basis of consent, freely and concurrently given, North and South, to bring about a united Ireland, if that is their wish.'

Moreover, the British conceded the Irish people's right to self-determination but only in the context of the Irish government's accepting that Irish unity required the backing of a majority of people in Northern Ireland. The text contained compromises by all sides. The British gave the commitment to 'encourage, facilitate and enable' agreement among the Irish people. The Irish government accepted 'that the democratic right of self-determination by the people of Ireland as a whole must be achieved and exercised with and subject to the agreement and consent of a majority of the people of Northern Ireland.'

Sinn Féin fudged its response to the Downing Street Declaration (DSD). It would have been difficult for Adams to stand up to support openly a document which acknowledged that, for Irish unity to be achieved, the participation and agreement of the unionist people was essential. But by not rejecting the document, Adams was signalling once more that he was prepared to compromise. The language of Irish republicanism was being rewritten and so too were core republicans beliefs. The idea of immediate British withdrawal was being pushed aside as Adams took his movement further down a road heading in the direction of a negotiated political settlement that would fall considerably short of Irish unity.

The DSD promised that parties that permanently ended the use of, or support for, paramilitary violence could 'in due course' enter the political process. During the negotiations, the British had sought a three-month quarantine period but the Irish government rejected the idea. Reynolds wanted Sinn Féin included in normal political life as soon as possible. Anything short of this commitment was unacceptable to Adams.

Over the following months, Sinn Féin made repeated requests for clarification on the DSD and, during this period, the IRA maintained its campaign of violence, including in London. In early 1994, IRA incendiary devices detonated in Oxford Street while mortar bombs were launched on Heathrow Airport. While the devices did not explode, the message about the IRA capability was obvious.

Not only was Sinn Féin seeking clarification of the Declaration but the party also wanted immediate direct talks with the British government. Adams told his party's 1994 Ard Fheis that the DSD was a significant departure in the attitude of the British government towards Ireland but, he added, 'one also has to ask, does anyone really expect the IRA to cease its activities so that British civil servants can discuss with Sinn Féin the surrender of IRA weapons after we have been "decontaminated"?'[39]

A three-day IRA ceasefire was announced at Easter 1994 to demonstrate that the organisation was sincere about the peace process. The British described the move as a cynical public relations exercise. There was some disappointment in Dublin that the IRA had not offered to go further but there was hope that more was to follow. Intensive dialogue was under way within the republican movement. The value of an unarmed strategy was being promoted by the Adams–McGuinness leadership axis.

The groundwork had been laid slowly and the participants were rewarded on 31 August 1994 when the IRA ended its campaign of violence. The IRA statement read:

> Recognising the potential of the current situation and in order to enhance the democratic peace process and underline our definitive commitment to its success the leadership of Oglaigh na hÉireann have decided that as of midnight, Wednesday, 31 August, there will be a complete cessation of military operations. All our units have been instructed accordingly. . . .[40]

The justification for an end to violence was clear. The Hume–Adams dialogue had created a unity within northern nationalism. By means of the Mansergh contacts, the government in Dublin had re-engaged with Northern Ireland in a comprehensive way not evident since 1922. This coming together of the various strands of nationalism in Ireland also had the support of the US Administration, which pledged to guarantee fair play. Nevertheless, the ceasefire had been called without the achievement of British withdrawal or even a timetable for a British withdrawal. The pragmatism of the Adams leadership had won out.

The IRA announcement did not use the word 'permanent' for ideological reasons, although other phrases were included to convey the republican commitment to the ceasefire. The British—and most unionists—were dubious about the IRA's intentions. They believed that the ceasefire was a tactical device. This issue dogged the Irish peace process for some time after the August 1994 ceasefire and was quickly joined by an even more enduring problem, arms decommissioning.

Decommissioning was an unresolved issue that lurked in the background as attempts to get a ceasefire were undertaken. In December 1993, Irish Labour Party leader Dick Spring had spoken of the need for the disposal of weapons, while Albert Reynolds had warned Sinn Féin that the arms issue would have to be dealt with expeditiously once peace had been established. Mansergh had raised the subject of arms when he met with the leadership of the Provisional IRA in the lead-up to the August 1994 ceasefire. One of those present at the meeting recalled: 'The question of arms was brought up but he was given a blank "no", and when the IRA says no, that's the end of discussion on the subject.'[41] A choice was made: the leading figures in Dublin were prepared to park the arms issue so as to consolidate the IRA ceasefire.

Sinn Féin's electoral advance quickened in the peace process era, making acceptance of the Adams-led compromises somewhat easier within the republican movement. But there were doubters within the IRA, and the lack of movement in establishing all-party political talks on the future of Northern Ireland led ultimately to a breakdown in the ceasefire, early in 1996. The peace process remained on hold until the summer of 1997 when elections in Britain and the Republic led to changes of government, with Tony Blair and Bertie Ahern taking office in their respective countries. The political landscape was changed. The New Labour government agreed to Sinn Féin's entry into talks without any precondition on decommissioning. The talks would convene in September, and Sinn Féin would be welcomed six weeks after a renewed IRA ceasefire.

Those talks climaxed in April 1998 when the Belfast Agreement was signed by the participating negotiating teams. The talks had been divided into three interlocking strands. The first strand concerned the parties in Northern Ireland. The second dealt with the relationship between Northern Ireland and the government in Dublin. The third strand addressed relations between the governments in Dublin and London.

The Belfast Agreement proposed a balanced constitutional settlement. The principle of consent was central to future relations on the island, while national self-determination would be exercised in Northern Ireland and the Republic separately but concurrently, and without British interference. On the institutional side, the agreement proposed a 108-member Assembly, which would work with the government in Dublin in a North–South Ministerial Council to progress co-operation on numerous areas of mutual interest. A new policing service, representative of the wider community, would be established. Arrangements for decommissioning of paramilitary arms and a commitment to demilitarisation were included in the deal. The governments also agreed to an early-release programme for prisoners convicted of terrorist offences.

Adams argued that the deal was transitional rather than a final agreement. The republican objective of Irish unity remained. Sinn Féin had secured North–South co-operation but, while the symbolism was potent, the range of activities covered was limited. Adams had secured the early release of prisoners but fault lines in republicanism were opening up. Republicans were on the road to membership of a new Assembly at Stormont, the IRA was on the road to decommissioning, and ultimately disbandment, while the British remained in Northern Ireland and Irish unity—despite the IRA's 25-year campaign—had not been achieved. There was more internal criticism of the Adams leadership than at any time previously.

A sister of Bobby Sands, Bernadette Sands-McKevitt, bluntly observed that her brother 'did not die for cross-border bodies with executive powers. He did not die for nationalists to be equal to British citizens within the Northern Ireland state.'[42] Some time later, a former leading IRA member, Brendan Hughes, said that there was declining enthusiasm in the movement 'not because people are war weary—they are politics weary . . . The political process has created a class of professional liars and unfortunately it contains many republicans.'[43]

The Real IRA emerged as an alternative military option for disgruntled republicans but, with no tangible political strategy, the dissidents won limited support. Alex Maskey, who was Sinn Féin's first mayor of Belfast City and encouraged closer relations with unionists, succinctly described the options faced by those who criticised the Adams leadership: 'My reply to those in our movement who are critical of our strategy is to say: "Well, find another one . . . give me a better one."'[44]

Adams had led his movement to accept a negotiated settlement that was well short of the long-standing and repeatedly stated republican goals. Pragmatism had won out. One senior republican and very close confidant of Gerry Adams neatly summed up the type of party Sinn Féin was evolving into when he spoke as far back as the November 1985 Ard Fheis. Tom Hartley was contributing to a one-hour Sunday afternoon debate on abstentionism and wanted the policy to be 'viewed as a tactic and not a principle'. The republican leadership was still twelve months away from directly challenging the issue but the 1985 debate was a dry run for the pragmatic decisions to come.

Addressing the Ard Fheis, Hartley declared: 'There is a principle rising above all principles and that is the principle of success . . . because we republicans have no right to commit further generations of young people to the graves and the jails if we don't know how we're going to win this struggle.'[45] At that stage, in 1985, the leadership cabal surrounding Adams decided that 'the principle of success' would drive its version of the Sinn Féin party. The Hartley declaration helps to explain the motivation underpinning the many changes in republican ideology sponsored by Adams during the peace process years. This was in keeping with the Adams strategy as outlined to Alex Reid—the republican leadership 'wanted some way of getting out of the IRA campaign honourably'.

FUNDING THE REPUBLICAN MOVEMENT

Thousands of mourners descended upon Belfast's Milltown Cemetery in July 2004. They came to pay their respects to the veteran IRA man, Joe Cahill. Leading members of the republican movement, including Gerry Adams and Martin McGuinness, took turns to carry the coffin. At the graveside, the folk singer, Frances Black, sang the republican song, 'The Bold Fenian Men'—'We may have brave men but we'll never have better/Glory-O, Glory-O/To the bold Fenian Men'.

The main oration was delivered by the Sinn Féin president, who had first met Cahill in the mid-1960s and went on to become a close friend. In praising Cahill and his long career in the IRA, Adams only hinted at the level of his involvement. There would, Adams said of Cahill's life, 'be stories told by Albert Reynolds, by Tony Blair, by Bill Clinton, and by Colonel Gaddafi.'[1]

Certainly, Cahill's life spanned the history of the modern republican movement. 'Joe was a physical force republican. He made no apologies for that,' Adams told the funeral mourners. Cahill was born in Belfast in 1920 just as the island of Ireland was partitioned into two separate jurisdictions. He spent his life trying to undo that partition, joining the IRA in his teens. 'You see, Catholics up the North felt left down by the government in the 26 Counties. They looked to them for support and help, and it wasn't forthcoming. Then when Fianna Fáil came to power [in 1932] they thought things would improve. Obviously it didn't. So the IRA were the only support for the people,' Cahill recalled in one of his final interviews.[2]

Cahill spent seven years in prison for the murder on Easter Sunday 1942 of a policeman in Belfast. By the mid-1950s, he was head of the Belfast IRA and was involved in the preparations for the border campaign, leading several raids on arms depots. As they attempted to stifle the IRA, the authorities in Northern Ireland sanctioned the internment of senior republicans. Cahill was arrested in 1957 and was interned for the next four years.

The Belfast man had little time for the left-wing political direction the IRA took in the 1960s as the republican leadership started a process of moving away from violence. 'There was a complete drift towards the political side of things and the military side of things was being run down,' Cahill complained. His involvement tapered off but he re-emerged at the time of the split in republican ranks that gave birth to the Provisionals.

As the campaign of violence wreaked havoc in Northern Ireland and beyond, Cahill became a senior figure in the IRA, serving for a time as the organisation's Chief of Staff. He later endorsed the dual strategy favoured by the Adams leadership, with continued support for the IRA campaign and backing for Sinn Féin's electoral participation. Martin McGuinness acknowledged the importance of Cahill's endorsement at the 1986 Sinn Féin Ard Fheis: 'If he had walked away, it would have seriously undermined the strategy we were attempting to put in place.' Indeed, until his death in 2004, Cahill was a source of advice and support for Martin McGuinness and, in particular, Gerry Adams.

Few people knew as many republican secrets as Joe Cahill. He was the movement's money-man with a deep knowledge of the fundraising operations of both Sinn Féin and the IRA. He was also a contact point for those seeking to smuggle arms into Northern Ireland, a role which in the 1970s and 1980s added to his pivotal position in the republican movement.

When the newly formed Provisional IRA sought to raise money and acquire weapons, responsibility was vested in Cahill. He travelled to the United States in the late summer of 1972 to help establish a fundraising drive for the IRA and to explore the possibility of getting weapons back to Northern Ireland. On an earlier trip in 1972, the Belfast man had rallied Irish-American support in cities like Chicago, Boston, San Francisco and Philadelphia. His second visit was, however, halted not far beyond the airport tarmac, when an American immigration official asked to see his passport and proceeded to stamp it 'null and void'.

Cahill was now a recognised IRA man and he was no longer welcome in the United States. But despite being refused a visa at every application until 1994, he still travelled there, illegally, over half a dozen times, using forged documentation. There was considerable publicity surrounding Cahill's detention in 1972. But all publicity is good publicity as his Irish-

American hosts saw it. '[They] would be ringing me up and saying, "Stay there Joe, don't get out, you're worth a million dollars to us locked up."'[3]

Cahill eventually made his departure from the United States but it was not too long before he was once more behind bars. In 1973, he travelled to Libya to meet Colonel Gaddafi. It was a profitable trip as he left the north of Africa aboard the *Claudia*, a Cyprus-registered steamer; the *Claudia* had a cargo of five tons of weapons and explosives. However, the Irish Navy intercepted the vessel as it approached the southeast coast of Ireland.

'You are bound at some time or another to have losses. You can't be successful all the time,' Cahill admitted.[4] He spent three years in prison for the failed Libya gun-running exercise, but there was no remorse: 'If I am guilty of any crime it is that I did not succeed in getting the contents of the *Claudia* into the hands of the freedom fighters in the country.'[5]

Cahill had an intimate knowledge of the IRA's fundraising operations. He was also joint treasurer of Sinn Féin. When asked about Sinn Féin's finances in the mid-1980s, Cahill declined to reveal anything about the party's fundraising arrangements, saying with a laugh: 'I don't want the taxman to know.'[6] Gerry Adams later recalled that Cahill's motivation as treasurer was 'to manage to spend a lifetime in struggle without spending a proverbial penny of republican money.'[7] Indeed, as Adams added, he 'was scrupulous and extremely stingy with party funds. In fact his stinginess was legendary.'

This financial thriftiness only augmented Cahill's reputation and credibility with Irish-American sympathisers in the United States. They knew that he would look after the money they were raising from dinners, dances, raffles and other fundraising events. While the annual totals varied, Northern Irish Aid (Noraid), which was set up after the start of the conflict in 1969, estimated that by the early 1980s it was raising an average of about $300,000 every year for republican causes.

Cahill was the principal contact point with the New York-based Noraid, which was the main US fundraiser for republicans in Northern Ireland. Correspondence from Noraid in March 1972 noted that:

Our funds are channelled through Joe Cahill of Belfast to be used for the advancement of the campaign in Ireland. Naturally, a great deal of it has to go to the relief of those who were burned out or driven out of their homes; to the families of men in jail, in the internment camps or 'on-the-run'. . . .[8]

The authorities on both sides of the Atlantic strongly believed that a large proportion of the Irish-American money was used to fund IRA activities. 'Money collected for Sinn Féin is Sinn Féin money, and money coming for prisoners goes to prisoners,' Cahill said in 1985.[9] There was no reference, however, to the money raised for the IRA, as well as the large undeclared sums of cash that were collected in Irish areas in the United States. Yet, despite their suspicions, the authorities on both sides of the Atlantic were unable to confirm where all the dollars went, with bank secrecy laws and cash donations aiding those who sought to operate clandestine fundraising arrangements.

The extent of the monies involved emerged in April 1982 when Cahill arrived at a coffee shop on Middle Abbey Street in Dublin. He had an arrangement to meet Ted Howell, another leading republican from Belfast and a known Adams supporter who had a particular brief to promote the organisation's international links. Howell had in the recent past been deported from both Canada and the United States, as well as having absconded in Paris.

Howell and four other men had been arrested in February 1982, trying to get into the United States illegally, near Buffalo. Interestingly, only a few weeks earlier, US immigration officers at Niagara Falls had detained two other leading republicans, Danny Morrison and Owen Carron. They were also travelling on false passports and were said to be trying to get to a republican fundraising event in New York.

The five members of the second group had lower public profiles but were well known to the authorities as leading IRA figures. Along with Ted Howell, another one of those detained was Dessie Ellis, who would later emerge as a leading Sinn Féin election candidate in Dublin. Ellis and Howell were suspected of planning the 1979 assassination of Lord Mountbatten, a cousin of the British monarch. The five men arrested near Buffalo were suspected of crossing the United States–Canadian border so as to travel to New York for a pre-arranged weapons deal. They were carrying the equivalent of €10,000 in cash and what was described at the time as a 'shopping list' of weapons.

Howell was sent back to Canada from where he was subsequently deported to Ireland. But during a flight change in Paris on 4 March 1982, he lost his Canadian escort. In the terminal building, he asked to use the toilet and then disappeared. Howell did not stay in Paris for long, and four weeks later he was swapping stories with Joe Cahill in a Dublin coffee shop.

The two men were both members of the Sinn Féin Ard Comhairle;

Cahill was the party's joint treasurer. They chatted in the Middle Abbey Street coffee shop but their rendezvous was about more than old friends catching up. As Howell made to leave and said goodbye, Cahill handed him a bag. Unknown to the two men, they were being watched by Garda Special Branch personnel. As Howell left the coffee shop, the undercover officers swooped. Howell and Cahill were both arrested. The bag they had exchanged was seized. Inside the bag, Gardaí discovered dollar notes which, when counted, totalled some $80,000 along with IR£646 and £250stg. Howell was later acquitted of IRA membership but subsequently returned to the courts in Dublin, looking for his money back.

Cahill told the court that the dollars had been donated to Sinn Féin, although he refused to name the individuals who had contributed the funds. The US money had come from donors in the United States. While the Irish currency was the proceeds from the sale of a republican magazine, Cahill said that it was intended to repay electoral debts run up by Sinn Féin in the Republic and also to fund the party's campaign for elections in late 1982 in Northern Ireland. The plan had been for Howell to lodge the money in a bank account in Dundalk, Cahill explained.

But the District Court judge did not accept the story and decided that the money should not be returned. The judge said that, 'in the balance of probabilities, the monies were for use by an illegal organisation. . . .'[10] Cahill and Howell were, however, not giving up that easily. Another four years of legal wrangles followed, but in July 1986, the money was returned.

By the standards of the early 1980s, the money that Cahill passed to Howell was significant. The dollar amount was a very large donation— no matter from how many unknown people—and that would have been the case for all political parties in Ireland. It was more particularly a substantial sum for a small fringe party with no national representation south of the border and scant established presence in Northern Ireland.

But then the republican movement—Sinn Féin and the IRA—has had a long tradition of securing access to substantial amounts of money, legal and illegal, from donors at home and abroad. Even today, doubts persist about the origins and allocation of monies controlled by republicans. Sinn Féin has faced repeated questions about its financial affairs. A series of revelations and policing activities after the Northern Bank robbery in December 2004 placed renewed focus on republican money.

Despite its many political and ideological transformations, Sinn Féin has, to a large extent, always been a party of money. A sum of £750 was spent during a by-election in North Leitrim in 1905, one of the first electoral outings of Arthur Griffith's Sinn Féin. The election fund was boosted by a donation of £150 from John Devoy in the US, a fact that illustrates how American money has been a long-standing feature of republican finances.

There was no electoral victory in North Leitrim in 1905 but, some years later, the party raised almost £1,300 for what was a famous win in the 1917 Roscommon by-election. One British government official wrote that Sinn Féin campaigners 'have a fleet of motor cars and are all put up in the best hotels and are spending money freely.'[11]

The third Sinn Féin, which emerged following the 1922 Treaty split, also received generous seed capital from the United States. The party's audited accounts for 1923/24 indicate income of around £26,000 which one historian notes was 'an impressive sum for an Irish political party at this period.'[12]

Throughout its history, Sinn Féin has had golden financial periods, although in the bleak wilderness years after the departure of de Valera in 1926 money was very tight and a loan was required to pay the rent due on the party's headquarters. Long-time activist and party president Margaret Buckley recalled Sinn Féin's precarious existence: 'We were left without resources—there being only about £26 left in the Treasury—and we soon had to evacuate the expensive headquarters in Suffolk Street and move to 16 Parnell Square. . . .'[13]

Political activity was a secondary priority for republicans for most of the half century that followed the 1926 split. When it was considered tactically beneficial, elections were contested, as on several occasions in the 1950s but, for the most part, the republican movement downgraded political and electoral action. What money was raised was used to fund military objectives.

The republican dilemma about linking participation in elections with recognition of the entire system continued to bedevil militant Irish republicanism. Only in the early 1980s could it be said that the issue was adequately aired and that the merits or otherwise of this facet of republican ideology were fully debated. This was to have an impact on how the republican movement was funded. During the initial course of the contemporary conflict in Northern Ireland, all the resources of the republican movement were directed into the military campaign of the IRA.

Money—like weaponry—was begged, borrowed and stolen. There was a multitude of sources: donations from supporters in Ireland and in the United States, money from illegal activities and funds secured from

IRA raids on banks and post offices. In the aftermath of an incident involving a cash transit van in Limerick in 1978, the Irish government, exasperated at the repeated occurrence of IRA raids, ordered Garda and army escorts for all significant movements of bank money.

With the Adams decision, after the 1981 hunger strikes, to allow political action to operate alongside military activity, there was considerable internal competition between the IRA and Sinn Féin for resources. The decision to rejuvenate Sinn Féin led to a questioning of the Adams leadership's commitment to the IRA campaign. Indeed, several leading republicans questioned the direction in which Adams was taking the movement, and in 1985 he faced a serious but short-lived challenge to his authority.

Danny Morrison was closely involved in the republican decision-making process at that time. He was also a very close confidant of Gerry Adams. Morrison confirmed the growth of this tension over the electoral strategy and the prioritisation of resources:

> There was an issue. Actually, there was trouble in the Belfast Brigade of the IRA in about April or May of 1985 . . . There were a group of people, very respected people, who felt that it was going too far and who, now I don't think it was an attempted coup or anything like that, but they had formed a little group inside the republican movement and were attempting to gather support against their comrades and were arguing about the politics. That could have led to a dangerous situation but the IRA sorted it out and put these people out of the organisation.[14]

Ivor Bell was the most senior of the individuals involved in what Morrison describes as 'a little group'. Bell's republican involvement paralleled that of Adams. The two men came to prominence in the early 1970s in the Belfast Brigade of the IRA. They spent time together in prison and spearheaded the IRA's reorganisation in the aftermath of the 1974–75 ceasefire. Within the republican movement, especially in Belfast, Adams and Bell were recognised as two of the brightest of the 'Young Turks'.

Bell succeeded Martin McGuinness as the IRA's Chief of Staff in late 1982, but the Belfast man had begun to hold reservations about the post-hunger-strike dual strategy favoured by Adams. From having been an early supporter of electoral interventionism, Bell now started to raise concerns about the impact of Sinn Féin's growth on the IRA's military campaign. He was unhappy about the internal competition for resources. Politics did not come cheap, and funds previously used exclusively for the military campaign were now also needed for electoral involvement. Building a political presence was a costly exercise, with money needed not just for election campaigns but also to open and staff the network of advice centres which would become the backbone of Sinn Féin's on-the-ground profile in Northern Ireland's electoral constituencies. Moreover, matters were not helped by a succession of elections in the 1981–84 period, on both sides of the border, which were a significant draw on resources.

Bell had another concern beyond money—he did not believe the leadership statements that the IRA campaign would not be affected by Sinn Féin political requirements. There were tensions about the level of IRA activity in and around election times, with the Bell group resentful that the campaign of violence was being turned on and off to suit the electoral needs of Sinn Féin.

Bell was arrested in September 1983, which ended his tenure as Chief of Staff, although he regained his position on the Army Council after his release the following year. Around this time, a decision was taken to move against the Adams leadership. Bell and a number of his close associates proposed calling a general army convention at which the dual electoral and military strategy would be challenged. But the plotters had underestimated the extent to which Adams and his supporters now dominated all sections of the republican movement. When word of the attempted coup emerged, the Adams group reacted swiftly. Bell and a handful of his supporters were threatened with execution if they did not go quietly. The message was heeded. Bell still lives in Belfast but he has long remained silent about the events of 1985.

The failed Bell rebellion was probably the most serious challenge to Adams's hegemony within Sinn Féin and the IRA. It was primarily an internal affair, which was dealt with with efficient ruthlessness. A similar message was conveyed to Ruairí Ó Brádaigh when he openly challenged the Adams strategy in 1986. Ó Brádaigh's influence had waned in the IRA and Sinn Féin by the early 1980s but he publicly took on Adams at the 1986 Ard Fheis over the abstentionism issue. When setting up his new organisation, Republican Sinn Féin, Ó Brádaigh was warned that any attempt to establish a military wing would be met with a bloody response. For that reason, the formation of the Continuity IRA, the military wing of Republican Sinn Féin, was concealed for some time.

In the mid-1980s, around the time of the failed Ivor Bell-inspired coup, it was estimated that the republican movement needed annual revenue in the region of £3m (€4.2m) in order to fund its military and political activities. A decade later, that figure had risen significantly, with the estimated running costs of the IRA alone being in the order of £1.5m (€2.1m). Estimates from the policing authorities put the IRA's annual fundraising capacity in the region of £5–8m (€7–11m). Given the secret nature of the IRA and the generation of funds from myriad legal and illegal sources, it is impossible to confirm these figures. Moreover, even within the IRA, few people have any real knowledge of the organisation's financial arrangements as the movement is structured in a way to ensure that the operations of the finance department are shrouded in complete secrecy.

Sinn Féin, as discussed below, has expenditure demands related to its political and electoral roles, on both sides of the border. The IRA, on the other hand, has had a variety of activities that require money, including its obvious need for weapons and communications equipment such as radio and mobile phones. In addition, the IRA has had to sustain its membership base with 'wages' for its Volunteers and other payments to those who provide safe houses and other forms of assistance.

The organisation also runs a welfare system for republican prisoners and their families, although these costs have fallen since the signing of the Belfast Agreement in 1998. Indeed, the IRA has in recent times benefited from a peace dividend of sorts. The freeing of IRA prisoners under the Belfast Agreement's early-release programme has brought a significant reduction in the welfare costs associated with prisoners and their families. Moreover, many of these released prisoners have been available to undertake revenue-raising activities. Despite its ceasefire, the IRA still had overheads, including administration, which were unrelated to the level of activity. Fundraising continued, especially in the absence of a final political settlement and with the possibility, however slim, that a military campaign may have restarted.

There is no way of knowing to what extent, if any, money raised illegally by the IRA was used to fund the political wing of the republican movement. No specific allegation has been stood up directly linking Sinn Féin to criminal activity, or proving that the party received money from illegal activities. This lack of evidence was confirmed in a 2003 Garda report, which noted:

> There is no specific intelligence available at this section to substantiate reports that illegal organisations [the Provisional IRA]

are involved in protection rackets, the setting up of dummy security companies and the drugs trade in this jurisdiction. However, individuals with connections to these organisations are known to be involved in these activities for personal gain.[15]

While these Garda comments do not cover activities in Northern Ireland, they do illustrate the difficult in substantiating allegations that IRA criminal activity funded Sinn Féin as an organisation. Individual republicans involved in illegal activities for personal gain are far removed from criminal activity bankrolling Sinn Féin's political activism. Opponents continue to point to the lack of financial transparency about the income and expenditure of local Sinn Féin organisations, although no political party in the Republic publishes accounts for its individual constituency operations.

In reporting on a series of robberies in Northern Ireland in 2004, the Independent Monitoring Commission concluded that while official internal sanction was given,

> It does not follow that if a particular operation is authorised by senior paramilitary figures the proceeds are only or mainly for the benefit of the group on that occasion. We believe that much of the proceeds of these operations—which may be very substantial—are for personal gain even through full advantage may be taken of paramilitary infrastructure, expertise and connections; indeed there are some paramilitaries who apparently view the material benefits of organised crime as the well-earned spoils of war.[16]

The evidence available, however, suggests that some proportion of the proceeds was likely to be passed on to the IRA itself. Whether or not Sinn Féin also benefited is unknown but the party came under huge pressure to deal with this matter in the aftermath of a series of high-profile robberies in 2004.

The raid at the headquarters of the Northern Bank in Belfast in December 2004 was an exceptional crime, regardless of the consequences for the peace process in Northern Ireland. As discussed previously, the operation was high risk and involved considerable planning. But sight must not be lost of the fact that the Northern Bank raid followed a number of other robberies that also netted handsome rewards for those responsible. These robberies were also characterised by considerable professionalism and extraordinary planning.

The first of these robberies took place in May 2004 when a 40-foot articulated truck pulled up at the security entrance to the Marko warehouse near Dunmurry in south Belfast. The driver bluffed his way past the security gates, saying that he had a late delivery for the warehouse which held a mixture of valuable electrical and consumer goods. As the truck came to a halt, night staff were beginning to arrive for the late shift which was just about to start. A gang of seven armed men in stocking masks emerged from the truck and, with military precision, set about implementing a well-planned operation. The security staff were rounded up and then, one by one, the arriving night workers were seized.

Many of these individuals were tied up and locked into the warehouse canteen, while others were forced to identify the location of specific goods in the vast warehouse. Making use of the warehouse forklift and electric trolleys, the gang members helped themselves to alcohol, cigarettes, fridges, washing machines and dishwashers. A significant number of television sets and DVD players were also amongst the goods loaded onto the articulated truck, which was eventually filled to capacity at around one o'clock in the morning. By the time the warehouse staff were able to set off the fire alarm in the canteen, the gang had a head start of several hours on the police. Goods with a total value in the region of €1.5m were taken in the heist which took about four hours to complete.

The warehouse robbery was one of the biggest of its type in Northern Ireland for many years. 'These people had the run of the place to themselves for over four hours. It was an extremely professional operation which required a fair degree of planning,' PSNI Chief Superintendent Gerry Murray said afterwards. He refused to rule out paramilitary involvement. There were few obvious clues but the police had their suspicions. The robbery was similar in its precision to a cigarette raid at Belfast docks in 2003 that had been attributed to the IRA.

In September 2004, four months after the warehouse robbery, the same type of professionalism was displayed by a ten-strong gang, which forced a manager at the Iceland supermarket store in Strabane to hand over thousands of euro in cash. The manager was at home with her husband and a family friend when the gang arrived at her home shortly before nine o'clock in the evening. The three people were hooded and taken across the border where they were held overnight. The gang was obviously aware that the woman had access to the supermarket's safe, as the following morning she was forced to go to work as normal, put the supermarket takings into a holdall and then take it to a prearranged location at a church in Lifford, again across the border in County Donegal. When the operation was completed, the gang released the two other hostages who were later located walking barefoot near the cash drop-off point.

The Iceland robbery was the fourth in twelve months in the Strabane area; all these robberies were similar in that an armed gang abducted people and forced them to retrieve money from their place of work. The same group of robbers was suspected of involvement; all were from republican paramilitary backgrounds, many from the IRA, although it was not clear to what extent these individuals were operating in a freelance personal capacity or to what extent the IRA benefited.

Just a week after the Iceland robbery, another significant raid took place, this time in Belfast. Late on a Friday evening, a gang of masked and armed men burst into the north Belfast home of an employee of the Gallagher tobacco company. The man, his wife and young child were held hostage overnight. The following morning, the man was ordered to go to work as normal at a Belfast warehouse. He was instructed to open the warehouse gates when a container lorry arrived. Cigarettes and other tobacco products worth around €3m were loaded into the lorry using the warehouse's forklift. The operation took about 90 minutes. As in the other robberies, nobody was physically injured but those held hostage were left severely shocked by their ordeal.

Professionalism and considerable attention to detail were the hallmarks of all these robberies. The raids netted those responsible goods and products with a market value of around €5m, although there would be an obvious loss in selling them on at black market prices. The meticulous planning, backed by apparent insider knowledge, was once more evident in late December 2004 when the Northern Bank in Belfast was robbed in spectacular fashion.

The question of responsibility for all these robberies remained contentious but the security forces on both sides of the border, as well as the governments in Dublin and London, strongly suspected IRA involvement. The Independent Monitoring Commission (IMC) in acknowledging the discipline within the IRA—and tight control exercised by senior personnel—observed that the IRA 'is more alert to the political consequences of demonstrable involvement in organised crime and at sensitive times can rein things back.'[17] It was against this background that the IMC concluded that the robberies mentioned previously, including the Northern Bank raid, had been sanctioned at a senior level within the IRA.

The scale of the Northern Bank robbery—over €30m—well exceeded the funds needed to maintain the organisational structure of the republican movement. Indeed, the value of the raids in Dunmurry in May, Strabane in September and Belfast in October would have been sufficient to meet all of the IRA's funding needs for 2004 and 2005. The IRA has long been considered the most financially sophisticated of the paramilitary organisations operating in Northern Ireland. For over 20 years, evidence has been available to the security authorities on both sides of the border to substantiate the IRA's financial muscle. But obtaining evidence that could sustain court convictions has never been easy.

In February 2005, the authorities in the Republic gave the go-ahead for a series of raids on businesses and homes which lifted the lid on a sophisticated money-laundering operation linked to individuals with known republican associations, which operation, it was claimed, benefited IRA coffers. There was considerable political and public outrage at the revelations, especially when it was alleged that some of the money seized might be linked to the Northern Bank robbery.

In truth, however, there should have been no surprise that the republican movement benefited from money laundering. Neither should there have been any great surprise at the scale of the money involved or the sophisticated international nature of the operation to shield illegally obtained money from the regulatory authorities. Almost two decades before the Northern Bank seizures, the authorities in Dublin had stumbled upon a war chest sourced to the Provisional IRA.

On Wednesday, 19 February 1985, the Fine Gael–Labour government was obliged to rush emergency legislation through parliament to deal with what the Minister for Justice described as 'a large sum of money which is the proceeds of criminal activity by the IRA—specifically extortion under the threat of kidnap and murder. . . .'[18]

Michael Noonan told the Dáil he was speaking about a 'seven-figure sum' and that he did not want anyone to infer that he meant 'the smallest possible seven-figure sum'. He confirmed that the money 'had already been moved across international frontiers and might, to an extent at least, have been "laundered"—to use a modern colloquial expression.'[19]

The money had been moved between at least two different foreign banks—in the United States and Switzerland—before being transferred into the Irish banking system in fictitious names. In explaining the necessity for his urgency, Noonan revealed that the Garda Síochána had received a tip-off about the funds and that the new legislation would give the authorities new powers 'to prevent the money becoming available to the IRA to fund its campaign of murder and destruction.'

The new legislation was used to immediate effect as an account at a Bank of Ireland branch in County Meath was immediately frozen. The IRA denied ownership of the funds: 'The money seized by the Dublin government this past week did not belong to the Irish Republican Army.' But not unlike the situation 20 years later, in the aftermath of the Northern Bank raid, the IRA statement left open the possibility that individual members of the organisation may have been responsible for the money. The similarities between the IRA denials of 1985 and 2005 also extended to the lack of elaboration about what the money was to be used for.

The 1985 seizure in the Irish banking system indicated that the IRA had a considerable ability to obtain money, especially as it was generally believed that the monies frozen had been raised only over the previous twelve months. At that time, the Associated Press quoted an unnamed senior Garda officer as saying:

> We're not talking about the Jesse James style outfit the IRA was a decade ago. They've turned to a much more sophisticated means of getting money than bank robberies and the like. Like the Mafia, they've moved in on respectable commercial enterprises ... But every once in a while, they find themselves short or need to raise a lot of cash quickly, say for an arms buy, and then they have to resort to the tried and true method of kidnapping or a big hold-up.[20]

The IRA has adopted a variety of approaches to fundraising over the years, ranging from the very simple to the highly sophisticated, involving methods that are both criminal and also apparently legitimate. Money has been raised from a variety of different sources, including robberies, kidnapping, fuel laundering and smuggling, as well as tax and welfare fraud. Republicans have long been innovative in sourcing cash. They have not had difficulty adopting straightforward scams to boost their coffers. For many years, they collected a percentage of the takings in certain pubs in Belfast and elsewhere, while the so-called 'prisoner's penny' resulted in a charge on every drink sold in pubs in republican areas. Slot machines in amusement arcades and pubs have also been a lucrative source of cash, with some machines said to net the republican movement up to €50,000 a year.

Throughout the 1970s and early 1980s, the IRA specialised in raising funds from banks and post offices. A decision to allow armed police and army officers to accompany payroll and other cash transfers—along with heightened security at individual bank branches—led the IRA to widen its finance-gathering net. The organisation moved more into kidnapping and extortion. The Associated Press quoted a police source as saying: 'The IRA regards kidnapping as the best and the most effective method of raising cash quickly.'[21]

Kidnapping was a lucrative but a risky undertaking as the IRA discovered in 1973 when it kidnapped a German businessman in Belfast. Thomas Niedermayer, who was also the West German consul to Northern Ireland, died from a suspected heart attack while being held captive. The prominent supermarket executive, Ben Dunne, was abducted in 1981 but released in South Armagh after five days. Despite denials, speculation still persists that Dunne's family paid a ransom of IR£300,000 for his safe release. Two years later, there was an unsuccessful attempt to kidnap Canadian millionaire Galen Weston, while later in 1983 a soldier and a garda were shot dead in a gun battle that followed the escape of businessman Don Tidey, who had been held for 22 days.

Kidnapping for a ransom had become less a feature of republican activity in recent years, although holding people against their will, as part of robberies, was a hallmark of the series of robberies in 2004, blamed on the IRA. Armed robbery was another long-standing way for the IRA to generate income, although there had been a change in the organisation's approach in recent times. Banks and post offices were no longer primary targets, with the high risks and relatively low returns involved in targeting local branches. The post office raid in Adare in County Clare in 1996 confirmed as much, with Garda Jerry McCabe shot dead in the hold-up. Instead, the focus switched to seizing electrical goods, alcohol and cigarettes, all of which were easily sold on the black market. The strategy saw republicans targeting warehouses and containers of goods, as one PSNI officer told the House of Commons Northern Ireland Affairs Committee:

> We had one incident at the dock side where something in the region of 4.2 million cigarettes were taken in one act of piracy because the container was off-loaded from a ship that was ready for sailing. That in itself would produce something in the region of £1million/£1.5million profit. So white goods and shipments of that nature, spirits, alcohol, a bonded delivery en route somewhere, are much more productive . . . and it does not embarrass them as much . . . then the argument arises as to whether they are on ceasefire or not.[22]

In spite of their stated aim of ending the partition of Ireland, republicans have long benefited in financial terms from the border between Northern Ireland and the Irish Republic. The existence of around 400 border crossing points facilitates the exploitation for profit of the various legal and taxation differences between the two jurisdictions.

The differentials in duty payable on road fuels on either side of the border encourage fuel laundering and smuggling. With higher duties in Northern Ireland, the incentive is to purchase fuel in the Irish Republic, and then smuggle it north for illegal resale at prices that undercut legitimate operators. On the other hand, cheaper rebated fuels such as red diesel are laundered. This lucrative activity involves treating and removing identifying chemical markers in red diesel before passing the fuel off as legitimate road-use diesel.

In border areas, diesel-laundering facilities process thousands of litres of fuel every week. This laundered diesel was never intended for use in motor vehicles and has the capacity to damage car engines. But this fact has not dissuaded many members of the public from purchasing laundered and smuggled diesel sold at illegal roadside sites, so-called 'hucksters', at prices cheaper than available at legitimate filling stations. In the late 1990s, it was estimated that up to two-thirds of petrol stations in Northern Ireland were selling laundered fuel, although there has been a significant behavioural change in recent times following a crackdown by customs and excise officials.

Alongside fuel smuggling, the other main products that generated cash-based income for the republican movement were tobacco and alcohol. Bottling plants turn out illicit alcohol that was then passed off for conventional drink brands. This alcohol was stored in recycled bottles with counterfeit labels from well-known vodka, gin and whiskey brands. Alcohol smuggling was less of a problem in Northern Ireland than smuggling of tobacco products, with the IRA generating considerable cash from the sale of stolen cigarettes. In recent times the IRA also hijacked a number of lorries carrying cigarettes.

The multi-million-euro black-market trade in tobacco, alcohol and fuel was obviously not confined to republican paramilitaries, with organised crime also gaining from these lucrative activities. Nevertheless, republicans specialised in raising revenue from black-market trading which had the obvious attraction of being a cash-based economy. The black-market sale of tobacco, alcohol and fuel, as well as counterfeit CDs and designer goods, grew because a willing market exists for these goods. There was ease in selling these goods, particularly within communities where sympathy for republican objectives already existed.

Thomas 'Slab' Murphy was identified as the most prominent republican figure involved in smuggling. In 2004, a BBC television programme described Murphy as the richest smuggler in Britain, with a personal wealth in excess of €50m. Murphy, who was long identified as a member of the IRA Army Council, had little involvement in Sinn Féin. According to Seán O'Callaghan, a former IRA member turned republican critic, 'the community of South Armagh depends on the benevolence of Thomas "Slab" Murphy for every single factor of their life. Nobody buys a farm, nobody builds a house, nobody does anything that Tom is not aware of, that is not referred to Tom. Everybody is doing very well. The community is awash with money.'[23]

There is a widespread perception that these black-market goods were sourced from 'victimless crime' but this viewpoint ignores the considerable cost to the conventional economy in Northern Ireland:

> We are well aware in terms of hydrocarbon fuel activities [that] some 120-odd petrol stations have gone out of business where petrol sales of a legitimate nature which raises money for the Exchequer have dropped significantly . . . you can roll that over into the tobacco activities as well, where again cigarettes costing £2 a packet as opposed to £4 are swamping the Northern Ireland market.[24]

This type of activity was not only profitable but also exposed the perpetrators to lower risks than traditional fundraising activities because of the relatively lower penalties. This was also true of counterfeiting, one of the areas where there was a blurring of the boundaries between paramilitary and criminal interests.

Republicans positioned themselves to take advantage of the huge public demand for replica branded goods at bargain prices. The production and sale of CDs, DVDs, computer games, perfume and designer clothing produced significant profits for paramilitary organisations in Northern Ireland. It has been estimated that some 80 per cent of intellectual property crime was undertaken by gangs with paramilitary links, while the IRA alone was said to earn over €1.5m annually from video and DVD piracy.

Paramilitary groups in Northern Ireland have also been active in the drugs trade, although it is interesting to note that, unlike for other republican and loyalist paramilitary groups, the Independent Monitoring Commission did not list drug income as a source of IRA revenue. Republican activists from the IRA and Sinn Féin have been prominent members of anti-drugs groups organised in socio-economically deprived areas, on both sides of the border. In the 1980s and 1990s, there were suspicions that republicans were using local anti-drugs committees to promote their own involvement in local communities. There were also allegations that known IRA members implemented heavy-handed treatment of drug pushers as the formal policing systems were by-passed.

There have been claims that republicans have constructed and operated an arm's-length drugs policy whereby they effectively 'license' their territories to drug dealers in return for a share of the proceeds of their illegal activity. 'In this way groups—but particularly the PIRA—have sought to benefit from deeply antisocial activity such as drug dealing while remaining distant from them,'[25] the House of Commons Northern Ireland Affairs Committee said. The former leader of the Irish Labour Party, Dick Spring, concurred in February 2002: 'They're up to their necks in peddling drugs in other parts of the island and on the other hand they're pretending they're going to save the country from drugs.'[26]

The republican movement used money obtained from illegal activities to gain entrance to the legitimate economy. The authorities on both sides of the border believe that money was laundered in taxi and security firms as well as courier services and public houses. The profits from these businesses were then available to the organisation.

The IRA does not have bank accounts or easily identifiable assets. The money it generated is hidden in complex financial arrangements developed and maintained to obscure the origin of the funds from the regulatory authorities. This financial system necessitated a network of professional advisers, including accountants and lawyers. The illegally obtained money was laundered to produce clean money, thereby throwing the regulatory authorities off the trail. According to the Northern Ireland Affairs Committee at Westminster:

They obscure the origins of the 'dirty money' by the use of complex money laundering schemes; they divide up and locate their assets in several jurisdictions—often those with bank, corporate or trust secrecy legislation—to make the work of regulators and investigators more difficult. This is the pattern of behaviour of organised criminals throughout the world. Those in Northern Ireland are no different.[27]

Investigation of these financial arrangements has been a complex process involving the unravelling of detailed paper trails developed to obscure the ownership of money and assets. The 2005 Garda investigation into alleged IRA money laundering was confirmation of the taxing and time-consuming nature of such inquiries.

The drama began on Wednesday, 17 February 2005, when the Cork to Dublin train arrived at Heuston Station in Dublin. Undercover gardaí were interested in one particular passenger travelling on the inter-city train. Don Bullman from Wilton in County Cork had no previous conviction but he was known to the Garda Síochána as a republican activist whose activities moved between the PIRA and dissident groups.

Bullman had an arrangement that evening to meet with two other men outside the railway station. They were waiting for the Cork man in a Northern-Ireland-registered jeep. The three men were talking inside the jeep when the gardaí knocked on the window. A Daz washing-powder box was on the floor of the vehicle. Inside, wrapped in cling film, there were three bundles of cash. The money totalled about €94,000. 'I suspected that the €94,000 was a money laundering operation on behalf of the IRA,' a garda officer told the court at which Bullman, who worked as a chef, was charged with membership of the IRA. The two other men were released without charge.

The railway station seizure was only the start of a series of dramatic events that would throw even further light on the clandestine world of republican finance, and cast doubts on Gerry Adams's denials that his movement was involved in criminality or benefited indirectly from the proceeds of criminal activities.

As Bullman and his two contacts were being escorted away from Heuston Station, two more arrests were made, this time in County Cork, while about £60,000stg (€87,000) was discovered in a house also in County Cork. The money was in several different denominations of Northern Ireland bank notes, beginning speculation that the authorities had seized upon a money-laundering operation involving cash from the Northern Bank robbery.

One of those arrested in County Cork was known to gardaí as a senior IRA member, while the second man was identified as Tom Hanlon, a former Sinn Féin councillor. Hanlon, an unsuccessful Sinn Féin candidate in the 2002 general election, was also centrally involved in the party's campaign in the following year's European Parliament elections in the Munster constituency.

The following morning, Thursday, 18 February 2005, officers from the

Criminal Assets Bureau and the Garda Bureau of Fraud Investigation arrived at a house at Farran on the outskirts of Cork city. The split-level bungalow was home to financial adviser Ted Cunningham and his partner, Cathy Armstrong. Fifty-seven-year-old Cunningham was a registered moneylender who generally operated from offices in nearby Ballincollig. He was the director of numerous companies and had done very well from property and other financial investments. During a search of Cunningham's home, detectives discovered some STG£2.3m in cash. They gleaned even more valuable information from the documents taken from the house and Cunningham's office.

While the raids were under way, gardaí swooped on other republicans whom they had been monitoring for some time. In all, seven people were arrested in the operation. Only hours after news of the money-laundering investigation had reached public attention, a man arrived voluntarily at a Garda station in Cork city. He handed over £200,000 in cash that he had been asked to mind by one of the people arrested earlier that same day.

Garda officers searched over a dozen premises in Cork, Dublin, Meath, Louth and Westmeath. They took away a considerable volume of documentation and computer equipment. An initial examination of the material pointed the officers in the direction of other business people who had dealings with one of Cunningham's main financial companies, Chesterton Finance Ltd. Over £100,000 was discovered when officers visited a businessman in Millstreet in County Cork, while another £20,000 was recovered in Rathmore in County Kerry.

Accountancy and legal firms were targeted as the gardaí began to unravel a complex money trail. Over the following days, another £250,000 was discovered after a raid on a house in Tullamore in County Offaly while inquiries in Dublin yielded a further £67,000. News of the money-laundering raids caused some people to panic. Sterling notes estimated to be valued at several hundred thousand pounds were burnt by one man in County Cork who believed his house was about to be raided by gardaí. Partially burnt notes were discovered. Despite the cash discoveries, the Garda authorities were initially reluctant to say publicly that the money could be sourced to the Northern Bank robbery, but a strong impression was given by political figures and in private media briefings that a link would be established.

Ted Cunningham was arrested and questioned by gardaí but subsequently released as the massive financial investigation continued. Central to that investigation was Chesterton Finance, which was involved in lending money secured on fixed assets. The company offered returns that were at a significant premium to commercial bank deposit rates. In 2003, Chesterton was offering a return of 10 per cent a year, compared to deposit rates of 3 per cent or less on offer from the commercial banks.

In the year to the end of February 2004, Chesterton made a profit of just over €32,000. The directors of the company were paid almost €120,000, according to the accounts. The inclusion of Phil Flynn on the list of Chesterton's directors added additional intrigue to what was already a dramatic tale.

Flynn was a pillar of the establishment in political and business circles in Dublin. He was chairman of Bank of Scotland (Ireland) and a board member of a state-owned health insurance company. He had had a senior trade union career but in more recent years had established a reputation as a troubleshooter, called in to resolve contentious industrial relations disputes. Flynn was well connected in political circles, having relationships with senior figures in all the main parties.

Flynn's earlier career as a republican activist was no secret. He was acquitted of being a member of the IRA in the 1970s when there was speculation that he was a central figure in organising republican finances. In the mid-1980s, he was a vice-president of Sinn Féin. He left the republican ranks as his trade union career developed but still held his 'unrepentant republican' views and maintained friendships established in earlier years. It subsequently emerged that when Brian Keenan, a leading IRA man with Army Council membership on his CV, was in Dublin for cancer treatment, he stayed at Flynn's house.

Flynn said that he was invited to get involved with Chesterton in late 2003. He had the financial viability of the company checked out by Daniel O'Connell, a former director of Bank of Scotland (Ireland). 'I am absolutely satisfied that Chesterton is OK. There's no-one saying anything is wrong with Chesterton,' Flynn said.

There were business opportunities in Eastern Europe. Flynn and Cunningham travelled to Bulgaria to explore investment opportunities in early 2004. They had lunch with the government minister with responsibility for inward investment as well as contacting lawyers and opening bank accounts. 'We did all the business in Sofia. We spent five days there and had 30 meetings and looked at a rake of options,' Flynn confirmed.[28] Daniel O'Connell was also on the trip, which he said was to investigate potential property investments. He said he was '100 percent innocent and had nothing to hide on the matter.'[29]

There was media speculation that plans were under way to purchase a commercial bank in Bulgaria, and that, with the proceeds of the Northern Bank raid, those responsible were set to buy in to the deal. Reports that there was a meeting with arms dealers were strongly denied. 'I didn't meet anyone selling arms in Bulgaria. It is absolute nonsense,' Flynn said.[30]

Sinn Féin strongly rejected claims that the party was funded from the activities of money launderers. Critics of the party, however, continued to allege that its activities were bankrolled by the proceeds of criminal activity, with the money-laundering investigation in early 2005 only confirming suspicions. But claims about IRA activities generating money for Sinn Féin were not new. They had been made at regular junctures by political opponents and in the media.

In late 2003, the Irish Minister for Justice said that he was 'certain' that IRA figures were still heavily involved in organised crime. He also described Sinn Féin as being 'morally unclean'. A month after those comments from Michael McDowell, former Taoiseach John Bruton responded to allegations that individuals in the IRA were involved in a €2.5m construction industry fraud. Bruton rejected the idea that Sinn Féin and the IRA should be treated as a separate movement or that the political party be treated separately from its individual members: 'If Sinn Féin has associations of this kind, nobody should vote for them. A party that is associated with crime doesn't deserve a single vote.'[31]

Sinn Féin vigorously contested the allegations as 'outdated republican bashing'. Caoimhghín Ó Caoláin said that party members were hurt and vexed at the suggestions. The Cavan–Monaghan TD declared that there was no such linkage between Sinn Féin and organised crime.[32] To counter the claims that its activities were part-funded by criminal activities, Sinn Féin released its audited annual accounts, although these figures related only to the financial activities of the party nationally.

Today, Sinn Féin runs a substantial political operation on both sides of the border. The national organisation owns two buildings on Parnell Square in Dublin which, along with its headquarters in Belfast, are conservatively valued by the party at more than €2m. In addition, local units of the party either own or rent some 47 premises on the island of Ireland. In several areas, local Sinn Féin activists pay the monthly mortgage or rent outstanding on party premises. The number of Sinn Féin buildings gives an indication of the political presence that the party has succeeded in developing across the island. These offices function as local advice centres that help to establish and maintain a near permanent Sinn Féin constituency presence.

Sinn Féin is by far the richest political party on the island of Ireland, although the events of 2004 and 2005 had a negative impact on the party's finances. Accounts for the year ended 31 December 2002 show a party with a total income of almost €1.6m, while overall expenditure was about €1.4m. Twelve months later, the income level had increased to just over €2m, with expenditure climbing to nearly €1.8m.

These income and expenditure figures related to the party's financial affairs at its central offices in Dublin and Belfast. The figures did not include the financial activities of local Sinn Féin branches in constituencies across Ireland. These branches tend to exist independently of head office so their income and expenditure are accounted for locally.

Sinn Féin employs over 60 people in a full-time capacity. Half of these employees are based in the party's offices in Dublin and Belfast. They receive a weekly gross salary of €500. Each of the party's public representatives has a designated full-time assistant although most of the latter personnel are paid by the Irish and British exchequers. Voluntary workers staff most of the party's local offices although, without the publication of the accounts of the local organisations, it is impossible to estimate what types of expense arrangements are in place.

The salary bill at Sinn Féin's central offices in Dublin and in Belfast hit half a million euro in 2003. The party also ran up considerable motoring and subsistence expenses—over €130,000 in 2003—while campaign, conference and election costs also made up a sizable chunk of the party's outgoings.

Given the scale and the cost of the Sinn Féin machine, it is not surprising that the party has a significant fundraising demand. The party receives money from a variety of sources—private donations, its own members and elected representatives, as well as from the Irish state and the United Kingdom government.

The bulk of the €2m income received in 2003 came from the Irish and British exchequers in the form of state assistance provided to all political parties with parliamentary representation. State funding in the Irish Republic provided almost €700,000, while exchequer funding in Northern Ireland added another €216,000. The difficulties in the peace process in 2004 and 2005 resulted in a curtailment in the money that Sinn Féin received from the British state. The party's allowances at Stormont and at Westminster were put on hold as a form of punishment for the alleged involvement of the IRA in several controversial incidents in 2004 and 2005. The financial sanctions pushed Sinn Féin into the red for the first time in many years in 2004.

On top of the figures from public sources, the party declared nearly half a million euro in private and business donations in 2003, while national party fundraising events and membership registration fees contributed another €120,000 to the Sinn Féin coffers. In addition, over half a million euro was received from Sinn Féin elected representatives who are mandated to hand over a portion of their parliamentary salaries for the party to spend on political activities.

Naturally, Sinn Féin public representatives were to the fore in rejecting allegations that the party benefited from criminal funding. 'I can state categorically that Sinn Féin is not a criminal conspiracy and we're not involved in criminality,' Mary Lou McDonald said, adding, 'Every penny and every cent is accounted for. We can stand over our accounts.'[33]

In the United States, its fundraising arm, Friends of Sinn Féin, represents the party. The organisation, which has offices in Washington and New York, actively promotes the Sinn Féin agenda in the United States, while also raising funds for the party. Sinn Féin has done very well since the 1994 IRA ceasefire, with several wealthy Irish-Americans deciding to help consolidate the peace process in Northern Ireland by donating to the republican cause. Among their ranks was the billionaire businessman, Chuck Feeney, who for several years after the first ceasefire donated $20,000 every month to Friends of Sinn Féin in Washington.

The peace dividend for Sinn Féin has been enormous in the United States. According to Larry Downes of Friends of Sinn Féin, the organisation has raised €5m in the US since 1997. There has been continuous growth in the money raised in the US in the period since the 1994 IRA ceasefire was called. Despite the party's left-wing policies and association with the communist bloc in the European Parliament, Irish communities across the United States—and American business people, in particular—continue to welcome warmly the presence of Sinn Féin leaders. These US trips revolve around dinners and other fundraising events for Sinn Féin.

For many Irish-Americans there is keen interest in meeting the visiting republicans who are very often perceived as men of peace and the originators of the peace process in Northern Ireland. For example, when Martin McGuinness arrived in Newport in September 2003, the local Irish-American community came to see him out of a mixture of support and curiosity. McGuinness was on a North American trip that included Sinn Féin fundraisers in New York, Boston and Toronto. One of those at the $100 a head dinner in Newport said that he thought the payment was 'money well spent', and admitted, 'I think everyone in this room feels that way or they wouldn't be here. This is money that will be spent to promote peace and a united Ireland.'[34]

Few people in this category of donor delve too deeply into the Sinn Féin policy agenda outside the peace process. These people do not worry that they are donating to a political party with a 'left, republican agenda'. Again, the Sinn Féin leaders trade on their celebrity appeal, universal recognition and association with peacemaking. One obviously awe-struck local in Newport told the local newspaper that the dinner 'was a great opportunity to see and meet one of the people primarily responsible for the peace in Northern Ireland'.[35]

Donations from the United States—and, to a lesser extent, Australia —account for the bulk of all private and corporate monies received by Sinn Féin, although new rules in the Irish Republic have placed restrictions on the ability of all political parties to raise money overseas. No such restrictions apply, however, in Northern Ireland, so Sinn Féin can legally fundraise in the United States and bring profits home to be spent on its activities north of the border.

Legislation in the Irish Republic requires public declaration only where a donation received exceeds €5,078, while the maximum annual donation from a single source cannot be greater than €6,348. Since 1997, Sinn Féin has declared non-foreign donations of about €250,000 which, given the fact that the party's support is still concentrated amongst working-class voters, may explain why the party in either part of Ireland has failed to attract significant business or personal financial support. Not unlike politicians in other parties, Sinn Féin candidates tend to receive small-scale donations from local businesses and supporters to fund constituency activities and to fight election campaigns. The sums involved are in the region of about €70,000 in donations spread over the period since 1997, although the bulk of this money was received after 2000.

Alongside money from private and business donors Sinn Féin has, as mentioned previously, been in receipt of sizable amounts of public money from the Irish and British exchequers. Electoral successes have given the party greater access to official state monies for parliamentary and political activities, and because of its activity in the Republic and in Northern Ireland, Sinn Féin has been able to dip into these funding sources in both jurisdictions.

In the Republic, all political parties with parliamentary representation are entitled to money from two state-funded schemes. A Party Leader's Allowance is paid for use on parliamentary activities, including research, and is calculated by reference to the number of TDs a party has in Dáil Éireann. Since 1997—with Sinn Féin for the first time formally implementing its post-abstentionist attitude to Leinster House—the party has received over €1m from this scheme. The annual amount now runs in excess of €250,000 because of the progress made by Sinn Féin in the 2002 general election.

In addition to the Party Leader's Allowance, state money is also paid to registered political parties that secure at least 2 per cent of the first preference votes at the most recent Dáil election. Sinn Féin qualifies for this money and the party has received almost €1.5m since this fund was established in 1998. The current annual amount exceeds €400,000. In all, the Irish taxpayer gives Sinn Féin in the region of €700,000 every year to fund its non-electoral activities, including policy research, the promotion of women's participation and organisation of political training schemes.

The ceasefire years have been good for the republican movement's financial coffers. Taking advantage of the peace process, Sinn Féin has gained in electoral terms and, with greater support at the ballot box, the party has benefited from greater access to official funding sources. In addition to the money Sinn Féin obtains for its parliamentary involvement in the Irish Republic, the party has also been in receipt of resources from the British state because it has MPs at Westminster. In keeping with Sinn Féin's abstentionist policy—which continues to exist for Westminster—none of the party's MPs take their seats, but until March 2005 they were entitled to claim expenses at the House of Commons.

Gerry Adams was first elected to the British Parliament in 1983 but he lost his seat in 1992. He was re-elected five years later, along with Martin McGuinness. In 2001, Adams and McGuinness were joined by two other Sinn Féin MPs, Pat Doherty and Michelle Gildernew. Conor Murphy joined his four party colleagues at Westminster after the 2005 British general election. It was only in the aftermath of the 2001 Westminster election that Sinn Féin was allowed to claim the financial benefits and use the facilities available to all members of the House of Commons.

Despite Sinn Féin's antagonistic attitude to the Westminster parliament and long-standing abstentionist policy, the party took considerable exception when in May 1997 the Speaker of the House of Commons decided that, 'those who chose not to take their seats should not have access to the many benefits and facilities that are now available in the House without also taking up their responsibilities as Members.'[36] The decision was directed at Sinn Féin and the party's MPs who were unwilling to swear or affirm to be faithful and 'to bear true allegiance' to the British monarch, as required under the Parliamentary Oath.

Sinn Féin challenged the 1997 ruling as far as the European Court of Human Rights. The case taken by Martin McGuinness was ultimately unsuccessful and the exclusion policy remained in place until December 2001 when, to advance the peace process, the Blair government decided to allow abstentionist MPs to claim expenses and use the facilities at the House of Commons.

The changes were passed on 8 January 2002 and, 13 days later, Adams and his colleagues went to Westminster to claim their entitlements, although as they still refused to take the oath of allegiance and their parliamentary seats, they were not paid their MPs' salary. At the time, Adams declared: 'There will never, ever be Sinn Féin MPs sitting in the British Houses of Parliament.'[37] It was left to Seamus Mallon of the SDLP to point out the hypocrisy of the Sinn Féin position in practising an abstentionist policy but taking money for involvement in parliamentary life at Westminster.

Despite its opposition to Westminster, Sinn Féin did well from the parliament whose authority the party rejected. After the January 2002 decision, the Sinn Féin MPs were each entitled to staffing allowances and other expenses worth a maximum of about £120,000 (about €170,000). Each MP could employ three full-time staff to help them with their parliamentary activities, while they were also in receipt of other allowances, including free stationery and telephone and postal services. Moreover, should any of the Sinn Féin MPs lose their seat at a future election, they will receive a resettlement grant to assist with the costs of adjusting to 'non-parliamentary life'. The amount paid is based on the age of the MP and their length of service but would exceed £30,000 (about €40,000).

In the year from April 2003 to March 2004, the four Sinn Féin MPs claimed allowances and expenses which totalled almost £440,000 (about €630,000). For example, Gerry Adams claimed a total of £110,000 in this period which included £18,268 as a reimbursement 'for necessary costs incurred when staying overnight away from their main home for the purpose of performing parliamentary duties'; £18,798 for office and equipment costs; £64,263 for employment of staff; £5,653 to cover the cost of travel on parliamentary business; and £554 to cover the cost of stationery and his use of pre-paid postage from Westminster.[38] Interestingly, the DUP leader Ian Paisley who participates fully in the life of the House of Commons claimed only £80,000 in the same period between 2003 and 2004—almost 40 per cent less than claimed by the Sinn Féin president.

In March 2005, the House of Commons passed a motion withdrawing these parliamentary allowances from Sinn Féin as a signal of displeasure with the controversies of the recent past. The action, according to one government minister, expressed: 'the profound disapproval of this House for the activities of the Provisional IRA and the responsibility which Sinn Féin shares for these activities in the estimation of the Independent Monitoring Commission.'[39]

The Independent Monitoring Commission had, a few weeks previously, reported on IRA involvement in criminality and the matter of who was responsible for the death of Belfast man Robert McCartney outside a bar in Belfast. A little over a year earlier, another IMC report blamed the IRA for the attempted abduction of republican Bobby Tohill, coincidentally also outside a bar in Belfast. Sanctions against Sinn Féin were recommended on foot of the 2004 report, and the party's allowances at Stormont were subsequently withdrawn for a 12-month period. On foot of the February 2005 report, those sanctions were expanded to include the party's parliamentary allowances at Westminster. The loss of the Stormont and Westminster money was a double whammy for Sinn Féin. The sanctions hit the party finances by not far off an annual amount of €1m.

But the criminality controversy hit the party's coffers in another way. Since he was first granted a US visa in early 1994, Gerry Adams has been a significant draw in the United States. Irish-Americans were drawn to Sinn Féin and its involvement in the peace process.

But the controversies in 2004 and 2005 damaged the party's image in the United States. There was considerable unease in Washington over the case of the so-called Colombia Three, with unconfirmed allegations of IRA links with the FARC rebel group in that South American country. In the post-9/11 world, greater attention was paid in the United States to Sinn Féin's associations with anti-system groups and regimes, which had least favoured status with the Washington government. Sinn Féin has long had links with the Castro regime in Cuba, but when Gerry Adams visited the island in December 2001, even some of the most public backers of the republican cause in the United States were upset. The Sinn Féin president had been advised by the White House and long-time supporters like Congressman Peter King not to travel to Cuba. In addition Sinn Féin's credibility took an obvious hit with the damaging revelations in the aftermath of the Northern Bank heist and the murder of Robert McCartney in Belfast.

When Adams travelled to the United States in March 2005, doors, which had opened to Sinn Féin in the aftermath of the 1994 IRA ceasefire, were firmly closed. But it was not just the lack of invitations from President Bush and Senator Edward Kennedy that illustrated the Sinn Féin predicament. Adams still had influential figures to meet and brief on the most recent developments in Northern Ireland. But all fundraising events were postponed. 'Initially, many of the planned events were to be fundraisers. However, the party leadership was concerned that fundraising could become a contentious issue and a distraction from the necessary work of rebuilding the peace process,' a Sinn Féin spokesperson explained.[40]

During the peace process years, the Sinn Féin political programme had been developed within a financial framework that included significant Irish-American backing and parliamentary allowances from the British exchequer. A reduction in those sources, even on a temporary basis, obviously had an impact as Sinn Féin discovered in 2004 when it was forced to use its reserves to maintain its established level of activities.

There are several other income sources that assist Sinn Féin in running its political activities throughout Ireland. The party has a policy whereby all Sinn Féin elected representatives hand over a portion of their parliamentary salaries. For example, in 2003, the party's twelve Assembly members in Northern Ireland and five TDs in the Irish Republic contributed just over €100,000 to Sinn Féin. In general, national political figures each give the party about €6,000 every year.

Sinn Féin also has the ability to generate money from its own commercial operations, including the weekly newspaper, *An Phoblacht*. It is the only political party to benefit from a weekly publication. For over 20 years, the party has sold a whole range of republican memorabilia in its shops and, more recently, on the Internet. Among the merchandise items that generate revenue are republican diaries and calendars, as well as party-produced videos of key events like the party Ard Fheis and the annual commemoration parade at Bodenstown in County Kildare.

Sinn Féin sells a wide range of material supportive of the IRA campaign. For example, every year a 'Republican Resistance Calendar' is produced. The calendar generally contains an array of republican images, mixing historical and contemporary events to create the seamless lineage to the past. So, IRA members in military dress, with their weaponry, feature alongside photographs from the War of Independence. Moreover, images of modern-day leaders like Adams and McGuinness are located near pictures of leading personalities from Irish history.

The advertising copy for the 1986 calendar provides an excellent example of the type of historical synergy propagated by the IRA and Sinn Féin. The 1986 calendar was produced to mark the seventieth anniversary of the 1916 Rising—'excellently produced and colourful'—and its selling points included:

> . . . the centrespread is illustrated with the Proclamation and photographs of the seven signatories. Full-colour photographs of republican murals in Belfast and Derry are featured on the other pages with quotations from the IRA, Padraig Pearse, James Connolly and Bobby Sands. Past republican events are remembered each day of the year and the back page has a full-size photograph of five armed Volunteers of the South Armagh Brigade, Óglaigh na hÉireann.[41]

This overlap between Sinn Féin and the IRA went well beyond the political organisation acting as a sales point for republican paramilitary memorabilia. There was membership overlap and strategic policy co-ordination between the two elements of the republican movement. What is less clear cut, however, is the financial relationship that existed between Sinn Féin and the IRA.

The IMC concluded in November 2004 that there was 'no fundamental change in the capacity of the organisation or in its maintenance of a state of preparedness, but we find no evidence of activity that might presage a return to a paramilitary campaign.'[42] Given this conclusion, the obvious question remains: why—and for what end—had the IRA been engaged in fundraising?

In a ceasefire environment, some people have exploited the relative inactivity to use their expertise to take advantage of opportunities to line their own pockets. There is mounting evidence that some republicans moved from what can be described as 'ideologically driven fundraising' into the arena of organised crime. The lines between the two had become increasingly blurred as paramilitaries pursued purely criminal activity.

Security authorities on both sides of the border describe these individuals as 'criminal entrepreneurs'—people who are willing to exploit criminal opportunities provided the profits involved are sufficiently high. Dissident republicans have been more open to sharing knowledge and operations with criminal elements, but IRA members also ventured into this lucrative world. The security forces continue to investigate links between known republicans and criminal activity. 'I am aware that the Garda has been investigating certain activities by people who may have connections with the Provisional IRA,' was how Bertie Ahern put it in December 2003.

Almost a year later, the Independent Monitoring Commission observed:

> It is also clear that some crimes are committed by individuals or groups of individuals from within a paramilitary group on their own behalf, whether for personal gain or in pursuit of grudges or revenge. These crimes clearly have paramilitary connections but may or may not have an organisational sanction. The result is that what constitutes a paramilitary crime is much less clear than might be assumed. . . .[43]

The financial side to the republican movement may be the greatest impediment to the full retirement of all IRA members as ordered by the organisation in its statement in July 2005. A vast financial network has been established over many years but not all the money raised by the republican movement found its way directly into its coffers. There can be no doubt but that individual republicans kept some of the money to fund lifestyles which would have been unsustainable from their legitimate income sources. Several years after the signing of the Belfast Agreement, the stark choice faced by the Adams leadership was whether or not these people were to be allowed to prevent the Irish peace process from transforming itself into a workable political process.

Sinn Féin's participation in democratic politics was totally incompatible with its links with an armed paramilitary organisation. The Provisional IRA may have been born with the objective of ending British rule in all parts of Ireland but, in the peace process era, the IRA was increasingly becoming an impediment to Adams building a political movement. In a post-IRA political environment, critics of the republican movement will obviously closely monitor Sinn Féin's financial position to see whether there is any change in the funds available for its activities on both sides of the border.

POLICY POSITIONS AND ELECTORAL STRATEGIES BEYOND 2005

S inn Féin sees itself as a party of opposition, a party of protest. It has successfully occupied the ground of the disaffected sections of Irish society, championing their causes but often without any serious scrutiny of the alternative republican policy prescription. Sinn Féin's self-image is that of a political party on the left of the political spectrum in Irish politics. Asked to characterise his party, Gerry Adams said: 'Sinn Féin in its entire philosophy is based on the 1916 proclamation. It's a republican party. Sinn Féin believes in equality and social issues as well as economic issues. It's a party of the left.'[1]

For many years, Sinn Féin described itself as a socialist republican party. The word 'socialist' still features in the Sinn Féin constitution. In more recent times, however, party leaders have dispensed with the term 'socialist' as a label of self-description. The phrase 'left' has become a more popular alternative, indicating a degree of self-censorship as the party repositions itself politically to garner increased electoral popularity. Mary Lou McDonald offered the following explanation: 'Very often people get into the semantics of the "ism's". But for us what the socialist agenda is about is fairness and equality in terms of access to services and a real sense of participative citizenship.'[2]

The Sinn Féin characterisation can obviously mean a variety of different things, as the terms 'republican' and 'socialist' operate on a variety of levels, according to one's ideological vocabulary. In the writings of Karl Marx, socialism is a phase that precedes the arrival of a communist existence. There is little in the writings of contemporary Sinn Féin or in the speeches of its principal figures to indicate that they see themselves on a journey to some communist utopia. Certainly, in the post-1989 fall of the Berlin Wall world, a political aspiration towards a communist state would be counterproductive as a political and electoral vote winner.

The difficulty, however, is that, outside its pre-communist existence, socialism is a very ill-defined concept. The term 'left' is also ill defined but can, in the context of Sinn Féin, be taken as meaning the creation of a government with very strong state control over all facets of life, including economic activity. There is considerable evidence across recent Sinn Féin policy documents to conclude that the party favours much greater state control in terms of economic planning and also direct ownership of industry and other sectoral activities.

A Sinn Féin policy document from 2003 posed the question—'what are "left policies"?' The answer provided by the party offers some indication of its own perception of its positioning on the political and ideological spectrum.

> As a left republican party, Sinn Féin believes that equality must be the cornerstone of our society and our economy. People should be treated as citizens with rights, not just consumers with more or less spending power. Government policies should be driven by the needs of citizens, not the demands of the market.[3]

When the cross-community power-sharing administration operated in Northern Ireland between 1998 and 2003, Martin McGuinness and Bairbre de Brún were the two Sinn Féin ministerial nominees. The party opted for big-budget ministerial portfolios—Health and Education—which allowed a focus on a socially reforming agenda. There were positive assessments of the performances of the two Sinn Féin ministers in the relatively short period during which the institutions actually functioned properly. But interestingly, the policy choices made by De Brún in particular illustrated just how pragmatic republicans could be. When it came to choices on locating a maternity hospital in West Belfast, the Sinn Féin health minister made a decision that favoured her electoral constituency.

The party is far more liberal on social and moral-type issues than its opponents in Northern Ireland or in the Irish Republic, although considerable internal differences do exist within Sinn Féin. Indeed, on several occasions, the liberal–conservative divisions within the party have been played out in public. But as republicans have traditionally been far from holding governmental office, and almost exclusively focused on constitutional issues, their lack of internal cohesion on other policy matters has attracted little attention. Sinn Féin backed the 1996 referendum to allow for divorce in the Republic, while the party has called for the introduction of legislation to allow same-sex couples to be allowed to marry and adopt children.

But liberalism within Sinn Féin has certain limits. Attitudes towards abortion have been as divisive within republican ranks as in the other political parties, on both sides of the border—parties which Gerry Adams likes to categorise as 'conservative'.

When the controversial subject consumed political and public life in the Republic in the 1980s, Sinn Féin formally remained outside the debate as the party did not recognise the 1937 Constitution. That fact, however, did not prevent Sinn Féin activists from participating in the referendum campaign or putting the subject of abortion on the agenda of their party's annual conference.

Party policy in the early 1980s was one of 'total opposition' to abortion but the Sinn Féin Ard Comhairle sought to strike a middle-ground position at the 1985 Ard Fheis. Delegates passed a leadership-sponsored motion which noted the party's opposition 'to abortion as a means of birth control, but we accept the need for abortion where the woman's life is at risk or in grave danger (e.g. ectopic pregnancy and all forms of cancer)'.

But this attempt at appeasing the diverse viewpoints on abortion backfired when, against the wishes of the party leadership, the conference delegates narrowly backed a motion recognising 'that women have the right to choose'. The vote was 77 votes to 73. A report in *An Phoblacht* noted, 'the vote on this motion was taken twice in an atmosphere of growing excitement as it became clear that the result would be close.'

But the policy—which identified Sinn Féin with a very liberal stance on abortion—did not remain in place for long. At the 1986 Ard Fheis, the party once more modified its attitude to abortion, adopting a position more in tune with that recommended by the party leadership. Like the wider public debate on abortion, Sinn Féin's policy has evolved but remains very much an accommodating consensus-seeking centrist position.

When the Northern Ireland Assembly debated the subject, there was near unanimity across the political spectrum in rejecting an extension of liberal British abortion laws to Northern Ireland. One Sinn Féin representative said:

Our party position is that we oppose abortion on demand or abortion as a form of birth control. We accept the need for abortion where a woman's life or mental health is at risk or in grave danger and in cases of rape and sexual abuse.[4]

A motion passed at the 2004 Ard Fheis mandated party representatives to push for the introduction of legislation in the Republic in line with the 1992 Supreme Court ruling in the so-called X-case. This would allow for the introduction of abortion procedures in certain limited circumstances. A similar motion appeared on the agenda of the 2005 Ard Fheis—one of 43 motions listed for discussion in the health session that was broadcast live on national television, although no delegate actually spoke to the abortion motion.

Sinn Féin sees itself as secular in its approach to social and moral issues although this has not prevented many of its leading members from openly identifying with the Roman Catholic Church. This dichotomy was illustrated in April 2004 when Martin McGuinness said:

I go to Mass every Sunday and I haven't found antagonism in Sinn Féin to the Church. Sure, people have different beliefs in all walks of life and all political parties but no one has ever questioned my religion within the Party . . . Gerry Adams, like me, regards himself as a Catholic, and finds solace in going to Mass as I do.[5]

Whatever about the Sinn Féin place on the liberal–conservative spectrum, the party would appear to have very well-defined economic policies. Three themes dominate Sinn Féin's economic thinking. Firstly, all the party's policies are, not unsurprisingly, couched in an all-Ireland framework, with continual reference to the need to create an island economy. Sinn Féin stresses the benefit of greater cross-border policy co-operation in areas like education, health, environment, agriculture, transport and tourism.

The Belfast Agreement provides for greater cross-border co-operation implemented through North–South institutional arrangements and bringing officials and politicians from Northern Ireland and the Irish Republic more closely together. Sinn Féin favours a significant expansion of the cross-border elements in the Belfast Agreement. 'Even at this embryonic stage the potential is obvious and it is clear that an all-Ireland economy would bring about considerable benefits to all of us living on the island.'[6]

There are political as well as economic motivations underpinning the enthusiasm that Sinn Féin shows for greater harmonisation of the various policy differences between the two parts of the island. This policy emphasis is consistent with the ultimate republican objective of a united Ireland, even if the possibility of such an eventuality coming about through enhanced North–South co-operation is in itself very slim.

The second dominant theme in Sinn Féin's economic outlook concerns the role of the state, which would be dramatically increased in all areas of economic life should the party's policy prescription be realised. For example, current moves to increase private-sector involvement in the provision of transport services in the Irish Republic would be ended by Sinn Féin. The party is opposed to 'any attempt to privatise public transport or our road network'. The privatisation of state assets would be excluded as a policy option—for example, Sinn Féin is very clear about its position on the future ownership of the Irish state-owned airline: 'Aer Lingus must not be sold but retained as a vital part of the state's transport infrastructure.'

Alongside preserving the status quo in relation to the public ownership of all state assets, Sinn Féin also wants greater state activism across a whole host of areas, including the construction of housing, the provision of pre-school childcare and oil exploration. This increased state intervention would prompt the third element of the Sinn Féin economic agenda—a massive expansion in government spending.

There has been little analysis of Sinn Féin policies and the priorities it would seek to include in any governmental programme in the Republic. This failure to scrutinise Sinn Féin to the same extent as other political parties with a possibility of involvement in government is partially explained by the peace process in Northern Ireland. Most of Sinn Féin's political attention has been devoted to resolving the troubles in Northern Ireland, and consequently much of the external focus on Sinn Féin has been concerned with its role in the peace process. Moreover, it is only since the party's electoral fortunes changed after the 1997 and 2002 general elections that political observers concluded that in a post-conflict environment Sinn Féin was emerging as a potential participant in government in the Republic.

The Sinn Féin policy agenda differs radically from that proposed by the other political parties with representation in Leinster House. The party envisages a world with huge amounts of public expenditure, considerable state control and restricted private enterprise. Moreover, it is impossible to determine the overall cost of the party's programmes and policies as Sinn Féin has failed to put financial figures on the alternatives that it proposes.

In a Sinn Féin idealised Ireland, the involvement of the private sector in Irish economic life would face strong government pressure and would ultimately play a significantly reduced role. This would be most evident in the banking, construction and health sectors, where a considerable expansion of the role of the state would be actively promoted.

Private banks and other financial institutions would be an early target. Sinn Féin believes that the people of Ireland should enjoy the benefits of banking profits, which the party claims, 'are siphoned out from the accounts of Irish people and Irish businesses'. The Sinn Féin solution is to bring the banks under state ownership and control— 'ultimately the banking sector should be nationalised so that the Irish people are the true beneficiaries of this vastly profitable business.'[7]

The party has little to say about how this nationalisation process would be organised and funded. The cost in public money would be enormous—just taking the four main financial institutions—AIB, Bank of Ireland, Ulster Bank and Permanent TSB—a buyer would expect to pay in the region of €40 billion.

In the economic system favoured by Sinn Féin, not only would the party seek to eliminate direct private-sector ownership in areas such as banking and transport, but the republican agenda would also oppose projects that involved co-operation between the private and public sectors. Sinn Féin has frowned upon the development of Public Private Partnerships, most particularly in the construction of the Irish road network. In explaining how its alternative policy preference would be funded, Sinn Féin points to borrowed money.

Sinn Féin in government would also target land ownership and the housing market, again with a series of interventions to increase the state's control over the sector. The state and its agencies would be given legal authority to acquire compulsorily any land deemed necessary for house building. The party predicts that there would be 'massive State investment in a new and comprehensive Social Housing Programme'.

The Irish constitution would be changed and new legislation enacted to change the behaviour of the private sector in the land market. Price controls would be introduced. A statutory ceiling on the price of land zoned for housing would—Sinn Féin claims—control the price of land which would end market speculation and reduce house prices. The private rented market would also be targeted with the introduction of rent controls.

The centrepiece of the Sinn Féin solution to the problems in the Irish health services would be the creation of a National Health Service similar to that already in existence in the United Kingdom. This Irish NHS would provide 'free care and medication for all who need it'. It would be funded exclusively by public monies and would be established in such as way as to allow the integration of the health systems in Northern Ireland and the Irish Republic. 'There can be no more important use made of taxpayers' money,' Sinn Féin claimed.[8]

Such a development would inevitably have a significant impact on the role of private medicine in the Irish health sector. Sinn Féin is very critical of the current public–private mix in the health services, arguing that 'the private sector is subsidised by taxpayers'. All tax incentives for private medical care would be ended, while medical consultants would find their ability to work in both sectors restricted.

> Consultants are being paid from the public purse for treating public patients while at the same time they profit from the thriving private health business. They are allowed to work unlimited private hours in public hospitals, using medical resources and public offices funded by the taxpayer for their business for personal private profit.[9]

The activist approach would be evident in other areas. Sinn Féin has proposed a massive expansion of spending at all levels of the education system, including the creation of a new national system of pre-school education. Access to this state-run education scheme would be guaranteed for all pre-school children, and it would be free. The management of potential oil and gas reserves off the Irish coast would also be fundamentally different under Sinn Féin. The party favours state-led exploration, with the establishment of a state-owned exploration company to undertake research and supervise the sector.

The various policy documents and pre-budget submissions prepared by Sinn Féin since 1997 confirm the classification of Sinn Féin as a 'spend and spend' party. There is no area of governmental activity where the party has not proposed a significant expansion of services, as well as the abolition of user charges. For example, in education, Sinn Féin opposes the re-introduction of fees for university-level tuition, while also proposing that registration fees be abolished and students' grants increased. In agriculture, the party wants low-interest loans for farm improvement and investment to encourage young farmers to stay on the land. Pensioners would do well from a Sinn Féin government—the party proposes linking the old-age pension to 40 per cent of the average industrial wage—an increase of about 35 per cent on its current level and a move that would cost in the region of €400m.

Spending plans are all very well but what of the ability to pay for this growth in public expenditure? In some areas—particularly in relation to capital projects—Sinn Féin has proposed extra government borrowing. While the party has not explicitly linked its ambitions for increased spending to a higher tax take, the implication is evident from the party's taxation proposals. Indeed, Sinn Féin has been very explicit about its plans for the taxation system. The party favours what it calls 'real tax reform and the creation of a just tax system'.[10]

The central plank of this system would be the introduction of what Sinn Féin calls a 'super tax'. This tax would be applied to the incomes of those described by Sinn Féin as 'super rich earners'. This new income tax would be levied at a 50 per cent rate and would apply to individuals with an annual salary that was greater than €100,000.

According to Sinn Féin, the current configuration of the tax system favours the better off, and the party believes that its tax proposals would reorient the system to the benefit of 'average workers'. The 'super tax' would be the first step in reducing this apparent imbalance, while a second line of attack would involve 'the elimination of tax avoidance measures which they ['super rich earners'] enjoy and which are out of the reach of the average worker'.

In the Sinn Féin-led restructuring of the tax system, all low-paid workers would be taken out of the tax system, with significant increases in their tax-free allowances. In its 2001 Pre-Budget Submission, the party proposed: 'doubling the single person's tax free allowance of £11,400. A single person would not pay tax unless he or she earned over £11,400 per annum and would not pay the higher rate of income tax until their earning exceeded £28,400 per annum.'[11]

In line with its approach to the private sector and the world of business, Sinn Féin is opposed to the current policy of low corporation tax. Sinn Féin would keep corporation tax at a 16 per cent rate, although a special rate would apply to financial institutions. Despite its wish to take the banking sector into public ownership, Sinn Féin favours increasing the level of corporation tax paid by Irish retail banks to a 30 per cent rate. Employer payroll taxes would be increased to 12 per cent. Capital Gains Tax would be restored to its 1997 level of 40 per cent.

Yet, despite the party's supposedly radical policies, Sinn Féin elected representatives actually send out far more consolidatory messages in terms of how they would operate if involved in governmental arrangements. Gerry Adams told the Dublin Chamber of Commerce in 2004 that he was 'reluctant to say that we would do A or we would do B. We are not in principle against tax increases, but we have no plans to introduce them. We just think that there should be a far, far better way of doing business.'

These comments tend to underline the weakness in Sinn Féin's policy outlook. The party's ideological outlook is not firmly cast. There is a radical voice that runs through the republican socioeconomic agenda but it is very muted by other party policies that indicate a strongly held pragmatism. The definition of 'left wing' offered by Mary Lou McDonald would seem to confirm a political outlook that is conscious of the need to appease a wider community beyond the current Sinn Féin core vote in the Republic:

> Obviously in any system you have to recognise the need to generate wealth. So its not that we're anti-enterprise or that we frown on ambition or wealth creation. We don't dislike wealth but we do have a difficulty with poverty. It's [left-wing politics] about the generation of wealth but then crucially it's a question of how you distribute it. And, yes, it is about public services. Access to public services is bound up with ownership of those services, and we believe that in certain essential areas the State has a legitimate role in terms of service provision.[12]

Many of Sinn Féin's current policies are obviously those of a party of opposition. The involvement of other radical protest parties in government has indicated that they do dilute their positions in return for tasting power. Moreover, the coalition governmental system in the Irish Republic—and the institutionalised cross-community power sharing in Northern Ireland—has to be built on compromise in order to function. The challenge facing Sinn Féin is to manage policy compromise while expanding its electoral base. The greater the compromise on current policy, the more the party risks losing its traditional support, but the evidence to date suggests that Sinn Féin has an excellent ability to retain its existing voter support as it develops a wider appeal.

The history of the Adams era has been marked by pragmatic decision-making. The end of abstentionism in 1986, the secret peace process talks with acceptance of the consent principle, the IRA ceasefire declaration without a British timetable to withdraw from Northern Ireland, taking seats in a Stormont assembly, appointing ministers to a government deriving its authority from Westminster, and weapons decommissioning. The substantial list has grown without a serious loss of republican political support and would appear to indicate an ability to make more u-turns and compromises in the socioeconomic policy area.

The 2002 Sinn Féin election manifesto indicated a degree of policy pragmatism, with the party shifting surprisingly somewhat towards the political centre. Proposals to support small and local businesses, which featured in the 2002 manifesto, would not be typical of a particularly left-wing policy approach. Moreover, the Sinn Féin concern with the need to tackle crime and drug addiction is more typical of parties on the more conservative end of the social policy spectrum.

One academic study of the various party manifestos in 2002 concluded that Sinn Féin was '. . . a party with a distinctive position on Northern Ireland, to be sure, but otherwise interested in moving into the territory of the mainstream Irish parties rather than marking out a distinctive position of the liberal left.'[13]

This assessment would be very much in keeping with the Fianna Fáil electoral ground that Sinn Féin wants to seize in the Republic. The strongly left-wing platform, which the party has articulated, will be an impediment to convincing significant numbers of middle-ground—and middle-class—voters to cast their ballots for republican candidates. When its time comes to enter government in Dublin, Sinn Féin may happily jettison some of its current policies.

The experience of the Irish peace process would tend to suggest that Sinn Féin might be politically flexible. The party has developed a strong trait of political pragmatism which it has displayed successively since the mid-1980s. The ending of abstentionism in the Republic in 1986 was a harbinger of further compromise to follow—IRA ceasefire, negotiations with unionism, involvement in cross-community government at Stormont, the decommissioning of weapons. Immediate British withdrawal has not been achieved; Irish unity has not been won. But Sinn Féin has continued to evolve pragmatically.

Similar pragmatism—and contradiction—has also been evident in the party's international links. During the 2003 Gulf War, the pages of *An Phoblacht/Republican News* were filled with negative comment on the role of the United States in the region. There was considerable criticism of the policies of US President George W. Bush. Gerry Adams, however, had no difficulty in meeting President Bush in the White House in March 2003. More significantly, when Adams delivered his annual leadership address at the 2003 Ard Fheis, he failed to mention the war in the Middle East. Once more, a strategy driven by pragmatism had been adopted by the Adams-backed leadership.

The United States has long played a role in the story of Irish republicanism. As discussed previously, seed money from America was important to the development of the early versions of the Sinn Féin party. Moreover, in the post-1969 period, funding from the United States sustained the IRA campaign and assisted in the development of Sinn Féin as a credible political party. But republicans were not above the occasional bit of self-censorship. The Sinn Féin message would often be adapted for different audiences with a softening of tone between Belfast and Boston.

Sinn Féin had a limited international reach in the 1970s but its leadership nonetheless attempted to forge links with what were considered like-minded causes, such as the separatist movement in the Basque region in northern Spain. At that time, caution was exercised in establishing links with leftist groups elsewhere in Europe, as the republican leadership avoided any possible contamination with Marxism or other radical ideological outlooks.

The emergence of the Adams leadership in the late 1970s and early 1980s brought a subtle reorientation in how republicans related to the external world. Many of those in the Adams group had read widely while imprisoned during the 1970s. Much of their reading material concerned left-wing politics and radical international affairs, as later confirmed when library material from the Maze Prison was released.

The Adams loyalist, Ted Howell, was to the fore in establishing common cause between the republican movement in Ireland and other self-styled international revolutionary groups engaged in so-called 'liberation struggles'. This positioning automatically opened up contact with groups in countries like South Africa, Cuba and Algeria.

Howell later observed: 'The importance of international work, of positively influencing international public and political opinion and of generating interest and the adoption of positive political positions and actions, has long been recognised as an integral and crucial part of the struggle for Irish independence.'[14]

In the 1980s, with members of the republican movement treated as outcasts in political circles in Ireland, efforts were made to win friends internationally. Indeed, during this period, Sinn Féin was intent on forging links with groups that shared a similar ideological outlook. Connection was also made with 'freedom fighters' in the other countries, especially those engaged in anti-imperialist conflicts. The presence at Sinn Féin conferences of representatives of the Palestinian movement, Basque separatists and the ANC served to develop these links. Moreover, republicans have become a familiar presence at international gatherings of anti-imperialist groups. As far back as 1985, a Sinn Féin representative was welcomed at a meeting in Palestine, where he diligently offered a message of solidarity with the people of Palestine.

If there was a common strand to the international circles that Sinn Féin representatives moved in, it was a Marxist orientation. For example, in 1983, Sean Halpenny, the party's head of foreign affairs, met with groups from the Soviet Union and North Korea.[15] Indeed, in the late 1980s, a deliberate policy was pursued to establish links with the communist regime in North Korea. In 1986, Sinn Féin sent a message of solidarity to the North Korean government. Twelve months later, while on a visit to Denmark, Gerry Adams took time out to visit the North Korean embassy in Copenhagen. He had accepted an invitation to a birthday reception from Kim Il Sung.[16] The peace process era has necessitated a Sinn Féin rethink on its international contacts and, today, it is unlikely the party would consider messages of solidarity with the North Korean regime.

Republicans also established and maintained relations with Fidel Castro's Cuba. For many years, Sinn Féin conferences passed motions of support with the Cuban regime. This position has been motivated by a sense of solidarity between Irish republicans and Cuba, based to a degree on a shared struggle—the self-perception was of small countries threatened by larger neighbours. The party, however, received considerable criticism for its continued relationship with Cuba. In late 2001, when Adams travelled to Cuba and met with Fidel Castro, the decision did not play well with senior political figures in Washington, including supporters of Sinn Féin's political strategy who put pressure on Adams not to travel. While in Cuba, the Sinn Féin president complimented the Cuban people who 'struggle despite all the difficulties, all the impoverished conditions and despite the hostility of the US Government, can survive and help others'. It was, he said, 'a big lesson to everybody.'[17]

The irony in Sinn Féin's international contacts with regimes in North Korea and Cuba has been the lack of ideological affinity. Sinn Féin has never espoused the hardline Marxist outlook promoted and practised in many of its ally countries. Indeed, it was probably convenient that the leaderships in these countries were unaware of Adams's denial in 1979 that there was a Marxist influence in his movement. Irish republicans were drawn to the themes of international struggle and anti-imperialism that provided them with a veneer of radicalism. They liked the 'them versus us'/big-country-picks-on-small-country similarities. In this regard, Sinn Féin was long to the fore in championing opposition movements in Central America, including in El Salvador and Nicaragua. This was especially so when these movements were perceived as fighting for national self-determination in the face of so-called US imperialism.

Much of the Sinn Féin interest in establishing international relations has been to legitimise the activities of the IRA. Bill Rolston's work on murals in Northern Ireland confirms this point, making reference to the implicit message in a Belfast mural that depicted woman militants from the PLO and SWAPO alongside Irish republican women. One mural depicts a PLO member and an IRA volunteer holding a rocket launcher underneath the slogan 'One Struggle'.[18]

The most obvious parallel was drawn with the struggle for freedom in South Africa. Writing in 1986, Adams stressed the similarities between the IRA and the ANC and noted that there was a 'natural, instinctive and deep affinity with the ANC and with the black majority who are oppressed in South Africa.'[19] Images of Nelson Mandela have featured in West Belfast murals, and his description of Sinn Féin as an 'old friend and ally' helped cement the relationship.[20]

Without doubt, from the Sinn Féin vantage point, the ANC connection also served to give legitimacy to the IRA campaign of violence. Adams first visited South Africa in 1995 and he has used the example of the ANC's peaceful transition into the democratic process as one that Irish republicans had to seek to replicate. Sinn Féin has copied several aspects of the ANC strategy including the public promotion of identifiable representatives and progressing the peace process at a pace that ensures continued and unified grassroot support.

In recent times, Sinn Féin's international alliances have been subjected to considerable scrutiny. The continued relationship with Basque separatists has been one source of controversy, especially in the aftermath of the breakdown in the 14-month ETA ceasefire in early 2000 and the subsequent banning of its political ally, Batasuna. But invitations to Batasuna representatives to attend the annual Sinn Féin Ard Fheis continue to be issued, and delegates continue to give their Batasuna guests a very warm welcome. Even after the 9/11 attacks in the United States in 2001, the invitation was issued and accepted.

Despite the obvious Sinn Féin support for 'armed struggles' elsewhere

—even when the IRA ceasefire was in place—the inconsistency and hypocrisy was by-passed, because to sever such connections would probably cause considerable internal unease within the republican movement.

A different insight into the wide-ranging international contacts established and maintained by the republican movement was provided after the arrest of three Irishmen in Colombia in August 2001. The central allegation was that the three men, travelling on false passports, were training anti-government rebels in urban guerrilla warfare. The FARC was reported to have been offering finance in return for the provision of this expertise. The fact that the FARC was known to have acquired much of its monies from drug trafficking seemed not to have disturbed the three Irishmen.

The IRA denied that the three men were on 'official' republican business in Colombia. Gerry Adams observed, 'they were not there to represent Sinn Féin. I would have to authorise such a project and I did not do so. Neither was I or anyone else asked.'[21] But two months later, Adams was forced to backtrack when it emerged that one of the men was the Sinn Féin representative in Cuba. All Adams could say was that the proper internal procedures had not been followed in the appointment of Connolly.

A huge Sinn Féin effort was put into defending the three men; securing their release—and, if possible, proving their innocence—was vital to preserve Sinn Féin's support in the United States. The reappearance of the men in Ireland in August 2005 closed the issue as far as Sinn Féin was concerned, notwithstanding continued questioning of what the men were doing in South America in the first place, and how they later came to abscond from Colombia.

But no single issue has been allowed to get in the way of the onward progression of the Adams-led transformation of Sinn Féin as the only element within the republican movement. Embarrassing episodes like that in Colombia, and even earlier allegations of gun running in Florida, were sidestepped. But the conclusion of the peace process necessitates an end to such controversies. The events of late 2004 and early 2005 finally brought matters to a point where excuses and delays from republicans were no longer enough to keep the process moving forward, even at a snail's pace. As on previous occasions, Adams decided that 'the principle of success' would determine the future of his strand of Irish republicanism. The 1985 Hartley declaration once more underpinned the strategic decision-making within the Adams-led leadership.

The Hartley declaration can also be used to describe the attitude and mind-set that Sinn Féin would apply to any negotiations on government formation in the Irish Republic. The party's agenda will be driven by the 'principle of success', and that ultimately means government and the acceptance of policy compromise. But how this is achieved will depend on the level of support obtained by Sinn Féin candidates in future elections. The larger the vote for Sinn Féin, and the greater the party's parliamentary representation, the more powerful Sinn Féin will be in getting its policy agenda implemented.

Sinn Féin has had a long history of antagonism towards electoral politics, as discussed in greater detail in Chapter 4. Those traditional attitudes have, however, been discarded under the Adams leadership. From the early 1980s onwards, the party tapped into a republican constituency in Northern Ireland but it is only since the 1994 IRA ceasefire was called that Sinn Féin's potential electoral strength in both parts of Ireland has become evident.

This potential was most recently realised in June 2004 when voters in the Irish Republic went to the polls in elections to the European Parliament and local councils across the country. The party had high hopes for Mary Lou McDonald, its Dublin candidate. McDonald attracted huge media attention given her middle-class background and her post-1994 IRA ceasefire entry into republican politics. The 34-year-old went to a fee-paying secondary school, studied literature at Trinity College, Dublin, and had a postgraduate degree in European Studies. She had joined Fianna Fáil before turning to Sinn Féin in 2000.

> It was very simple. I was just in the wrong party. I didn't feel that Fianna Fáil had within it the capacity to deliver on the things I felt were very important—on the national question, in terms of driving national reunification but also, and equally important, in terms of issues of equality and issues of social justice.[22]

McDonald is typical of the new generation of recruits into Sinn Féin since the 1994 ceasefire was called and particularly since the party signed up to the Belfast Agreement in 1998. Interested in republicanism but with no lived experience of the conflict in Northern Ireland, they have injected renewed energy into Sinn Féin ranks, while also allowing the party to push new non-IRA candidates in elections in the Republic. With her background, it was little wonder than Sinn Féin pushed McDonald so strongly in the Dublin constituency.

When the first count results were declared in the small hours of the morning, McDonald danced a 'wee jig' in celebration. Her victory in Dublin and a raft of other results across the country confirmed the speculator growth in the Sinn Féin vote over the previous decade and also that the party was bedding in for the long haul. It would seem that the 'long electoral campaign' pursued by Sinn Féin was on the verge of replacing the IRA's 'long military campaign'.

There was a certain irony that the Sinn Féin breakthrough came in elections to the European Parliament. The party had actually boycotted the first direct European elections back in 1979. That contest was, however, the only time Sinn Féin stood aside from elections to the parliaments in Strasbourg and Brussels because by the time the next campaign came around, five years later, in 1984, there had been a near historic change in party policy.

In the early 1980s Sinn Féin was re-examining its 60-year-old policy of refusing to take seats won in the parliaments in Dublin, London and Belfast. This abstentionist policy went to the very core of Irish republicanism—built, as it was, upon the refusal of Sinn Féin and the IRA to recognise the legitimacy of any of these parliamentary institutions. The performance of the prisoner candidates in elections in 1981 convinced the Adams leadership that the traditional policy had little strategic merit in the Irish Republic where the majority of the population looked to Leinster House as the legitimate parliament. The republican policy in relation to any assembly in Northern Ireland and in relation to Westminster remained unchallenged.

The overhauling of this fundamental principle in relation to the parliament in the Irish Republic came after several years of internal debate. One harbinger of the political and ideological transformation that was under way was the party's 1983 Ard Fheis when delegates opted to contest on an attendance basis all future elections to the European Parliament. Indeed, the European Parliament became the first significant assembly in 60 years that Sinn Féin committed its candidates to taking their seats in should they be elected. The move was also the first tangible indicator of the bitter dispute being fought within republicanism over Sinn Féin's future direction—it was one of the reasons why veteran republican Ruairí Ó Brádaigh stood down as party president at the 1983 Ard Fheis.

Despite the new policy, Sinn Féin in 1983 still held on to its protest position, declaring that any party MEPs would follow an anti-imperialist policy of opposition to the European Economic Community, as the European Union was then known. Moreover, any Sinn Féin MEP would sit in the parliament only 'with the declared intention of working for the disbandment of the EEC as a European capitalist bloc.'[23]

It would, however, be 21 years before Sinn Féin would be in a position to test this mandate in the European Parliament. By the time Sinn Féin MEPs arrived in Brussels, the party's policy was the most anti-European of the Irish political parties although the language used by Sinn Féin had moderated considerably.

In any event, for most of those years, voters in the Irish Republic were not interested in sending a Sinn Féin political representative to Brussels and Strasbourg, with the party suffering successive defeats in the polls. The Sinn Féin European performance in Northern Ireland was somewhat better, but with John Hume as the SDLP candidate, the single seat that nationalists could realistically hope to secure was never likely to be won by Sinn Féin.

Given the poor electoral history of the party in the Irish Republic from the mid-1980s through to the early-1990s, the transformation in recent elections has been substantial. The success in the European Parliament elections in 2004 was the most visible sign of the electoral arrival of Sinn Féin, although the party's performance in the local elections in the same year may well be the real signal for further growth over the coming years.

The celebratory scenes at count centres in Dublin and Belfast in June 2004 continued a pattern of electoral advance for Sinn Féin in the decade since the first IRA ceasefire in August 1994. The beginning of this Sinn Féin electoral advance in the Republic was clearly evident in the 1997 general election results. The average Sinn Féin candidate support increased to 3,041 votes (compared to 678 votes in 1992) while 12 of the party's 15 candidates won sufficient support to hold on to their election deposits, something candidates representing Sinn Féin had not been very good at. More important, however, was the fact that in 1997 Sinn Féin won its first post-abstentionist seat in Leinster House.

Caoimhghín Ó Caoláin topped the poll in the Cavan–Monaghan constituency. He was the first Sinn Féin TD to be elected to Dáil Éireann since 1957. But the important difference in 1997 was that Ó Caoláin would take his seat in Leinster House. The significance of his election was not lost on the former bank official who had been a Sinn Féin activist since the 1981 hunger strikes: 'People are accustomed now to the flag waving and air punching reaction of the Sinn Féin team when success is delivered. It [the 1997 victory] was quite a unique moment and everybody was clearly euphoric.'[24]

The end of the broadcast ban against republicans in early 1994 allowed the Irish public for the first time to hear Adams and his colleagues on the airwaves. The party garnered huge profile—and goodwill—on account of the IRA's cessation of military operations in August 1994. But while the terms of Sinn Féin's involvement in the 1997 electoral contest had been dramatically altered, the campaign was conducted in a period when the IRA was off-ceasefire. The first ceasefire was ended in February 1996 although the IRA campaign had not been renewed with anything like the same ruthlessness as previously. There was also an expectation that a second cessation could be secured during the summer months of 1997. Nevertheless, the Irish electorate was fully aware that violence was again an option to be exercised by the republican movement, and lives were going to be lost.

In this 'vote-for-peace' environment, Sinn Féin polled well. The 1999 local elections in the Republic allowed Sinn Féin to consolidate and build on its promising electoral position in various parts of the country. The party trebled its local government representation, winning 21 seats across 10 of the 34 councils, with an important showing in Dublin where the four Sinn Féin councillors all looked like potential Dáil winners.

The emergence of Sinn Féin was evident in the opinion polls undertaken during the life of the 28th Dáil. After the 1997 general election, Sinn Féin had a poll rating of 2 per cent but by the time the last *Irish Times*/MRBI poll was undertaken prior to the calling of the 2002 general election, that figure had risen to 8 per cent. Facing into the 2002 general election in the Republic, the practical electoral benefit from that trebling of Sinn Féin's council seats in the Republic was matched by the psychological boost of overtaking the SDLP as the largest nationalist party in Northern Ireland in the 2001 Westminster elections.

In the 2002 general election in the Republic, Sinn Féin concentrated on a number of target constituencies, with party officials believing that three to four seats could be added to the Cavan–Monaghan seat first won in 1997. As in previous elections since the ending of the abstentionist policy, Sinn Féin had two key constituencies that it tapped for support—people living in poorer urban communities who had not benefited from the economic boom, and people living mainly in rural areas, where there was a traditional republican vote. The strategy—while limited to a handful of constituencies—paid dividends.

The results of the 2002 and 2004 elections in the Irish Republic indicate that Sinn Féin is now in transition from being a party of protest to potentially being a substantial player on the political scene in Ireland. The sense of celebration south of the border was matched in Northern Ireland where Sinn Féin added to its 2001 Westminster success by becoming the largest nationalist party in elections to the Northern Ireland Assembly, in November 2003. There were more gains in the 2005 elections with a fifth Westminster seat and an even greater Sinn Féin presence on local government councils across Northern Ireland.

The SDLP has been relegated into a secondary position as the Adams electoral project has gone from success to success. In the Republic, Sinn Féin support has not only widened but it has also deepened. The typical Sinn Féin voter in 2004 was male, under the age of 35 and came from a working-class background. Whereas previously the typical Sinn Féin voter was out of work, now the party has more supporters who are employed than unemployed.

The typical voter who supported Mary Lou McDonald in the Dublin constituency in 2004 was from this background. McDonald attracted support from 20 per cent of all male voters, compared to only 11 per cent of all female voters. She received the backing of 22 per cent of voters in the 18-to-24 age group compared to only 11 per cent of those over 50 years of age. Moreover, almost one in five of those from a blue-collar background cast their ballot for the Sinn Féin candidate. This voting pattern was repeated for the other Sinn Féin European candidates and could also be seen in the Sinn Féin support in the local elections, which took place on the same day in June 2004.

A number of false myths surround the increased Sinn Féin electoral position in the Republic. Firstly, it is not true to claim that Sinn Féin garners huge support only from new voters and from the ranks of the disillusioned. One in ten of those who backed Mary Lou McDonald in the Dublin Euro-constituency had not voted in the 2002 general election. The figures for other party candidates are not hugely different from the Sinn Féin level. Similarly, while Sinn Féin won the highest level of support from first-time voters, the level is also only marginally greater than that received by the other parties and it is at a level to render reaching definite conclusions utterly useless.

The experience from the 2002 general election and 2004 European election would tend to suggest that Sinn Féin is actually cannibalising Fianna Fáil's working-class vote and making this constituency its own. This is also the pool of votes from which the Labour Party looks to gather significant support. But the future for Sinn Féin is to be found in a single statistic produced in the RTÉ/Lansdowne exit poll—one in four of those who backed McDonald in 2004 had, two years previously, voted for Fianna Fáil.

The experience in recent elections shows that Sinn Féin has always taken votes from Fianna Fáil, but the numbers have become more dramatic recently. The poll data indicates that 8 per cent of those who voted for Fianna Fáil in 1992 switched to Sinn Féin in 1997; the figure for former Fine Gael voters was 2 per cent. Sinn Féin also attracted 9 per cent of its new support from 1992 Labour supporters, while there was no movement from either the PD or Green voters in 1992 to Sinn Féin in 1997.

The Sinn Féin threat to Fianna Fáil became much clearer at the 2002 general election. Of those who voted for Sinn Féin candidates in 2002, some 31 per cent had moved from Fianna Fáil at the previous election in 1997. The figures for the 2004 European and local elections produced a similar result in explaining where Sinn Féin's vote came from—Fianna Fáil. This evidence confirms that there is some validity in the fear in Fianna Fáil circles about the damage that could be done to the party's future electoral prospects by the emergence of Sinn Féin.

While a sizable electoral and parliamentary gap still exists between Fianna Fáil and Sinn Féin, the evidence suggests that Sinn Féin is the party in the ascendant. Even from a low base, the party has the capacity and the capability to be a huge danger to Fianna Fáil and perhaps even to the Labour Party. Sinn Féin is hoovering up support among the young employed working class, precisely the constituency that both Fianna Fáil and Labour need to win if either of those two parties is to hold its current Dáil representation.

The exit poll data for the 2004 European and local elections suggests very strong voter attraction to Sinn Féin as a party, over its policies and choice of candidate. Without doubt, Mary Lou McDonald was the most personable and media-friendly of the Sinn Féin candidates in the Republic for the European elections. Yet of those who backed the party's Dublin candidate, only 15 per cent said their decision was based on the candidate's personality, while 30 per cent admitted that their choice had been determined by policy choice. The vast majority of those who voted for Sinn Féin in Dublin did so because of their attraction to the party itself—a sizable 47 per cent of the overall party vote.

So, almost half of those who backed the Sinn Féin Dublin candidate did so not because they wanted to support Mary Lou McDonald, but rather because they wanted to vote for the Sinn Féin party. This attraction to the political party itself in voter behaviour was higher for

Sinn Féin than for any other political party in the June 2004 European elections in the Republic.

In the local elections, the main issue identified by Sinn Féin supporters was the presence of candidates on the ground in their constituency. Voters turned to Sinn Féin for its local political activism, with some 23 per cent saying that candidates' presence in their community and an involvement in local activities were the main issues determining their voting choice.

This level was second only to Fianna Fáil, which has a long-established and formidable local organisational network across the country and is famed for the ability of its candidates to mop up all surplus support. Sinn Féin, it would seem, is moving in on the territory so long the domain of Fianna Fáil, again confirming that the fiercest political battle in the years ahead may well be fought between these two parties. In constituency organisational terms, Sinn Féin is very much the modern-day Fianna Fáil and, ironically, Sinn Féin is challenging Fianna Fáil using the very tactics and strategies devised by Fianna Fáil itself.

Outside this local presence, crime emerged in the summer of 2004 as the next biggest determination of the voting intentions of potential Sinn Féin supporters. The condition of the health services and the cost of living were the other two main issues in the local elections for Sinn Féin supporters.

One common misconception about support for Sinn Féin in the Republic is that policy on Northern Ireland is one of the reasons why people vote for the party. Certainly, Northern Ireland is strongly identified by Sinn Féin voters, more so than by those who back any other political party. But the evidence from several election studies is that Northern Ireland is far from the most important issue for Sinn Féin supporters in the Republic. In 2002, among those who backed Sinn Féin, only 9 per cent rated the North as the main policy area that determined their voting intentions. Health was mentioned by 13 per cent of the exit-poll respondents, crime by 12 per cent, while honesty in public life and drugs were each mentioned by 8 per cent respectively.

In terms of policy having an impact on the direction of a person's vote in 1997, the analysis undertaken by Marsh and Sinnott indicated that taxation—a major issue of the campaign in 1997—was not a factor in supporting Sinn Féin. It would seem that at that time national policy issues and Sinn Féin were not yet considered as co-existing, a situation which may have pertained because most people—even, perhaps, Sinn Féin voters—did not then see the party as a party of government. That situation has obviously changed if voter preferences in recent elections are anything to go by.

Sinn Féin has another electoral asset that may help the party as it expands its representation in the Republic—voter loyalty. Nearly three-quarters of those who backed Mary Lou McDonald decided to give her their first preference vote two-to-three weeks out from polling day. For all the other main candidates, the voters' decision to support them came much closer to the day of the election.

Another notable feature of the Sinn Féin vote is the party's ability to retain its support base. This is very clear from an analysis of voter behaviour data contained in a 1997 exit poll compiled by RTÉ/Lansdowne. The poll indicated the Sinn Féin success in retaining its 1992 vote—some 71 per cent of those who voted for the party in the 1992 general election also backed Sinn Féin candidates five years later.

The experience of the 2004 elections confirms this pattern. Recent experience indicates that Sinn Féin loses support to a lesser extent that the other political parties. In 2004, some 77 per cent of those who voted for Sinn Féin in 2002 again voted for the party in 2004. This attribute in retaining voters was not matched by the other parties. For example, in 2004, Fianna Fáil and Labour held on to only 65 per cent and 67 per cent respectively of their 2002 general election vote. This retention feature has to be a very positive outcome for Sinn Féin given the considerable number of concessions and compromises agreed in the 1992–2004 period by the leadership of the republican movement.

Two decades ago, Gerry Adams received cheering endorsement from crowds of supporters at a republican commemoration ceremony when he declared, 'The IRA needs no electoral mandate for its armed struggle . . . .'[25] Today, the rules of the game have been fundamentally changed. Sinn Féin now actively seeks out an electoral mandate and recent election results confirm that the party seems to be good at this task.

Irish voters are no longer embarrassed to say that they will give their support to Sinn Féin. The party name has strong brand identification and generates considerable public allegiance. There is a striking demographic profile to the typical Sinn Féin voter—young, male and working class. This voter support has fuelled the election of the first raft of Sinn Féin public representatives.

Not surprisingly, the urban areas where Sinn Féin is currently strongest and most active are those where crime and drugs are the issues of greatest concern to local communities. In turn, these are the issues identified by Sinn Féin voters as their main concerns. Sinn Féin is viewed as an alternative to the established political parties. The empirical evidence suggests that there is further scope for Sinn Féin to develop in urban and rural Ireland. The party took 12 per cent of the urban vote in the 2004 local elections, compared to 25 per cent for Fianna Fáil, 20 for Fine Gael and 17 for Labour. It is likely that the gap between Sinn Féin and the other parties will narrow over time.

Significantly there is also huge scope for Sinn Féin to broaden its appeal in rural areas. In the 2004 local elections, some 7 per cent of rural voters backed Sinn Féin, compared to 40 per cent for Fianna Fáil, 31 per cent for Fine Gael and 7 per cent for the Labour Party. These figures suggest that in both urban and rural Ireland, the main political parties stand to lose from the rise of Sinn Féin—especially Fianna Fáil and Labour in urban Ireland, and Fianna Fáil and Fine Gael in rural Ireland. Overall, the biggest loser from the advance of Sinn Féin into the political mainstream may well be the party that emerged out of a split in the Sinn Féin ranks back in 1926—Fianna Fáil.

But there is one factor that may act as a brake to the development of Sinn Féin—the IRA. The structure of the electoral system in the Republic, where a proportional representation system is used in national elections, may be an impediment to the party's growth. Transfers are vital to the political parties if they are to maximise the number of seats they can win. The evidence from the 2002 general election indicates that many voters are still unwilling to give lower-preference votes to Sinn Féin candidates.

Even with an end to the IRA and its arsenal of weaponry, this pattern is likely to persist. The fallout from the Northern Bank robbery and the money-laundering investigations in the Irish Republic may still place a limit on the current voter expansion enjoyed by republican candidates. The end result may cost Sinn Féin in terms of the number of seats the party can win. In effect, the recent history of the IRA and links to 'dirty money' may act as a self-inflicted ceiling to the growth of the political wing of the republican movement, in the short to medium term.

Nevertheless, the confidence of senior republicans in their ability to grow Sinn Féin as a significant political force remains undimmed. Gerry Adams is not alone among the republican leadership in sensing power:

> I actually think for the first time, certainly in my lifetime, we actually have a strategy which is a political strategy. There were always strategies but they tended to be military strategies or military tactics. Here we have something which is based upon building political

strength. And electoralism is a very key part of all of that although it isn't in its entirety. So we do have a strategy—it's peaceful, it's democratic, and it's working.[26]

However, this strategy has so far not delivered the long-stated republican objective of a united Ireland. The IRA campaign has ended, weapons have been decommissioned, Sinn Féin has a parliamentary presence in Leinster House and at Stormont, while republicans are edging to acceptance of police arrangements in Northern Ireland. The strategy applauded by Adams sidesteps the slogans of 'Brits Out' and 'Not a bullet, not an ounce'. Republican critics see the compromises as evidence of a sell-out. But there may be another assessment of the Adams-sponsored pragmatism that now defines Sinn Féin as its still aspires towards Irish unity.

The record of the Adams era shows that everything in the republican code is now a tactic in pursuit of the principle of Irish unity. He has displayed a total disregard for traditional republican dogma and has refused to be hamstrung by historical principles like abstentionism and decommissioning, preferring to see them as tools in a tactical approach to achieving progress. The loss of human life over the 30 years of the IRA campaign remains, however, the brutal consequence of this strategy. The replacement of the 'long war' with the 'long peace' does little for those caught up in the mayhem of this violence.

Sinn Féin is still defined by its traditional republican agenda—the party's all-Ireland structures and all-Ireland approach to politics and policy-formation mark it out from other parties in parts of the island that also aspire to Irish unity. The changes since Bobby Sands was nominated as a prisoner candidate in the Fermanagh–South Tyrone by-election in 1981 have combined to move Sinn Féin closer to being a normal political party.

This normalisation process will be concluded when the IRA is finally laid to rest as an active organisation. The campaign of violence failed to achieve Irish unity, and in that regard the republican movement failed. Some of Adams's supporters argue that the post-Agreement Northern Ireland is one without institutionalised sectarianism, but a considerable price was extracted in achieving equal status for all the people in Northern Ireland. However, by settling for the terms of the Belfast Agreement—even taken as a transitional arrangement—acceptance has been signalled that violence did not succeed.

Even before the peace process went public in the early 1990s, Adams was prepared to say that he could envisage a future without the IRA. Nothing has been sacred in the Adams era and the end result of the compromises and concessions he has sponsored has been the defeat of the IRA itself. Sinn Féin has now emerged as the dominant force in the century-old Irish republican tradition. This is as Arthur Griffith would have wanted it.

NOTES

Chapter 1 (pages 1–21)
1. *An Phoblacht*, 9 May 2002.
2. McKittrick et al., 1999, p. 1,483.
3. English, 2003, pp 162–63.
4. Aengus Ó Snodaigh, interview with author, November 2004.
5. Gerry Adams, interview with author, 20 July 2004.
6. Aengus Ó Snodaigh, interview with author, November 2004.
7. Ibid.
8. Today FM, 10 December 2003.
9. *The Irish Times*, 21 February 2005.
10. *An Phoblacht*, May 1976.
11. Martin McGuinness, interview with author, 3 February 2005.
12. Gerry Adams, interview with author, 20 July 2004.
13. Ibid.
14. Ruairí Ó Brádaigh, interview with author, 19 February 1997.
15. *See* English, 2003, p. 383.

Chapter 2 (pages 22–37)
1. *An Phoblacht*, September 2003.
2. *An Phoblacht*, 23 September 1982, p. 8.
3. *The Irish Times*, 29 August 2001.
4. *An Phoblacht*, April 1998.
5. IRA statement, 13 April 2003.
6. Sinn Féin, 22 October 2003.
7. *The Irish Times*, 10 January 2005.
8. Martin McGuinness, UCD, 3 February 2005.
9. Dolours Price, 17 January 2005, http://lark.phoblacht.net/phprint.php.
10. Independent Monitoring Commission, 2005, p. 5.
11. Martin McGuinness, interview with author, 3 February 2005.
12. *Guardian*, 11 March 2005, G2 Section, pp 2–4.
13. Joe Reilly, interview with author, 4 March 2005.
14. *Village* magazine, 26 March 2005, pp 21–3.
15. *Guardian*, 11 March 2005, G2 pp 2–4.
16. *Village* magazine, 26 March 2005, pp 21–3.
17. Ibid.

Chapter 3 (pages 38–61)
1. *See* Hibbert, 2001, pp 437–8.
2. *United Irishman*, 31 March 1900.
3. *See* Hibbert, 2001, p. 438.
4. *Cork Examiner*, 3 August 1903.
5. *The Times*, 22 July 1903.
6. *United Irishman*, 18 April 1903.
7. *See* Paseta, 1999.
8. *The Irish Times*, 19 May 1903.
9. *See* Ellmann, 1982, p. 237.
10. *See* Ellmann, 1982, p. 236.
11. O'Hegarty, 1924, p. 93.
12. *See* De Buitléir in Ward, 1996, pp 14–15.
13. Ibid.
14. *Sinn Féin*, 29 February 1908.
15. Garvin, 1981, p. 105.
16. Laffan, 1999, p. 70.
17. Ibid.
18. *See* Laffan, 1999, p. 53.
19. O'Hegarty, 1924, p. 5.
20. *See* Laffan, 1999, p. 77.
21. Greaves, n.d., p. 6.
22. Ibid.
23. Ibid.
24. Laffan, 1999, p. 82.
25. O'Hegarty, p. 34.
26. Garvin, 1981, p. 118.
27. *Irish Independent*, 1 May 1917.
28. *See* Laffan, 1999, p. 100.
29. Quoted in Laffan, 1999, p. 182.
30. Quoted in Kee, 1982, p. 35.
31. *Nationality*, 5 January 1918.
32. Greaves, n.d., p. 10.
33. O'Hegarty, 1924, p. 22.
34. Hopkinson, 2004, p. 201.
35. Quoted in Cronin, 1972, p. 103.
36. Quoted in Cronin, 1972, p. 101.
37. Hennessey, 1997, p. 11.
38. Hennessey, 1997, p. 17.
39. Smith, 1997, p. 41.

Chapter 4 (pages 62–96)
1. Uí Buachalla, 1956.

2. Regan, 1999, p. 52.
3. Quoted in Regan, 1999, p. 56.
4. Sinnott, 1995, p. 30.
5. Garvin, 1981, p. 133.
6. *See* Regan, 1999.
7. Pyne, p. 6.
8. Bowyer Bell, 1990, p. 53.
9. *An Phoblacht*, 15 January 1926.
10. Greaves, 1954, p. 10.
11. Smith, 1997, p. 61.
12. *An Phoblacht*, 3 June 1927.
13. Buckley, 1956, pp 59–60.
14. *An Phoblacht*, 23 July 1992, p. 14.
15. Laffan, 1999, p. 442.
16. Uí Buachalla, 1956.
17. Manning, 1972, p. 90.
18. *See* Laffan, 1999, p. 446.
19. *United Irishman*, December 1949.
20. Dáil Debates, 20 March 1947, VOL. 104, 2537.
21. Uí Buachalla, 1956.
22. Dáil Debates, 16 April 1947, VOL. 105, 740.
23. Dáil Debates, 11 March 1947, VOL. 104, 1755.
24. *Irish Press*, 15 June 1949.
25. With the exception of 1953–54, MacLogain held the position of Sinn Féin party president until 1962. In the fallout from the futile IRA border campaign, MacLogain, like other republican veterans, found himself sidelined from both strands of the republican movement. He died from self-inflicted gunshot wounds in 1964.
26. *See* Rafter, 1996.
27. Hennessey, 1997, p. 105.
28. *Belfast Telegraph*, 16 May 1955.
29. Quoted in Bowyer Bell, 1990, p. 291.
30. Ruairí Ó Brádaigh, interview with author, 19 February 1997.
31. Ibid.
32. Uí Buachalla, 1956.
33. Ibid.
34. MacStiofain, 1975, p. 81.
35. *Irish Independent*, 27 February 1962.
36. *New York Times*, February 1962.
37. Laffan, 1999, p. 444.
38. *Irish Independent*, 9 December 1970.
39. Gerry Adams, interview with author, 20 July 2004.
40. MacStiofain, 1975, p. 104.
41. Ibid.

42. RTÉ, *This Week*, 31 July 1970.
43. *An Phoblacht*, February 1970.

Chapter 5 (pages 97–138)
1. *An Phoblacht*, 4 February 1982, p. 1.
2. *An Phoblacht*, 25 February 1982.
3. Seán Crowe, interview with author, 23 July 2004.
4. Adams, 11 October 1975. *See* www.cain.ulst.ac.uk.
5. Ibid.
6. Adams, 14 August 1976. *See* www.cain.ulst.ac.uk.
7. Drumm, 18 June 1977. *See* www.cain.ulst.ac.uk.
8. Jim Gibney, interview with author, 16 July 2004.
9. *An Phoblacht*, 23 June 1979.
10. *An Phoblacht*, 28 October 1978.
11. Jim Gibney, interview with author, 16 July 2004.
12. Danny Morrison, interview with author, 16 July 2004.
13. *An Phoblacht*, 6 November 1980.
14. *An Phoblacht*, 14 March 1981, p. 12.
15. *An Phoblacht*, 11 April 1981.
16. Jim Gibney, interview with author, 16 July 2004.
17. Martin McGuinness, UCD, 3 February 2005.
18. Owen Carron, interview with author, February 2005.
19. Ibid.
20. Jim Gibney, interview with author, 16 July 2004.
21. *Andersonstown News*, 9 April 2001.
22. Owen Carron, interview with author, February 2005.
23. *An Phoblacht*, 30 May 1981.
24. *Iris: The Republican Magazine*, November 1981.
25. Owen Carron, interview with author, February 2005.
26. *An Phoblacht*, 5 November 1981.
27. Ibid., p. 1.
28. Ibid.
29. Ibid., p. 7
30. Aengus Ó Snodaigh, interview with author, November 2004.
31. Caoimhghín Ó Caoláin, interview with author, 21 July 2004.
32. *An Phoblacht*, 25 February 1982, p. 5.
33. Ibid.
34. *An Phoblacht*, 4 March 1982.
35. *An Phoblacht*, 11 November 1982, p. 4.
36. *An Phoblacht*, 4 November 1982, p. 2.
37. *An Phoblacht*, 23 September 1982, p. 2.
38. *An Phoblacht*, 23 June 1983, p. 7.
39. *An Phoblacht*, 17 November 1983.

40. Ibid.

41. Ibid.

42. Ibid.

43. Ibid.

44. *See An Phoblacht*, 4 November 1982, p. 5.

45. *An Phoblacht*, 7 November 1985, p. 9.

46. *Ibid.*, p. 11.

47. *An Phoblacht*, 7 November 1985.

48. Ibid.

49. *An Phoblacht*, 2 January 1986.

50. Ibid.

51. *An Phoblacht*, 29 May 1986, p. 7.

52. Aengus Ó Snodaigh, interview with author, November 2004.

53. *An Phoblacht*, 26 June 1986, pp 8–10.

54. *An Phoblacht*, 7 August 1986, p. 12.

55. *An Phoblacht*, 14 August 1986, p. 1.

56. *An Phoblacht*, 18 September 1986, p. 12.

57. *An Phoblacht*, 16 October 1986, p. 12.

58. *An Phoblacht*, 23 October 1986.

59. *An Phoblacht*, 30 October 1986, p. 12.

60. *An Phoblacht*, 14 October 1986.

61. *An Phoblacht*, 18 September 1986, p. 11.

62. Ibid.

63. *Sunday Press*, 2 November 1986, p. 1.

64. *Sunday Press*, 12 October 1986, p. 13.

65. *Sunday Tribune*, 26 October 1986, p. 6.

66. *An Phoblacht*, 6 November 1986.

67. Ibid.

68. Ibid.

69. Ibid.

70. Ibid.

71. *The Irish Times*, 3 November 1986, p. 1.

72. *An Phoblacht*, 6 November 1986, p. 2.

73. Gerry Adams, interview with author, RTÉ *This Week*, 24 February 2002.

74. *An Phoblacht*, 6 November 1986.

75. *An Phoblacht*, 6 November 1986, p. 2.

76. Arthur Morgan, interview with author, 23 July 2004.

77. *An Phoblacht*, 30 September 1982, p. 12.

78. Sinn Féin, 10 May 1998.

79. Gerry Adams, interview with author, 20 July 2004.

Chapter 6 (pages 139–69)

1. Christy Burke, interview with author, 19 July 2004.

2. Ibid.
3. Aengus Ó Snodaigh, interview with author, November 2004.
4. *An Phoblacht*, 11 February 1982, p. 6.
5. Caoimhghín Ó Caoláin, interview with author, 21 July 2004.
6. Christy Burke, interview with author, 19 July 2004.
7. Aengus Ó Snodaigh, interview with author, November 2004.
8. Mary Lou McDonald, interview with author, 4 March 2005.
9. Christy Burke, interview with author, 19 July 2004.
10. Ibid.
11. Ibid.
12. Ibid.
13. Ibid.
14. Ibid.
15. Aengus Ó Snodaigh, interview with author, November 2004.
16. Horgan, 2002, p. 379.
17. Comments by Garret FitzGerald, 10 November 2004.
18. Caoimhghín Ó Caoláin, interview with author, 21 July 2004.
19. Seán Crowe, interview with author, 23 July 2004.
20. Gallagher, in Laver, Mair and Sinnott, 1987, p. 80.
21. Ibid.
22. Caoimhghín Ó Caoláin, interview with author, 21 July 2004.
23. Gallagher, in Gallagher and Sinnott, 1990, p. 77.
24. Ibid.
25. Aengus Ó Snodaigh, interview with author, November 2004.
26. *See* Marsh and Sinnott, in Gallagher and Sinnott, 1990, pp 109–10.
27. Gallagher, in Gallagher and Laver, 1992, p. 67.
28. Gerry Adams, interview with author, 20 July 2004.
29. Seán Crowe, interview with author, 23 July 2004.
30. Arthur Morgan, interview with author, 23 July 2004.
31. Ibid.
32. Gallagher, in Gallagher and Laver, 1992, p. 67.
33. *An Phoblacht*, 23 September 1982.
34. *An Phoblacht*, 30 September 1982.
35. Jim Gibney, interview with author, 16 July 2004.
36. Gerry Adams, interview with author, 20 July 2004.
37. Michelle Gildernew, interview with author, 4 March 2005.
38. Ibid.
39. Caoimhghín Ó Caoláin, interview with author, 21 July 2004.
40. Gallagher, in Marsh and Mitchell, 1999, p. 135.
41. Ibid.
42. Marsh and Sinnott, in Marsh and Mitchell, 1999, p. 172.
43. Aengus Ó Snodaigh, interview with author, November 2004.
44. Gallagher, 2003, p. 101.
45. Mary Lou McDonald, interview with author, 3 March 2005.

46. Gerry Adams, interview with author, 20 July 2004.
47. Mary Lou McDonald, interview with author, 3 March 2005.
48. Danny Morrison, interview with author, 20 July 2004.
49. Ibid.
50. Mary Lou McDonald, interview with author, 3 March 2005.
51. *An Phoblacht*, 22 July 2004.

Chapter 7 (pages 170–87)
1. Alex Reid, interview with author, 15 October 2002.
2. Elliott, 2000, p. 404.
3. Adams, 2003, p. 33.
4. Adams, 2003, p. 29.
5. *Guardian*, 12 September 1998.
6. Quoted in *The Times*, 28 March 1987.
7. Mary Holland in the *Observer*, 12 April 1998.
8. Alex Reid, interview with author, 15 October 2002.
9. McElroy, 1991, p. 63.
10. Quoted in O'Connor, 1994, p. 294.
11. *Irish Press*, 16 January 1978.
12. *Sunday Times*, 29 May 1988.
13. Quoted in McElroy, 1991, p. 63.
14. McElroy, 1991, p. 63.
15. *Pastoral Ministry and Political Violence. Providing a 'Tearmann'—A Sanctuary Setting.* Mission statement of Clonard Peace Ministry c.1988. Private papers of Fr Alex Reid.
16. The author wishes to thank Fr Alex Reid for releasing this material for use.
17. Alex Reid, interview with author, 15 October 2002.
18. *Pastoral Ministry and Political Violence. Providing a 'Tearmann'—A Sanctuary Setting.* Mission statement of Clonard Peace Ministry c.1988. Private papers of Fr Alex Reid.
19. Ibid.
20. Ibid.
21. Alex Reid, interview with author, 15 October 2002.
22. Ibid.
23. Ibid.
24. Alex Reid, interview with author, 17 April 2002.
25. Ibid.
26. Ibid.
27. The first meeting with Mansergh remains one of Reid's most vivid recollections from his involvement in the peace process. It was a key moment, according to Reid: 'What does the bible say, "There was a man sent by God"; I thought "Cometh the hour, cometh the man." Martin was the ideal person for conducting a debate with the republican movement, which aimed at taking

the gun out of Irish politics. You wonder if it would have succeeded without him.'

28. Mansergh, 1995.
29. Alex Reid, interview with author, 17 April 2002.
30. Untitled document c.1989. Private papers of Fr Alex Reid, previously unpublished.
31. Ibid.
32. Ibid.
33. Ibid.
34. Mitchell McLaughlin, interview with author, 21 March 2002.
35. Untitled document c.1989. Private papers of Fr Alex Reid, previously unpublished.
36. Ibid.
37. Ibid.
38. McKittrick et al., 2001, p. 1,328.
39. Quoted in Bew and Gillespie, 1999, p. 288.
40. IRA statement, 31 August 1994, quoted in *An Phoblacht*, 1 September 1994.
41. Rafter, 2003, p. 230.
42. *The Irish Times*, 8 January 1998.
43. *Fourthwrite*, No. 1, 2000, p. 7.
44. See *Labour Left Briefing*, June 1996.
45. *An Phoblacht*, 7 November 1985.

Chapter 8 (pages 188–218)
1. *An Phoblacht*, 29 July 2004.
2. Ibid.
3. Ibid.
4. *Christian Science Monitor*, 17 January 1985.
5. Ibid.
6. United Press International, 3 July 1984.
7. *An Phoblacht*, 29 July 2004.
8. *Christian Science Monitor*, 17 January 1985.
9. Ibid.
10. *The Irish Times*, 2 July 1982.
11. Laffan, 1999, p. 100.
12. Pyne, p. 41.
13. Uí Buachalla, 1956.
14. Danny Morrison, interview with author, 20 July 2004.
15. Northern Ireland Affairs Committee, 62.
16. Independent Monitoring Commission, November 2004, p. 29.
17. Ibid., p. 28.
18. Dáil Debates, 131–150, 19 February 1985.
19. Ibid.

20. Associated Press, 24 February 1985.
21. Ibid.
22. Northern Ireland Affairs Committee, 62.
23. O'Callaghan, 1998, p. 63.
24. Northern Ireland Affairs Committee, 29.
25. Ibid., 37.
26. *The Irish Times*, 4 May 2002.
27. Northern Ireland Affairs Committee, 153.
28. *Irish Independent*, 19 February 2005.
29. *Examiner*, 25 February 2005.
30. *Irish Independent*, 19 February 2005.
31. *The Irish Times*, 2 December 2003.
32. Caoimhghín Ó Caoláin, interview with author, 21 July 2004.
33. Mary Lou McDonald, interview with author, 3 March 2005.
34. *Cincinnati Enquirer*, 10 September 2003.
35. Sinn Féin fundraising in the United States has been adversely affected by new rules in the Irish Republic, which preclude political parties from accepting all donations from individuals (other than Irish citizens) who reside outside the island of Ireland. Moreover, corporate donations can now be accepted only from businesses that have an office in the island of Ireland from which one or more of its principal activities is directed.
36. House of Commons, sn/pc1667, p. 2.
37. Ibid., p. 17.
38. Information provided by House of Commons Press Office.
39. *The Irish Times*, 11 March 2005, p. 10.
40. *Daily Ireland*, 2 March 2005.
41. *See An Phoblacht*, 7 November 1985.
42. Independent Monitoring Commission, November 2004, p. 13.
43. Independent Monitoring Commission, Third Report, November 2004.

Chapter 9 (pages 219–43)
1. Gerry Adams, interview with author, 20 July 2004.
2. Mary Lou McDonald, interview with author, 3 March 2005.
3. sf document, 'No Right Turn', September 2004. See www.sinnfein.ie.
4. Northern Ireland Assembly, 20 June.
5. *Irish Catholic*, 22 April 2004.
6. sf Pre-Budget Submission, 2001.
7. sf Pre-Budget Submission, 1999.
8. sf Pre-Budget Submission 2002.
9. sf Pre-Budget Submission 2003.
10. sf Pre-Budget Submission, 2001.
11. Ibid.
12. Mary Lou McDonald, interview with author, 3 March 2005.

13. Benoit and Laver, 2002.

14. Quoted in Irvin, 1992, p. 81.

15. *See* Frampton, 2004.

16. Ibid.

17. *The Irish Times*, 15 December 2001.

18. Rolston, 1992, p. 50.

19. Adams, 1986, p. 131.

20. *The Irish Times*, 3 October 2001.

21. *The Irish Times*, 29 August 2001.

22. Mary Lou McDonald, interview with author, 3 March 2005.

23. *An Phoblacht*, 17 November 1983, p. 7.

24. Caoimhghín Ó Caoláin, interview with author, 21 July 2004.

25. *An Phoblacht*, 23 June 1983, p. 7.

26. Gerry Adams, interview with author, 20 July 2004.

BIBLIOGRAPHY

Newspapers consulted included *An Phoblacht, Andersonstown News, Irish Times, Irish Independent, Sunday Press, Sunday Times, Sunday Tribune, Belfast Telegraph, Christian Science Monitor, Cincinnati Enquirer, Daily Ireland, Examiner, Fourthwrite, Guardian, Iris: The Republican Magazine, Irish Catholic, Nationality, New York Times, Observer, The Times, United Irishman, Village* magazine. Lansdowne Market Research in Dublin provided the opinion poll data and exit poll information. Sinn Féin policy documents and material relating to the peace process are available at www.sinnfein.ie and www.cain.ulst.ac.uk. For various reports of the Independent Monitoring Commission, see www.independent monitoringcommission.org.

Adams, Gerry, *The Politics of Irish Freedom*, Brandon, 1986.

Adams, Gerry, *A Pathway to Peace*, Brandon, 1988.

Adams, Gerry, *Before the Dawn*, Brandon, 1996.

Adams, Gerry, *Hope and History*, Brandon, 2003.

Benoit, Kenneth and Michael Laver, *Estimating Irish Party Policy Position Using Computer Wordscoring: The 2002 Election, A Research Note*, TCD, 2002.

Bew, Paul and Gordon Gillespie, *Northern Ireland: A Chronology of the Troubles, 1968–99*, Gill & Macmillan, 1999.

Bishop, P. and Eamon Mallie, *The Provisional IRA*, Heinemann, 1987.

Bowyer Bell, J., *The Secret Army: The IRA 1916–1979*, Poolbeg, 1990.

Bric, Maurice and John Coakley, *From Political Violence to Negotiated Settlement*, UCD Press, 2004.

Buckley, Margaret (*See* Uí Bhuachalla, M. Bean).

Cox, Michael, Adrian Guelke and Fiona Stephen (eds), *A farewell to arms? From 'long war' to long peace in Northern Ireland*, Manchester University Press, 2000.

Cronin, Seán, *The Fenian Movement*, 1980.

Dixon, Paul, *Northern Ireland: The Politics of War and Peace*, Palgrave, 2001.

Elliot, Marianne, *The Catholics of Ulster*, Penguin, 2000.

Ellmann, Richard, *James Joyce*, Oxford, 1982.

English, Richard, *Armed Struggle: The History of the IRA*, Oxford University Press, 2003.

Frampton, Martyn, '"Squaring the Circle": The Foreign Policy of Sinn Féin, 1983–89', *Irish Political Studies*, 19: 2, 2004.

Gallagher, Michael, 'Stability and Turmoil: Analysis of Results', in M. Gallagher, M. Marsh and P. Mitchell (eds), *How Ireland Voted 2002*, Palgrave, 2003.

Gallagher, Michael and Michael Laver (eds), *How Ireland Voted 1992*, Folens, 1992.

Gallagher, Michael and Richard Sinnott (eds), *How Ireland Voted: 1989*, Centre for the Study of Irish Elections, 1990.

Garvin, Tom, *The Evolution of Irish Nationalist Politics*, Gill & Macmillan, 1981.

Garvin, Tom, *Nationalist Revolutionaries in Ireland, 1858–1928*, Oxford University Press, 1987.

Garvin, Tom, *The Birth of Irish Democracy*, Gill & Macmillan, 1992.

Greaves, Desmond (ed.), *Father Michael O'Flanagan, Republican Priest*, Connolly Association, n.d.

Hennessey, Thomas, *A History of Northern Ireland 1920–1996*, Gill & Macmillan, 1997.

Hennessey, Thomas, *The Northern Ireland Peace Process: Ending the Troubles?*, Gill & Macmillan, 2000.

Hibbert, Christopher, *Queen Victoria: A Personal History*, Harper Collins, 2001.

Hopkinson, Michael, *The Irish War of Independence*, Gill & Macmillan, 2004.

Horgan, John, 'Journalists and Censorship: A Case Study of the NUJ in Ireland and the Broadcasting Ban 1971–94', in *Journalism Studies*, 3: 3, 2002.

Kee, Robert, *The Green Flag: A History of Irish Nationalism*, Penguin, 1982 edn.

Laffan, Michael, *The Resurrection of Ireland: The Sinn Féin Party, 1916–1923*, Cambridge University Press, 1999.

Laver, Michael, Peter Mair and Richard Sinnott, *How Ireland Voted 1987*, Poolbeg, 1987.

McElroy, Gerald, *The Catholic Church and the Northern Ireland Crisis, 1968–1986*, Gill & Macmillan, 1991.

McGarry, Fearghal (ed.), *Republicanism in Modern Ireland*, UCD Press, 2003.

McIntyre, Anthony, 'Modern Irish Republicanism: The Product of British State Strategies', *Irish Political Studies*, 10, 1995.

McKittrick, David et el., *Lost Lives: The Stories of the Men, Women and Children Who Died as a Result of the Northern Ireland Troubles*, Mainstream, 2001 edn.

MacStiofain, Seán, *Memoirs of a Revolutionary*, Gordon Cremonesi, 1975.

Manning, Maurice, *Irish Political Parties*, Gill & Macmillan, 1972.

Mansergh, Martin, 'The Background to the Peace Process' in *Irish Studies in International Affairs*, VOL. 6 (1995).

Marsh, Michael and Paul Mitchell, *How Ireland Voted 1997*, Westview Press, 1999.

O'Callaghan, Seán, *The Informer*, Bantam Press, 1998.

O'Connor, Fionnuala, *In Search of a State: Catholics in Northern Ireland*, Blackstaff, 1994.

O'Hegarty, P. S., *The Victory of Sinn Féin*, 1924 (reprinted in 1998, UCD Press).

Paseta, Senia, *Before the Revolution*, Cork University Press, 1999.

Pyne, Peter, 'The third Sinn Féin party: 1923–1926', *Economic and Social Review*, 1: 1 and 1: 2, 1969–70.

Rafter, Kevin, *The Clann: The Story of Clann na Poblachta*, Mercier, 1996.

Rafter, Kevin, *Martin Mansergh: A Biography*, New Island, 2002.

Rafter, Kevin, 'Priests and Peace: the role of the Redemptorist Order in the Northern Ireland peace process', in *Études Irlandaises*, 2003.

Regan, J.M., *The Irish Counter-Revolution 1921–1936*, Gill & Macmillan, 1999.

Reid, Alex, *Pastoral Ministry and Political Violence. Providing a 'Tearmann'—A Sanctuary Setting*. Mission statement of Redemptorist Peace Ministry c.1988. Private papers of Fr Alex Reid.

Reid, Alex, *Untitled document*, Redemptorist Peace Ministry, c.1989, Private papers of Fr Alex Reid. Unpublished.

Rolston, Bill, *Politics and Painting: murals and conflict in Northern Ireland*, Farleigh Dickinson, 1991.

Rolston, Bill, *Drawing Support: Murals in Northern Ireland*, Beyond the Pale, 1992.

Sinnott, Richard, *Irish Voters Decide: Voting Behaviour in Elections and Referendums Since 1918*, Manchester University Press, 1995.

Smith, M. L. R., *Fighting for Ireland? The Military Strategy of the Irish Republican Movement*, Routledge, 1997 edn.

Tonge, Jonathan, *The New Northern Ireland Politics*, Palgrave, 2005.

Uí Buachalla, M. Bean, *Sinn Féin: 1905–1956: A Proud History*, Sinn Féin, 1956.

Ward, Margaret, *Unmanageable Revolutionaries*, Pluto Press, 1996.

INDEX